Re-Shaping Learning: A C

Re-Shaping Learning: A Critical Reader

The Future of Learning Spaces in Post-Compulsory Education

Edited by

Anne Boddington
Jos Boys

University of Brighton, UK

SENSE PUBLISHERS
ROTTERDAM/BOSTON/TAIPEI

A C.I.P. record for this book is available from the Library of Congress.

ISBN: 978-94-6091-607-6 (paperback)
ISBN: 978-94-6091-608-3 (hardback)
ISBN: 978-94-6091-609-0 (e-book)

Published by: Sense Publishers,
P.O. Box 21858,
3001 AW Rotterdam,
The Netherlands
www.sensepublishers.com

Printed on acid-free paper

TABLE OF CONTENTS

List of Illustrations vii

Acknowledgements ix

Reshaping Learning - An Introduction xi
Anne Boddington and Jos Boys

PART 1: WHERE ARE WE NOW?

1. Doing Learning Space Evaluations 3
   Brett Bligh and Ian Pearshouse

2. Methods for Understanding the Relationships between Learning
   and Space 19
   Clare Melhuish

3. What do We Know About What is Being Built?: New Typologies
   of Learning Spaces 33
   Jos Boys and Hilary Smith

4. Where is the Theory? 49
   Jos Boys

PART 2: WHAT KIND OF SPACE IS LEARNING?

5. Between the Lines: The Transitional Space of Learning 69
   Olivia Sagan

6. What Matters About Space for Learning: Exploring Perceptions
   and Experiences 81
   Clare Melhuish

7. Research Spaces 93
   Maggi Savin-Baden

8. Fragile Constructions: Processes for Reshaping Learning Spaces 105
   Susan Sherringham and Susan Stewart

PART 3: LEARNING SPACES AND INSTITUTIONAL IDENTITIES

9. 'Learning Landscapes' as a Shared Vocabulary for Learning Spaces 121
   Angela Thody

10. Learning Spaces as Social Capital 137
    Paul Temple

11. Some Models for Re-Shaping Learning Spaces 147
    Fiona Duggan

12. Learning beyond the University: The Utopian Tradition................155
    David Anderson

PART 4: RESHAPING THE FUTURE OF LEARNING SPACES

13. Configuring Learning Spaces: Noticing the Invisible....................167
    Ronald Barnett

14. Designing Education and Reshaping Learning...............................179
    Anne Boddington

15. Social Learning Capacity: Four Essays on Innovation and Learning
    in Social Systems 193
    Etienne Wenger

List of Contributors...211

Index..217

LIST OF ILLUSTRATIONS

FIGURES

Figure 3.1. Interior of Idea Store, Whitechapel, London.
Photograph: Jos Boys 39

Figure 3.2. Masters course facilities, White Space, University of Abertay.
Photograph: Jos Boys 41

Figure 4.1: Learning space framed through the patterning of binary
associations and oppositions (re-printed from Boys, 2010, p. 5) 49

Figure 4.2. Learning space framed as the patterning of socio-spatial
practices (re-printed from Boys 2010, p. 7) 51

Figure 4. 3: Analysing socio-spatial practices (adapted from Lefebvre,
1991 and re-printed from Boys 2010, p. 81) 56

Figure 6.1. InQbate Creativity Zone, University of Sussex. Photograph:
Clare Melhuish 82

Figure 6.2. Centre for Excellence in Learning and Teaching through
Design (CETLD). Photograph: Clare Melhuish 85

Figure 6.3. The Creativity Centre, University of Brighton. Photograph:
Clare Melhuish 86

Figure 8.1. Early development and testing of tools and models -
'Day in the Life' exercise, Scaffold Workshop, Sydney 2009.
Photograph: Susan Sherringham 113

Figure 8.2. An activity-scape being developed - 'The Parallel University'
game, Scaffold Workshop, Interdisciplinary and Social Sciences
Conference, Cambridge, 2010. Photograph: Susan Sherringham 113

Figure 8.3. Persona Development - Scaffold Workshop, Sydney, 2010.
Photograph: Susan Sherringham 115

Figure 12.1. A studio workspace, with associated computer facilities
at the Sackler Centre, V&A Museum, London. Photograph: Hilary Smith 161

LIST OF ILLUSTRATIONS

TABLES

Table 3.1. Examples of informal learning design in the UK (reprinted from Boys, 2010 pp. 20–21) 34

Table 3.2. Example pattern of citations of UK learning space examples................35

Table 15.1. Configuring social learning capacity - structural interactions between governance and accountability..208

Table 15.2. Configuring social learning capacity - creating patterns of vertical and horizontal accountability..208

ACKNOWLEDGEMENTS

This book developed out of the work of Centre for Excellence in Teaching and Learning through Design (CETLD). This was a 5-year partnership between the University of Brighton, the Royal College of Art (RCA) the Victoria & Albert Museum (V&A) and the Royal Institute of British Architects (RIBA), funded by the Higher Education Funding Council for England (HEFCE) that ran from 2005 to 2010. We would like to thank all our colleagues at these institutions, who were central to the research and development behind this book, both in their engagement with the group and through their associated projects and activities. Particular appreciation is due to Anne Asha, Debbie Hickmott, Philippa Lyon, Jane Devine-Meja, Hilary Smith, Beth Cook, Catherine Speight, Rebecca Reynolds, Sol Sneltvedt, Clare Chandler, Sina Krause and Roland Mathews at CETLD; Irena Murray and Paul Snell at the RIBA, Morna Hinton at the V&A and Professor Alan Cummings and Chris Mitchell at the RCA. We would also like to thank the many people who gave their time on various occasions to discuss learning spaces: these have included Sian Kilner, Tom Hamilton, Diane Brewster, Jon Rimmer, Lars Wieneke and Noam Austerlitz. As part of developing our overall ideas and individual chapters we undertook a conference at the University of Brighton in July 2009 entitled Reshaping Learning. We would like to thank the many delegates who participated in this event for their valuable contributions to the learning spaces debate.

In addition, many people have been involved in supporting and undertaking the research that underpins each chapter. Chapter 1 draws upon work funded by JISC's e-Learning programme. Brett Bligh and Ian Pearshouse would like to thank Mike Sharples for his helpful comments on an earlier draft. Chapters 2 and 6 summarise research funded through CETLD and the InQbate Centre for Excellence in Teaching and Learning in Creativity (a partnership between the Universities of Sussex and Brighton.). Clare Melhuish would like to thank all the staff and students at the Universities of Sussex and Brighton who kindly agreed to participate in her study, for their support and input. Funding for the research described in Chapter 8 has been provided by the Australian Learning and Teaching Council Limited, an initiative of the Australian Government Department of Education, Employment and Workplace Relations. Susan Sherringham and Susan Stewart would also like to thank to DEGW for permission to use their Culture Cards in the initial development and testing of ideas for the ALTC project. The research in Chapter 9 by Angela Thody was undertaken as part of 'Learning Landscapes' based at the University of Lincoln, funded by HEFCE and completed in 2010. Fiona Duggan would like to acknowledge all the participants who were involved in the learning spaces development projects which form the basis of Chapter 11. Anne Boddington would like to thank Professor Bruce Brown for persuading her to develop the CETLD and as the co-author of the original bid; and Professor Jonathan Woodham and Dr Catherine Harper for their patience, feedback, reading and re-reading of drafts for chapter 14. Etienne Wenger would like to thank the leaders of the EQUAL initiative, Ana Vale and Gerhard Braunling, for involving him in their interesting challenge; and many EQUAL participants for their conversations and from their comments on Chapter 15, especially Beverly Trayner and Maria do Carmo Nunes.

Finally, The editors would like to thank Etienne Wenger for his permission to include 'Social learning capacity: four essays on innovation and learning in social systems' (2009), the unpublished report from his research for EQUAL, an initiative of the European Social Fund. This essay is also available for download free from http://ewenger.com.

ANNE BODDINGTON AND JOS BOYS

RESHAPING LEARNING - AN INTRODUCTION

BACKGROUND

The impetus for gathering the authors and essays for this publication was our growing recognition of an emerging and complex field that resides under the collective title of 'learning spaces'. This is situated at the confluence of a number of disciplines including education, museum studies, architecture, estates planning, human-computer interaction, and policy and management; so although there are many shared concerns, participants come to their engagement with the field from varied perspectives and with very different methodologies. All the papers touch upon and contribute to our understandings of learning spaces in post compulsory education – which in the UK and Australian contexts covered here - means further, higher and adult education post-16. Where contributors are writing about a specific part of this sector they will talk about education in universities, colleges or museums. We believe, however, that many of the examples are more generalisable, to a wider international audience and context. This includes the schools sector, other settings where learning takes place and a consideration of learning spaces in the context of a productive and fulfilling workplace. Our initial review of learning spaces revealed that much high quality research was being undertaken in and across different disciplines, but that its different 'locations' has prevented the consolidation and distillation of ideas, and made it hard to develop a picture of the field as a whole or to communicate this work easily to its many audiences. In addition, and despite considerable interest, the quality of many reports remain uneven and few are linked to contemporary research in either education or design. This has resulted too often in a reiteration of many simplistic divisions between 'old' formal teaching spaces and 'new' informal and social learning space. Our main aim, then, was to connect the work of disparate disciplines in one place, bringing together a substantive body of learning spaces research which could inform the future development of the field.

In the UK, the first decade of the new millennium saw significant public investment in the physical and digital spaces and educational infrastructure of universities, colleges and related environments. In turn this stimulated a growing interest in the re-examination of learning and the spaces in which learning takes place; to try and ensure their fitness for purpose, and to see whether they meet the needs of 21st century learners, academics and other related publics. This has opened up interesting questions, first, about the lack of any theoretical under-standing as to how such spaces should be conceived or designed; and second, about the shifting purposes of post-compulsory education and the institutional role of the University. Pragmatically it has also revealed a lack of effective frameworks for either the development of contemporary learning spaces or for assessing their impact on learning and research. Each of these areas urgently needs more knowledge-sharing and constructive dialogue across disciplines, and more rigorous research into the appropriate conceptual frameworks and methodologies for analysing and improving learning spaces.

The book is therefore designed as a'critical reader' which can enable researchers, academics, students and managers across the fields of post compulsory education, estate management and architecture to share and engage with some of the key academic ideas, issues and texts from many different places. It is intended for anyone interested and wanting to think more about learning spaces, whether as users, clients or managers or with a more general interest in relationships between the social and the spatial (for example, anthropologists, architects, designers, sociologists, sociolinguists, geographers and human-computer interface designers). *Reshaping Learning - the future of learning spaces in post-compulsory education* intends to both problematise and to develop a constructive critique of the current assumptions about learning space. It offers examples of cross-disciplinary research by leading scholars in the field, as they grapple with the complexities of understanding the intersecting interrelationships between space and the learning, teaching, research and management that happens within it. Taking a variety of perspectives, these essays begin to map that field and to question what kinds of reshaping – conceptual, social and/or physical – may be brought to bear on post-compulsory learning, teaching and research.

As already noted, the experts chosen for this collection come from many different fields. Education is well-represented (Ronald Barnett, Paul Temple, Etienne Wenger, Maggi Savin-Baden, Olivia Sagan and Angela Thody) since so little research about learning spaces is being undertaken from this perspective. But there is also research and writing from architecture and design (Anne Boddington, Jos Boys, Susan Sherringham and Susan Stewart), from anthropology (Clare Melhuish), from estates management (Fiona Duggan), from museums education (David Anderson), and from computer science (Brett Bligh and Ian Pearshouse). Each discipline thus has the opportunity to engage with ways of looking 'outside' of their usual frameworks. In this way, the book hopes to increase the number of fruitful cross-disciplinary connections and debates.

In addition, contributors use a variety of voices and references. Some are most interested in unravelling what happens in particular learning encounters, others are more concerned to address the institutional agenda, and others again explore the potential of articulating learning through its spatial 'conceptualisations'. Thus this work, as a collection, begins to both open up the field of learning spaces to its many complexities and difficulties, whilst also offering the developing clarity that different kinds of focus can bring. What the contributors share is an understanding that learning is always *situated* and *embodied*, not just in material space but also in individual, social, cultural, economic and political contexts. Space can only be viewed in relation to its occupation, that is, as *socio-spatial practice*. This means that learning spaces are not so much a matter of aesthetics or innovative design, as about the processes of learning, teaching and research and the ways in which relationships between these are categorised, organised and connected (that is, in what is 'named' and identified and what is not; what is revealed, what is kept together and what is disaggregated and dispersed) both conceptually and materially.

'Talking Back' from a Design Perspective

The development of this book was supported by the Centre for Excellence in Teaching and Learning through Design (CETLD), a partnership led by the Faculty of Arts at the University of Brighton in collaboration with the Victoria and Albert Museum (V&A), the Royal Institute of British Architects (RIBA) and the Royal College of Art (RCA) which ran from 2005–2010. Though the locus of the CETLD was design and learning, learning spaces was a key theme from the beginning and the developing research programme aims for a much wider influence on other, more mainstream, educational and professional learning theories and practices. Superficially at least this may appear an unexpected step. Art and design education is rarely aligned to much that is written about post-compulsory teaching and learning. Teachers within these fields often find little connection with pedagogic theory and many do not see much use or value in the concept of 'learning space' itself (Boys, 2010 p. 8). Very infrequently do the 'commonsense' arguments in favour of more informal learning spaces make any sense to art and design teachers who are already dealing with the complex overlays of 'creative subjects' and the wide range of spaces they utilize (including conventional lecture theatres and seminar rooms, studios, workshops and laboratories). Yet, at the same time, art and design education is often cited as an innovative paradigm for contemporary learning. This is because it is multidisciplinary, problem, project and often professionally-based and developed around collaborative critique and self-reflective iteration. We believe that the creative disciplines can offer an alternative and distinctive perspective on learning from much of the contemporary literature, and throw a different light on pedagogy more generally. We want it to 'talk back' constructively and creatively to ideas both about the formation of learning and about space. So, although the authors represented here come from a wide range of disciplines there are considerably more from design subjects than would usually found in such collections. This is deliberate; it situates design as a kind of ghost at the heart of the educational machine.

CHAPTER STRUCTURE

The book is divided into four sections:

Part 1: Where are we now? – brings together key reviews and critiques of the field of learning spaces; clarifying and discussing what it is that we already 'know' and reflections on how to develop and method for analysis.

Part 2: What kind of space is learning? – presents examples of the latest research exploring how to analyse learning as an activity that is socially and spatially embedded

Part 3: Learning Spaces and institutional identities – examines the issues for considering learning spaces strategically within an institutional context

Part 4: Reshaping the future of learning spaces –explores how we might re-think the 'shape' of learning in the post-compulsory sector, conceptually, socially and physically.

Part 1: Where are We Now?

In chapter 1 Brett Bligh and Ian Pearshouse set the scene with a critical analysis of the current learning space evaluations methods in post-compulsory education across the UK. Given the significant value of the estate for the majority of institutions this chapter reveals the limitations of short-term methods of analysis that fail to provide objective methods from which to gather data and feedback about the role space has in affecting learning. In chapter 2 Clare Melhuish reviews the different ways in which relationships between learning and space can be analysed and explores some useful approaches, with particular reference to architectural studies, social anthropology, geography and environmental psychology. She argues for methods that elucidate the participant's view, rather than that of the researcher, and that build on a rapport between participant and researcher to reveal insights that could not be achieved through established, objectified and behaviourist methods. In chapter 3 Jos Boys and Hilary Smith present a critical review of the current design of learning spaces in the UK. They examine what is being presented as innovative and 'good' learning space (irrespective of supporting evidence) and the kinds of spaces that remain less visible. Importantly they argue that the current tendency to use metaphor and to make analogous links between learning and its formal and visual representation (e.g. informal learning equates to bright colours and soft furnishings) maybe be considerably more problematic than it first appears because such actions mask or invert key relationships between the social practices of learning and the design of the associated spaces. Jos Boys closes this first section. Chapter 4 explores what kinds of contemporary theories and ideas drawn from education and architecture might better inform our understanding of the relationships between learning and space. The aim here is to see how theory can begin to advance practice and the debates about learning spaces, by providing ways to address the complexity, diversity and fluidity inherent in such a subject.

Part 2: What Kind of Space is Learning?

In chapter 5 Olivia Sagan applies the concept of transitional space (Winnicott, 1971) to the question of precisely where learning takes place, suggesting it happens in the 'space' between the taught and the learned. She challenges an educational discourse already saturated with spatial descriptors, such as notions of 'top' and 'bottom' grades, of 'under' graduate, 'foundation' level, and 'higher' education. As a counterpoint she examines the place of learning in which 'aspects of the self are created and transformed in relationships with others and with the matrices of culture' (Day-Sclater, 2003 p. 326). This relational process is both fraught and gifted with emotional investment and risk. Her chapter explores the constituent elements of such a place, and considers how these might be provided for, within an educational environment that is increasingly constrained. In chapter 6, Clare Melhuish applies some of the ethnographic methods outlined in chapter 2 to the study of three new learning spaces in post-compulsory education. Her aim is to examine individual participants' perceptions (students and staff) of particular physical spaces and the perceived impact on their learning. The study focused on two specific issues: on participants' understandings of the institutional agenda, and on their interpretations and experiences of the spatial, material and sensory qualities of each space. Her research demonstrates how, if asked specific questions participants can engage with physical space in a rich and multi-layered way that extends across, social, spatial symbolic, functional and experiential interpretations. In chapter 7 Maggi Savin-Baden usefully moves into a discussion of what kinds of the learning spaces support research. She suggests that in the UK, as public funding for higher education reduces, student numbers expand and research demands and aspirations increase, there has been relatively little attention given to the nature and needs of research space. Yet, she argues, like learning spaces, it is essential that spaces and places for research are recognized and developed because they are vital for the sustenance and wellbeing of the higher education community. In chapter 8, which concludes this section, Susan Sherringham and Susan Stewart also argue that the relationships between space and learning are fragile and constructed, personally, culturally and institutionally. The chapter outlines their research, supported by an Australian Learning and Teaching Council (ALTC) Priority Project Grant, which centres on mapping the relationships between curriculum, pedagogy, technology, learning activities, learning stances and spatial affordances, to develop more informed insights as to how and if space supports learning. They have designed and tested a set of tools and techniques, which enable participants to articulate and negotiate their understandings of learning through mainly visual means, which, the authors argue, opens up debate and development both creatively and productively.

Part 3: Learning Spaces and Institutional Identities

In chapter 9 Angela Thody explores what general agreement there is on meanings of 'learning landscapes' as a concept to unite an understanding of learning spaces at the institutional level. Her aim is to find a shared vocabulary between different constituencies and perspectives, as well as to propose methods to support this understanding, with particular reference to both university conceptualisations past and present, and to participatory ways of working. In chapter 10 Paul Temple outlines the complexities of assessing the effectiveness of learning spaces for the educational institution and focuses on how visual and spatial design, at the level of the campus, can communicate "messages" both internally and externally. Intuitively, he notes, it does appear that some learning spaces and campus designs work "better" than others and are for instance, more welcoming, on a human scale. The lack of empirical evidence however arises from the challenges of designing studies that could demonstrate convincingly a cause-and-effect relationship where there are multiple variables. Here Temple demonstrates how concepts such as 'encounter management' and 'social capital' may help to articulate the interactions that occur and can begin to create a sense of belonging and institutional identity. As a complement, in chapter 11, Fiona Duggan offers practical insights for learning space development projects by educational institutions. She outlines a series of ways of working that constructively bring together different perspectives on space, and presents some models for articulating different kinds of spatial and learning values across organisations, each developed pragmatically from particular educational contexts and leading to the design of new post-compulsory learning spaces. Concluding this section, in chapter 12 David Anderson extends these ideas beyond the campus and considers learning spaces in the museum. He outlines how galleries and other spaces in museums, although less structured as learning environments than in schools and universities, are relatively more formal, structured and rich in material culture than daily life. Articulating these places as micro-utopias, he argues that such learning spaces are vital and distinctive as public spaces and can actively contribute to cultural and social dialogue. Drawing both on theoretical and cultural ideas he also examines the development and ethos of the new Sackler Centre for arts education at the V&A Museum in London (opened in 2008) and some related public and cultural collaborations for the local area.

Part 4: Reshaping the Future of Learning Spaces

This final section explores future propositions from a range of different perspectives. In chapter 13 Ronald Barnett problematises the potency of the metaphor of space in the phrase 'learning spaces'. He suggests that though seductive it invites many questions. He focuses on the scope of learning spaces, their connectedness and their depth, visibility and invisibility and the implications in the idea of learning spaces of spaciousness, particularly its connection with the expansiveness of outlook that universities in particular have long been felt to provide. This invites pertinent questions for the contemporary period. He asks what are the available and appropriate spaces within which to learn, and what is or should be their scope, for the future of education and to further disciplinary knowledge. In chapter 14 Anne Boddington reflects on the experiences, ideas and research findings from the Centre for Excellence in Teaching and Learning through Design (CETLD), to posit ideas about the potential position of designerly activity in the shifting roles of academe. She also examines how potential convergence and/or collaborations with other cultural and learned institutions might reposition and present new possibilities for supporting citizen-learners, scholars and researchers in the 21st Century. Chapter 15 is the concluding chapter, written by Etienne Wenger. It provides some reflections on his involvement with the EQUAL Initiative, a European Social Fund project designed to support the spread of social innovation and collaboration across groups and activities. Here Wenger uses the case of social innovation to explore four key elements of social learning capacity: social learning spaces, learning citizenship, social artists and learning governance. Interest in these factors reflects a significant shift in the way education is understood. He goes beyond learning as something acquired through a fixed curriculum, to a process inherent in our participation in social systems. He concludes by suggesting that increasing the learning capacity of these social systems is becoming an urgent concern in a world where we face daunting learning challenges.

CONCLUSION: FUTURE CHALLENGES FOR RESEARCH AND PRACTICE

By bringing these authors together it has been possible to see, within and across the diversity of concerns represented, a series of underlying key themes beginning to emerge. Learning spaces remains an under-developed field, and we suggest that each of these themes presents opportunities for important future research, discussion and development.

Opening Up Different 'Angles of View'

Throughout this collection there is an awareness of the considerable complexity of interrelationships between learning and space. This serves to demonstrate the need to resist reductive or over-simplified approaches. To grapple with the difficulties of exploring such complexities, authors have taken a variety of positions in relation to theory and practice. The essays gathered here draw principally from three theoretical pillars. These are, first, Lefebvre (1991), who has suggested methods for investigating the interactions between occupation and space, and has had a considerable influence across both architecture and the social sciences (including psychoanalytic theory) where these are concerned with space. Second, many authors draw in some way from Latour's Actor Network Theory (2008), which incorporates into its frame-work both human and non-human conditions, so ensuring that any analysis captures detailed contextual understanding. Third, is the considerable impact of Wenger and Lave's Communities of Practice model (1991), as well as Wenger's later work (1998), is having on ideas - particularly in education -about learning as a long-term journey, centred on the making of social meanings.

It is also interesting to see different intellectual trajectories and values being played out across different contributors, disciplines and locations. For example, 'within' architecture, Lefebvre and other writers in this (mainly Marxist) tradition such as Foucault (1977, 1984), De Certeau (1984) and Bourdieu (1984) are currently influencing understanding of spaces as socially constructed and embedding problematic power relations. From 'within' education there is a stronger tendency to refer to researchers such as Hillier (1996/2007), Hutchinson (2004) and Dovey (2008). These latter authors - who tend to come from a scientific and humanist background- focus more on the potential of material spaces to incorporate 'universal' qualities, such as a sense of place (ideas that are eternally unstable, and often questioned within architecture). An important value of the book is in making available these different approaches in one place, so that cross-comparison becomes easier. But, in bringing together a variety of voices concerned with the emerging field of learning spaces, we must also take the opportunity to have - and set up frameworks for - more explicit, critical debates about both our various theoretical positions and our 'commonsense' assumptions.

From Solution to Illumination

Not surprisingly, the variety of theories 'brought to bear' on the subject of learning spaces inevitably lead to different ontologies that serve to conceptualise and construct arguments and to form conclusions. What is more, some disciplines will tend to emphasise bespoke, site-specific designed solutions, focusing on the detailed specificity of each situation and context, while others will be more interested to attempt generalisable conclusions. This is particularly clear in the first chapters where the very situatedness of Melhuish's anthropological case study methods raises issues about what kinds of wider conclusions can be drawn; whilst the more structured and comparative methods offered by Blight and Pearshouse can suffer - as they appreciate - from being unable to achieve any such fine-grain analysis. This problem also appears later in, for example, the differences between the pragmatic, case-by-case customised work of Duggan and the more abstract and theoretical conceptualisations of Barnett and Boys.

Similarly, contributors vary as to the 'slice' of learning spaces they investigate. The different sections in this collection highlight the various foci this tends to produce. So Part 1: *Where are we now?* concentrates on detailed modes of analysis, particularly in relationship to learning encounters in real environments, while Part 2: *What kind of space is learning?* also examines learning encounters but from a more theoretical perspective. The questions asked in Part 3: *Learning Spaces and Institutional Identities* tend to be of a different scale and type - mainly engaging with issues of organisation and identity. Finally Part 4: *Reshaping the future of learning spaces* looks both at learning as an activity, and at institutions as learning providers, but tends to expand how these aspects of learning spaces might be imagined, both conceptually or - in the widest sense - politically. Some authors attempt to provide ways of articulating these different 'levels' from direct learning encounters to societal conceptualistions, which are explored by different essays; for example Barnett's division of learning spaces into material space, educational space and the student's 'interior' space; or Boys's adaptation of Lefebvre's spatial triad as everyday socio-spatial learning routines, designed environments, and individuals perceptions and experiences of both learning routines and the spaces in which they take place.

Of course, we can learn many lessons from all these different kinds of examination of learning space, at whatever scales and granularity they are framed. Given the complexities we have revealed, it is vital that we develop both theory and practice with the many kinds of both rigour and richness being offered here. We need *both* better conceptual frameworks and more appropriate methods that enable some degree of summative analysis and a range of methods and tools that reveal, assist and inform rather than dictate and fix the management and construction of learning spaces, whether physical, digital or intellectual. Again though, as with different academic positionings, the underlying issue is to make sure that we are comparing like-with-like and are providing relevant supporting evidence. Most contributors agree on a few key points. First, examinations of learning spaces are best constructed as 'thick descriptions' (Geertz, 1973), which capture the complexity of social and spatial relationships. Second, whatever methods we use, the overall aim should be to assess *value* (however that comes to be defined). Bligh and Pearshouse, and Duggan in this volume both deal at length with this issue of value. And, third, the outcome of proposing conceptual frameworks, making arguments, and gathering data - whether to inform a learning space project or to evaluate it - is not to provide easy solutions but to *illuminate* our understanding of learning spaces (Parlett and Hamilton, 1972).

Recognising the Ambiguity of Space

Of critical concern is the ambiguity of space as a category. It is evident throughout the various chapters that in the context of learning spaces, there is considerable slippage in the use of terms between the conceptual, the physical and the metaphorical; between individual, community and public space; and between personal and imaginary space, institutional spaces (whether digital or physical), and the public realm. While partially caused by the varied use of language in different disciplines it is nevertheless vital to unpack and understand the many assumptions about, and meanings given to, learning spaces as they are used in this anthology. While space is already clearly ambiguous as a category in terms of the material world, we should also note that, with the recent 'spatial turn' in cultural theory more generally (Deleuze and Guattari, 2000), it is increasingly used as a means to explore or communicate at the level of *ideas*, what we have called socio-spatial conceptualisations of learning. Whilst this is opening up debate in a potentially very exciting and enlightening way, we need to be clear about how - and if - such spatial conceptualisations of learning connect with either actual material spaces, or individual and group embodied perceptions and experiences.

The other central ambiguity of space is in the different ways it is assumed to 'translate' educational ideas and learning practices into built form. So there is, for example, a tension throughout the collection around the usefulness of metaphor in general as a way of generating ideas about space, and/or in making actual environments; and also differing emphases on space as a representational medium (expressing, for example, identity) and as an events-based process (that is, as a kind of choreography). As before, explicitly exploring these differences is potentially a very creative and constructive way to open up and progress debate and development.

Developing a Relational Understanding of Learning Spaces

We started the book with the clear understanding that learning spaces is a deeply complex and as yet under-researched field. As these chapters have been drawn together, two things became increasingly clear. First, we still do not have a generally shared language for articulating what is distinctive about post-compulsory learning as an activity. We remain poor at explaining how learning at this level *works*, either to those within or to those beyond the academy. However, overall, this book shows some emerging similarities in understanding and descriptions of post-compulsory learning that can be usefully developed. As many of these authors show, in educational theory, learning spaces are increasingly understood as moments of transition between different states of learning, with many boundaries and thresholds to be negotiated (Meyer and Land, 2006; Lave and Wenger, 1991; Wenger, 1998). Many essays therefore explore how students (and staff) can both be supported in their learning journeys and enabled to take risks; and how both conceptual and material space is implicated in that process. This has been voiced in a variety of ways - as recognition and validation, as belonging and as being challenged. Second, and growing out of this first point, the design and development of learning spaces requires a relational understanding of individual and collective learning, within and beyond the physical boundaries of institutions. Learning spaces are therefore not about seeking singular solutions to particular problems. They are about patterns of learning, teaching and research, the development of knowledge as a generative and shared activity; and the role of different kinds of spaces (conceptual, personal, social, material) in this process. In seeking to create a shared understanding and to articulate the important characteristics of learning spaces a number of descriptors have been proposed such as 'learning landscapes' or 'learning ecologies.' These are indicative of continuous and more dynamic spatial relationships although it is not entirely clear whether these ultimately serve to confuse by overlaying metaphors one upon another. What has become obvious is that learning spaces bring together existing socio-spatial practices, designed places and individual perceptions of both practices and actual places and their place alongside institutional processes/ relationships and societal ideas.

What has also become apparent is that what is fixed and revealed and what remains transient, impermanent and relational are critical decisions that can clearly be transformative and/or destructive. Refining our knowledge of how to establish optimal conditions for investing in learning spaces is vital given the scale of the investments and how little we really know about the educational process and practices or about how these intersect with the conceptual, physical or aesthetics of space. This realization alongside Savin-Baden's parallel and related observations about the spaces of research, reveal important issues and opportunities for future research particularly in the changing contemporary context in the UK.

Envisaging the Future of Education

Space, then, cannot be separated from its occupation; changing learning spaces for the better is thus about understanding and improving the *socio-spatial practices* of education. Second, the design of learning spaces is not so much about providing solutions as enabling the optimal *conditions for learning*. Each social and spatial aspect requires detailed understanding and a relational tolerance that enables designers of (physical and virtual) spaces and designers of learning (be they teachers or students) to both generate and complete the learning space between them through embodied encounters. Learning spaces are only 'completed' through this inhabitation, and will only work well when this is understood and where there is a relational and conceptual alignment between physical spaces, the invisible governance systems of the institutions, and the conceptualisations of learning that underpin the educational process (and so that the potential for creative learning is not obstructed).

Moving towards such an alignment challenges the very nature of learning institutions themselves as well as the 'shape' of education more generally (what is learnt, where, by whom?). It suggests that universities, colleges and adult education providers will need better ways of dynamically modelling what they do, and of acting flexibly and creatively in adapting and transforming their learning provision through time. Post-compulsory educational institutions need to learn how to learn and evolve, and how to embed responsive mechanisms within their governance structures. As UK further and higher education undergoes a significant transformation over the coming decade there are challenges to its role, to the idea of 'learning for its own sake' and for personal intellectual development. Post-compulsory education has become increasingly focussed on and driven by professional formations and on its direct benefit and service to the economy. This is, then, a critical moment to reflect upon how the interrelationships between the academic infrastructures for learning, teaching and research can be developed alongside and in tandem with more responsive and intelligent models and systems of management and governance. This collection and its diverse range of authors bring together a series of perspectives in this emerging field and we believe it offers some initial essential steps in responding to these important and urgent questions.

REFERENCES

Barnett, R. (2007). *A will to learn: Being a student in an age of uncertainty.* Maidenhead: McGraw-Hill/ Open University Press.
Barnett, R. (2010). *Being a university.* Abingdon: Routledge.
Bourdieu, P. (1979/1984). *Distinction: A social critique of the judgement of taste.* London: Routledge.
Boys, J. (2010). *Towards creative learning spaces: Re-thinking the architecture of post-compulsory education.* London and New York: Routledge.
Day-Sclater, S. (2003). What is the subject? *Narrative Inquiry, 13,* 317–330.
De Certeau, M. (1979/1984). *The practice of everyday life.* Berkeley, CA; London: University of California Press.
Deleuze, G., & Guattari, F. (1988). *A thousand plateaus: Capitalism and schizophrenia.* London: Continuum.
Dovey, K. (2008). *Framing places: Mediating power in built form.* Abingdon: Routledge.
Foucault, M. (1977). *Discipline and punish: The birth of the prison.* London: Allen Lane.
Foucault, M. (1984). *Of other spaces (1967) heterotopias.* Retrieved from http://foucault.info/ documents/heteroTopia/foucault.heteroTopia.en.html
Geertz, C. (1973). Thick description: Toward an interpretive theory of culture. In *The interpretation of cultures: Selected essays* (pp. 3–30). New York: Basic Books.
Hillier, B. (1996/2007). *Space is the machine.* London: Space Syntax.
Hutchinson, D. (2004). *A natural history of place in education.* New York: Teachers' College Press.
Latour, B. (2008, September 3). *A cautious prometheus? A few steps towards a philosophy of design* (with special attention to Peter Sloterdijk). Keynote lecture for *Networks of Design,* meeting of the Design History Society, Falmouth, Cornwall.
Lave, J., & Wenger, E. (1991). *Situated learning: Legitimate peripheral participation.* Cambridge: Cambridge University Press.
Lefebvre, H. (1991). *The production of space* (D. Nicholson-Smith, Trans.). Oxford: Blackwell.

Meyer, J. H. F., & Land, R. (Eds.). (2006). Threshold concepts and troublesome knowledge: Issues of liminality. In *Overcoming barriers to student understanding: Threshold concepts and troublesome knowledge*. Abingdon: Routledge.

Parlett, M. R., & Hamilton, D. (1972). *Evaluation as illumination: A new approach to the study of innovatory programmes*. Workshop at Cambridge, and unpublished report Occasional paper 9, Centre for research in the educational sciences, University of Edinburgh.

Savin-Baden, M. (2008). *Learning spaces: Creating opportunities for knowledge creation in academic life*. Maidenhead: Open University Press/McGraw-Hill.

Temple, P. (2007). *Learning spaces for the 21st century: A review of the literature*. York: Higher Education Academy. Retrieved from http://www.heacademy.ac.uk/ourwork/research/litreviews

Temple, P., & Barnett, R. (2007). Higher education space: future directions. *Planning for Higher Education, 36*(1), 5–15.

Wenger, E., (1998). *Communities of practice: Learning, meaning and identity*. Cambridge: Cambridge University Press.

Winnicott, D. W. (1971). *Playing and reality*. London: Tavistock/Routledge.

PART 1: WHERE ARE WE NOW?

BRETT BLIGH AND IAN PEARSHOUSE

1. DOING LEARNING SPACE EVALUATIONS

In this chapter we argue that evaluating learning spaces is a valuable activity that can generate operational insights into *how physical space affects learning*, and can thus feed into processes of learning space design. The broader context is a desire to improve learning by designing better spaces within post-compulsory education. However, while it is clear that the configuration of space profoundly impacts human activity generally (Hillier, 1996/2007), Learning Space evaluation (LS·e) must contend with the reality that explicit links between space and theories of learning remain poorly explored and that theories of learning themselves rarely emphasise the importance of space (Jamieson, 2003; Neary et al., 2010). Thomas (2010), for example, has argued that 'in short, our difficulty in understanding and articulating the nature of learning is *partly brought about by our inability to articulate where learning takes place*' (p. 502, our emphasis).

If learning theories fail to discuss physical space explicitly, they nonetheless profoundly affect it by suggesting new forms of learning activities, which many existing spaces in post-compulsory education are manifestly not designed or configured to support; as Van Note Chism (2002) has noted, recent developments 'have challenged the adequacy of traditional learning spaces' (p. 9) and on this basis the creation of new learning spaces is seen to be much more crucial than in the past. Thus, LS·e must make reference to theories of learning if it is to have explanatory power and we argue that evaluations, suitably constructed and diss-eminated and in sufficient numbers, can allow us to start constructing an under-standing of the links between theory and physically embodied learning through aggregated experience. Melhuish (Chapter 2) echoes these concerns, arguing that the anthropology of education needs to become more spatially aware, and can begin to better understand spatial practice by using ethnographic methodologies and constructing Geertzian 'thick descriptions', understood as academic fictions.

Yet, in addition to coming to a contextualised understanding of Learning-Space relations, evaluators are routinely tasked with representing that understanding in ways which are convincing to funders and other stakeholders, are useful in future planning, propose design solutions to be implemented in other locations, and which suggest ways to improve current spaces. Thus, as we shall argue in this chapter, LS·e tends to balance a set of core values about what is (or is believed to be) important about the space under evaluation against a set of more pragmatic constraints, often related to institutional context. In our view, it is the management of this balance that discriminates good evaluations, which generate useful insights, from mediocre ones, which fail to do so.

A. Boddington and J. Boys (eds.), Re-Shaping Learning: A Critical Reader: The Future of Learning Spaces in Post-Compulsory Education, 3–18.

At least some of the problems with LS·e we wish to outline have their roots in learning space *design* limitations. Reasonably, given the lack of available theoretical guidance, design teams base decisions on their (limited) understanding of spatial purpose (Temple, 2008, p. 231). Furthermore, timescales of estates refurbishment and decommissioning within Higher Education (HE) mean that many spaces, or elements of spaces, outlast learning theories' prevalence even where attempts are made by designers to embody such theories (Thomas, 2010, p. 503). So evaluating spaces in terms of pedagogic intent is difficult because such intent either was never explicit in the mind of the designer or evidence of the intent was not available to the evaluators. Thus, success criteria for LS·e have usually been derived from other sources, including space evaluation practices used outside the education sector. Roberts and Weaver (2006) describe how, even as late as the early 1990s, LS·e was seen 'only in relation to stock and weeding policies, not clients and certainly not 'learners'!' (p. 97). In the UK context, Temple (2008, p. 230) points out that the University Grant Committee's quantitative, traditionalist spatial 'norms' from the 1960s and 1970s continue to influence university planners' judgements of building size and design, notwithstanding that they have ceased to have official recognition. These spatial norms are 'traditionalist' in the sense that they evaluate what we here call *demand*, and have limited explanatory power since they do not take into account the factors generating utilisation or occupancy and nor refer to pedagogical principles. Yet 'space management' certainly *impacts* on pedagogy, despite being based on such quantitative blunt instruments, because it affects the relative availability of space types and thus privileges chosen learning activities. Here, we suggest that, since LS·e carries implications for learning and also impacts upon institutional identity, there is an urgent need to develop more subtle instruments than space allocation metrics alone. Partly we draw upon our Joint Information Systems Committee (JISC)-funded study of these issues, *A Study of Effective Evaluation Models and Practices for Technology Supported Physical Learning Spaces* (hereafter 'JELS', Pearshouse et al., 2009), which investigated what methods and tools were already being used to evaluate the contribution *to learning and teaching* of physical Learning Spaces (ibid., p. 6). This project concluded that, despite the existence of some plausible *models* in the literature, most *actually existing* examples of LS·e were of modest ambition compared with the spaces they were examining, were often fragmented and often only aspirational. Mainly utilising data such as footfall and surveys to establish demand or satisfaction, most evaluations we reviewed failed to consider learning as an activity, while others seemed content that new ways of learning and teaching were 'enabled' (ibid., pp. 12–14). Furthermore, links between LS·e and design were not usually explicit and the dissemination of project outputs was poor (ibid., pp. 14–16). Our conclusions – that future practice for LS·e should seek to build flexibility into design, relate design to intended pedagogy, consider infrastructural provision including spare capacity, better relate to established professional guidelines, and better understand the context and legibility of proposed designs – were thus focussed on the *shortcomings* of existing evaluations across the UK.

This chapter follows on from that research by seeking to unpack what kind of evaluations *can* be plausibly undertaken. It offers a typology of evaluation types, contrasting the benefits and drawbacks of different models relative to common evaluation contexts. We then draw attention to factors that crucially affect LS·e practice – such as initiation and timescale, relationship to design, the identity of the evaluators, and data gathering methods. We conclude by emphasising the interdisciplinary nature of LS·e, by recognising the relative merits of the available evaluation models, and by arguing that the scholarly potential of LS·e has been insufficiently recognised. The quality of evaluation should ultimately be judged by the *insights* gained into the ways spaces *support learning* and the ways in which these insights are shared within a community of interested practitioners.

A TYPOLOGY OF LEARNING SPACE EVALUATIONS

Aiming to classify LS·e into types privileges certain properties as fundamental. We contend that it must also operate at a suitable level of detail for practitioners, who should be able to place their current practice into context and re-examine their assumptions. Previously, Powell (2008, p. 28) has sought to distinguish *appraisal* evaluations, which seek to validate a learning space's 'success' in a manner reminiscent of many examples uncovered by JELS - outlined below - from *design studies*, which seek greater detail about which facets of a design can be linked to useful outcomes. These latter thus more closely resemble academic research. While this distinction is useful and perhaps necessary, since it demarcates a genuine boundary line between different approaches to LS·e, it is nonetheless insufficient for our purpose, since each category could be applied to a large number of heterogeneous evaluations. Roberts and Weaver (2006, pp. 96–97), on the other hand, begin their discussion of LS·e by setting out a list of potential *insights* which evaluation might provide – demonstrations of interactivity, approaches to learning technology development, supporting the needs of diverse learners, researching impact on learning, and so on (p. 96) – and subsequently provide a (lengthy) list of the *reasons* why an evaluation might occur. Examples include providing evidence for return on investment, to assist with future planning, and to connect project outcomes to institutional contexts. Unfortunately, the relations between these insights and reasons are not made explicit, and while we acknowledge that these attributes can be applied to many of the evaluations we have encountered, we consider that this model operates at a level *too* fine-grained to distinguish usefully between models of evaluations. Similarly, some practitioners define evaluations in terms of their sources of data (especially if these are innovative, for example utilising a Web 2.0 platform), but we argue that this factor is also not fundamental since innovative data collection leads to better evaluation outcomes only when linked to appropriate evaluation questions and analytical methods (Pearshouse et al., 2009, pp. 11–12). Instead, we begin by examining the *values* (success criteria) of the evaluations themselves, since we

5

believe these offer insights into the assumptions of the evaluators, and suggest clustering LS·e models as follows:

- **Demand model**: quantitative analysis of conventional space metrics (occupant density, booking statistics), or financial income (external bookings, internal market calculations), etc.;
- **Outcomes model**: evaluating changes in learning outcomes;
  Satisfaction model: collecting data about the *experiences* and satisfaction of space users;
- **Scenario provision model**: examining space *provision* (technology, configuration, size, etc.), in light of *judgments* about the *activities* which need to be supported;
- **Activity support model**: evaluating activities undertaken within a space *in practice*, often using observation-based methods;
- **Spatial ecology model**: examining configurations of, and relationships between, the variety of spaces available;
- **Brand model**: evaluating spaces' contribution to institutional image, as projected to entities including media, external partners, prospective and current students and staff, etc.

These LS·e models describe *ideals* (archetypes) that may not be mutually exclusive in practice. For example, evaluation programmes may encompass several models for 'triangulation' purposes (to construct a more holistic picture or to reach more confident conclusions). Or one evaluation may give rise to another as a *reaction*; Powell (2008) notes a common need to defend innovative new learning spaces against charges of being 'space hungry' (p. 30). This might involve deploying a Satisfaction or Activity Support model to challenge Demand Model conclusions (even though the outputs generated by the different models are not likely to be directly comparable). In addition, the values of LS·e are often constrained by the context, which affects what kinds of study are achievable.

Our assumption above of a relation between the values of an LS·e programme and those of the evaluators themselves also needs to be clarified. The JELS project encountered many cases of evaluations whose conclusions precisely met expectations, trumpeted success or even justified decisions to *cease evaluating* on the grounds that success had been achieved (Pearshouse et al., 2009, pp. 14–15). We found little evidence of genuinely problematic evaluation conclusions, leading us to suspect at the time 'that reports which contradict initial expectations were unlikely to be publicly acknowledged' (ibid., p. 53). More insidiously perhaps, the very construction of LS·e frames of reference itself serves to render negative results unlikely, and thus problematic reports are rarely written. Here we use reverse engineering to focus on those values for which evaluation programmes appear to demonstrate high regard. If contextual demands have constrained LS·e to the extent that the programmes do not reflect the values of those undertaking the evaluations, then this discrepancy deserves to be underlined so that the evaluation processes, institutional constraints — or even the values themselves — become open to challenge. Starting points for such challenges could be: whether the values and assumptions of the evaluators are appropriate, whether the evaluation carried out

matches the values from which it claims to proceed, and whether the evaluation has the resources needed to ensure a usable outcome. LS·e strategies are typically affected by factors including:
- Pragmatics of data availability in order to generate 'quick wins': data that already exists, or that can be gathered using automated techniques, is often preferred to data which must be gathered manually (Pearshouse et al., 2009, p. 11);
- Resources available to undertake an evaluation (timescale, budget, staff allocation);
- Externally imposed funding timescales or project staging guidelines which impose 'decision gates' (Radcliffe, 2008, p. 14) on an evaluation.

We continue by providing a brief overview of each of the models outlined above.

Demand Model

The Demand Model for LS·e arises because university estate is a resource with large associated costs – typically the second largest cost overall borne by an institution within HE behind staff costs (NAO, 1996). This model proceeds from the basis that such a resource should be used, above all, *efficiently* (Neary et al., 2010, p. 46). The UK Space Management Group (SMG, 2006, p. 3) defined space utilisation, a measure of how space is used, as a function of frequency (proportion of time a space is in use) and occupancy (proportion of a space's capacity taken up when in use). Alternate models measure space per student or space per staff member (ibid., p. 6). The model addresses issues such as what size of estate is affordable, whether resources deployed in support of under-consumed space should be re-directed, and the opportunity costs of supporting inefficient spaces (ibid., p. 3). This model is overwhelmingly dominant across Higher Education LS·e (Pearshouse et al., 2009; Neary et al., 2010, p. 32). The advantages of Demand Model LS·e are that it can be:
- Holistic, developing a picture of provision across a variety of spaces;
- Benchmarked, and linked to estimates of what an institution can afford;
- Suggestive, since it can be used to set utilisation targets, emphasise spaces that may need to be marketed more widely, or suggest priorities for investment;
- Analysed and presented in formats which influence policymakers (ibid., p. 4).

However, the model also presents considerable drawbacks:
- Change in utilisation rates over time tends to be minimal, so meaningful comparison can be difficult;
- Measuring demand is reactive, and does not suggest innovative solutions;
- Objective measures can correlate poorly with the perceptions of staff and student about overcrowding or lack of available spaces;
- Differing measures (such as calculating space per full-time equivalent (FTE) instead of utilisation) highlight different trends, and it is unclear which of these delivers more insight (SMG, 2006, p. 6);
- Data collection is inconsistent and often of dubious quality, consistency and sample size, which in turn can render comparisons between institutions problematic (SMG, 2006, p. 7);

– The method does not discriminate between the factors that cause a space to have given levels of utilisation or occupancy (ecological properties, technology provision, popularity etc.).

Such a model can also be criticised because it does not relate to teaching and learning. The SMG's (2006) own work acknowledges the need to 'balance' minimising cost against 'meeting the pedagogical and research needs of staff and the learning and support needs of students' (p. 3). The latter places a greater emphasis on social and pedagogical aspects of space rather than efficient use (Neary et al., 2010, p. 46), and it is clear that the Demand Model can provide little guidance with regard to such issues. We therefore contend that such a model is necessary for institutional space management, but certainly not sufficient.

Outcomes Model

Discovering causal benefits between space design and learning outcomes would perhaps be the best way of raising the profile of the learning spaces agenda across the post-compulsory education sector. But we contend that identifying such tangible links in practice is difficult, and probably implausible, because they are weak, indirect and easily 'masked' by other factors (Temple, 2008, p. 237). Nonetheless some authors do argue that we cannot shy away from these issues. Warger and Dobbin (2009), for example, argue that 'ultimately learning success must lead these evaluations: what contributes to students' mastering academic content, finishing courses, and completing degrees?' (p. 11). In making such comments, Warger and Dobbin imply that LS·e should focus on issues more traditionally associated with the theory of Student Involvement (Astin, 1984/1999), which is indeed connected with space in that it emphasises 'environmental influences on student development' (p. 518). Yet the institutional evaluation programmes which do exist, informed by Student Involvement theory, necessarily take the form of wide surveys of student experiences whose conclusions cannot be taken as support for notions of spatial causality.

To gain insight into the kind of work that needs to be undertaken to establish the impact of learning spaces on learning outcomes, it is useful to consider the quasi-experimental work of Brooks (in press). Brooks *isolates* the effects of space by controlling (keeping constant) confounding factors such as time of day, course materials, assignments, instructor behaviour, and so on and is thus able to demonstrate a statistically significant difference between the predicted and actually achieved grades of different groups of students whose teaching occurred in two classrooms with different designs. As a piece of research, this work is useful in demonstrating that physical space *can* improve learning, yet as a technique for LS·e this work is problematic both in its construction (we design learning spaces with the understanding that tutor behaviour, teaching session duration etc. *will* change) and in its intensiveness of labour (it seems impractical for institutions to conduct such pair-wise comparisons of spaces separately for each learning scenario they wish to evaluate, at the scale that would be necessary to answer Warger and Dobbins' Student Involvement-inspired challenge).

A further illustration of the difficulties in operationalising Outcomes Model ideas can be found in the work of Hunley and Schaller (2006, 2009). In 2006, these authors set out an Assessment Framework for Learning Spaces, focussing on institutional growth, quality of person-environment interaction, learning outcomes and personal engagement (Hunley and Schaller, 2006, p. 13.3). Within this framework, the possible aggregation of learning outcomes with student evaluations of teaching quality is discussed (ibid., pp. 13.1–13.2). However, writing three years later, Hunley and Schaller (2009) advocate using *engagement* as a proxy measure for learning 'due to the complexity of assessing specific learning outcomes' (p. 28). Ultimately, while we agree with Warger and Dobbin (2009, p. 12) that student outcomes constitute a quantitative measure of success for the whole institution as a 'learning environment', we believe that direct measurements of these outcomes within LS·e are unlikely to be fruitful. Instead, we advocate accepting proxy measures for learning outcomes, as other models do below, and ensuring that LS·e is appropriately co-ordinated with other, complementary institutional evaluations such as those investigating retention or the student experience.

Satisfaction Model

The JELS project found that a strong driver of LS·e – especially of internally initiated service evaluation programmes – was to respond to the demands of the UK National Student Survey (NSS) (Pearshouse et al., 2009, p. 4). Thus, to align with the focus of that survey, many LS·e programmes value occupants' *satisfaction* with the spaces they encounter. Furthermore, *students'* satisfaction is privileged, not that of academics or support staff. One such example asked 'how people perceived the space and the impact it had on them as individuals, learners' (ibid., p. 11). This model often uses data collection tools such as surveys, interviews and focus groups, and we concluded (ibid., pp. 3–4) that the apparent success of these tools in addressing NSS concerns acts to prevent other forms of evaluation from flourishing. Within the UK literature, for example, the SOLSTICE centre's common evaluation framework (Roberts and Weaver, 2006) invokes the language of the 'student experience' (p. 104) in defining its central aims, but this framework commendably complements this by emphasising the importance of obtaining staff viewpoints.

Associated drawbacks include the fact that many other factors influence satisfaction in HE *more* than (or despite the) properties of spaces (Temple, 2008, p. 238), which may confound response validity. Students may also lack the confidence to project their 'voice' with regard to spatial experiences, and may need support to do so (Neary et al., 2010, p. 29). Finally, ostensibly related issues – such as the engagement between a space and its occupants (Thomas, 2010, p. 503) and the effects of spaces on 'how students feel about their *place* in the institution' (Temple, 2008, p. 233, our emphasis) – point towards a need for deeper understanding of the affective experience of space, which can only ever be partly addressed by constructing a narrative around student satisfaction.

Scenario Provision Model

A prominent focus within LS·e is the *enabling* of new teaching and learning *scenarios*, particularly 'ensuring that spaces are being utilised, and utilised in an exploratory and innovative manner, in line with design ambitions' (Pearshouse et al., 2009, p. 12). Compared with the models above, this model is innovative in that it explicitly refers to spatial design and thus implies a link to design processes. What this model usually involves in practice is making judgements about which activities (scenarios) a space needs to support and ensuring that the space, its contents (furniture, technology) and its basic infrastructure are appropriate for such activities – and, in some cases, keeping logs of the activities which occur in the room over time.

Anticipating the activities a space needs to support is crucial in design (Watson, 2007, p. 258) and linking evaluation to these considerations is similarly crucial to understand how students and staff engage with designed space. Such a model runs into the problems we outlined in our introduction, that many designs are informed by (often dubious) assessments of what a space is required to do and are not related to well-developed pedagogical models. Furthermore, the language of 'learning styles', often invoked to underpin design (Neary et al., 2010, p. 42) in the absence of more convincing guidelines, can be used to justify predetermined conclusions independent of context and thus to imply a minimal role for LS·e in suggesting design solutions. Instead, we need to design spaces with a clear understanding of their pedagogic purpose, and subsequently *evaluate* whether our aims were achieved. With regard to the implications of learning styles, perhaps a more appropriate response is to 'design for diversity but with the aim of resourcing individuals to explore alternative modes of learning – rather than only reinforcing entrenched preferences' (Crook and Mitchell, submitted).

Evaluating Scenario Provision often involves collecting data on 'occupancy, usage and scenarios' (Pearshouse et al., 2009, p. 13) rather than examining the activities actually taking place. While useful, this model thus operates with in-sufficient granularity to take into account the 'design gestures' (deliberately designed affordances, ibid., p. 25) which support the scenarios. Used alone, we consider the Scenario Provision Model to be in danger of allowing *spatial determinism* – generous resourcing (of technology, for example) is claimed to have supported innovative pedagogy by an evaluation process which cannot theorise *how* this support occurs and whose analytical framework would not be able to refute such claims were they untrue. Similar problems have been noted with strategies sometimes used to evaluate collaborative learning technologies (Bielaczyc, 2006, p. 308), which we argue can best be overcome by evaluating activity within the space in which it takes place.

Activity Support Model

Activity Support LS·e investigates the learning interactions of students and staff and locates those within physical space. This often involves mapping *back* to physical and cultural affordances (for example the configurations of students, teachers and machines within space, or how the social identities of the actors within the space are understood by those present), as opposed to Scenario Provision LS·e, which establishes activity checklists from design assumptions and maps these forward to occupancy. Such a mapping would ideally constitute a *dialogue* between design and evaluation through time. However, this dialogue is often thwarted by both the problems of theoretical contributions to design which we have already noted, and a lack of institutional memory about design principles (as the intentions behind a space are not understood by its occupants, and may be increasingly forgotten by support staff due to factors like staff turnover even if designers originally articulate their intentions well through staff presentations or brochures). Furthermore, many evaluators utilising detailed observations and other ethnographic data-gathering techniques may be influenced by theoretical traditions that disapprove of *a priori* assumptions - such as designers' suggestions about what a space is designed to accomplish - and wish instead to identify relevant themes from the data, as outlined by Melhuish (Chapters 2).

So Activity Support LS·e usually starts with observation, formulates conjectures about learning activities and attempts to map these back to spatial properties. When using these methods in the context of LS·e (as opposed to fundamental research), the idea is to subsequently compare findings against (reverse engineered) ideas about a space's design purpose. Such processes fit well with the *exploratory and descriptive evaluation of space* of our own Framework for the Evaluation of Learning Spaces (Pearshouse et al., 2009, p. 19). Such a model for LS·e closely borders scholarly research into teaching and learning, with a number of plausible models detailed within the literature (Radcliffe, 2008; Powell, 2008; Fraser, 2009; Pearshouse et al., 2009; Bielaczyc, 2006; Sandoval, 2004; Melhuish, Chapter 6). Yet at present, the Activity Support model is relatively uncommon in practice (Pearshouse et al., 2009, pp. 12–14), being heavily outnumbered by Scenario Provision programmes even where evaluators claimed to be investigating learning activities. Activity Support approaches allow for close examination of what Temple (2008, p. 234) terms micro-design, as well as designed flexibility (Watson, 2007, p. 260). The opportunities for design insight mean that Activity Support LS·e should be coupled with actual design processes so as to iteratively improve designs. Many of these approaches place emphasis on *coming to understand* the design objectives of the space, since they may be lost or only implicitly understood for reasons we have already seen. The Framework for Evaluating Learning Spaces (FELS), for example, encapsulates *what* is being evaluated through its Context, Practice and Design dimensions (Pearshouse et al., 2009, p. 21). The Theory of Change model used by Levy (cited in Pearshouse et al., 2009, p. 16) to evaluate spaces in the Sheffield Information Commons, negotiates theories about space to determine whether it 'met those targets through the routes expected' (Fraser, 2009, pp. 9–11). The Social Infrastructure Framework explicitly embodies conjectures within educational designs and identifies and refines those conjectures through research (Bielaczyc, 2006). If the methodology chosen does not allow *a priori* assumptions, then the coupling between processes will be necessarily looser, but it is still essential that conclusions are communicated back to designers in as accessible a manner as possible.

Within the literature, Bligh and Lorenz (2010, pp. 18–22) provide a micro-level spatial description of teaching within a small group seminar series, drawing attention to the physical affordances for teaching of space and technology. Crook and Mitchell (submitted) use an array of methods including audio diaries, scan sampled ethological observation, on-task conversations and focus groups to examine student behaviours within a technology-rich library setting. The methodological challenges of such approaches include:

– How can evaluations focussed on micro-design provide guidance broad enough for institutions to utilise?
– How can non-academic staff be supported in undertaking activities they may regard as 'research' and therefore the domain of academics? (Pearshouse et al., 2009, p. 4)
– How can links between design and evaluation processes be operationalised?
– What kind of knowledge is produced by these research-like evaluations?

This latter problem is particularly important, since significant problems are often encountered when *transferring* Learning Space designs to new locations. As Neary et al. (2010, p. 27) have noted, such problems are often derived from a failure to appreciate the wider contextual factors, which contribute to a design's success *in situ*, resulting in problems of conservatism as design ideas are superficially re-used again elsewhere without attempting either to recreate the wider original context or to adapt the design to its new setting. Evaluating situated activities produces knowledge that is inherently specific and *local* (Sandoval, 2004, p. 213), raising questions about the generalisability of LS·e conclusions and whether particular designs can ever be directly transferred to other contexts.

Spatial Ecology Model

Spatial Ecology LS·e highlights the fact that spaces derive much of their value from physical context and connectedness with other spaces. An *ecology* of Learning Spaces cannot be understood by simply evaluating each space individually, since it is likely to be affected positively or negatively by other provision within the ecology. For example, Temple (2008, p. 232) argues that centrally driven plans to increase space utilisation may reduce opportunities for informal learning. So a space provides benefit to students if its affordances complement other surrounding spaces (such as an informal area surrounded by lecture theatres), a fact which smaller scale, more intensive LS·e models such as the Activity Support model can fail to capture. Writing about *campuses* as learning spaces, Jamieson (2003) states that: 'Overall, a university campus needs spaces designed to generate interaction, collaboration, physical movement, and social engagement as primary elements of the student learning experience' (p. 121). Students also need a variety of space types which provide different opportunities; Wilson (2008, p. 20) suggests a suitable model of space types for post-compulsory education.

A prominent tool that takes into account this view is the Campus Mapping Profile of Neary et al. (2010). The tool evaluates campus expression, efficiency, and effectiveness – asking questions about identity and branding, condition and maintenance, circulation and permeability, flexibility, way-finding and orientation properties, effective use, and security. From an LS·e perspective, the tool provides a 'spatial framework within which the performance of the learning landscape can be considered' and a ''supply' side analysis of the estate against an institution's vision, allowing for a new method of 'Gap Analysis' [to] support prioritisation of possible areas of intervention' (ibid., p. 34). Another ecological method to analyse space is Space Syntax (Hillier, 1996/2007), a model based upon quantitatively understanding space as a *movement economy*, which operates at a variety of scales. Though we have yet to see examples of such work appear in the learning spaces literature, examples by Kaynar (2005), operating within open plan museums, provide a glimpse of how such techniques could be used to understand ecologies of spaces within post-compulsory education.

Brand Model

The fact that innovative learning spaces are sometimes conceived as grand architectural statements is often viewed negatively within the literature (Temple, 2008, p. 230), since architectural prestige is often seen to take precedence over learning and teaching considerations. Yet an emphasis on strong design image need not be counterposed against teaching and learning if it acts as a crucible for innovative new teaching and learning methods (instead of the more usual conservative reproduction or reactivity), if it demonstrates respect for students and staff, if it acts as a showcase for the pedagogical aspirations of management, and so on. From a US perspective, and perhaps more cynically, Graetz and Goliber (2002) argue that a central function of the 'brand' of a post-compulsory education institution is to generate student 'place attachment to their college' (p. 16), implying that greater student alumni contributions in the future will be the result. The Learning Spaces field needs to better problematise branding and identity considerations, but to retain our focus here on LS·e we restrict ourselves to a few brief points:
- Genuinely innovative new spaces may initially 'perform' less well than more conventional facilities (which reproduce well-understood socio-spatial cultural relations). Evaluating the institutional *prestige* of a new and innovative space may offset negativity and encourage a willingness to take risks which, it has been argued, is much needed in the field of learning spaces design (Watson, 2007, p. 256);
- It is important to link teaching and learning sites and campus master plans to institutional values and aspirations (Neary et al., 2010, p. 7);
- Attractive architecture plays a role in attracting prospective students, thus indirectly impacting on teaching and learning climates;
- Valuing space's 'iconic' status foregrounds maintenance issues, which may have a large impact on learning (Temple, 2008, p. 238).

FACTORS AFFECTING LEARNING SPACE EVALUATIONS

While this chapter divides LS·e into categories according to the ways in which they value space, there are cross-cutting factors, and we address a range of these here.

Initiation and Timescale

Many LS·e programmes seem to be initiated at the post-occupancy stage, are designed to catalogue 'quick wins' (Pearshouse et al., 2009, p. 11) and are conceived as one-off processes (ibid., p. 14). Though funding bodies and stakeholders may stipulate evaluation milestones (Roberts and Weaver, 2006, pp. 101–102), we would suggest that evaluations would be improved if they were:

- Undertaken at the proposal stage for learning spaces, as part of a process of competitive funding decisions (Powell, 2008, p. 28);
- More longitudinal, to better distinguish between 'factors arising out of novelty' and those remaining once a space is established (Roberts and Weaver, 2006, p. 102);
- Related to the life-spans and *capacity for change* (Watson, 2007, p. 257), of the different elements of the building (site, building structure, cladding, internal design, decoration, furniture, etc.);
- Ongoing, and *accessible* to those undertaking design projects (Neary et al., 2010, p. 21);
- Constructed to allow enough time for the necessary *trajectories of change* (Bielaczyc, 2006, p. 322) to occur.

Yet conversely, proposals for extensive, time-consuming evaluation need to be balanced against institutional needs for conclusions within practical timescales, especially if they are to inform policy and subsequent designs.

Relationship to Design Process

To produce better spaces, robust LS·e should be used as a basis to inform designs for other learning spaces (Powell, 2008, p. 27). As well as timescale co-ordination between evaluation and design processes, the literature points to the need for common language so that disparate, interdisciplinary teams can communicate successfully (Neary et al., 2010, p. 22; Thody, Chapter 9). Watson (2007, p. 261) has argued for the use of *metaphor* to describe learning spaces, giving examples such as 'the busy city', 'the airport departure lounge' and the 'domestic living room', which act to support rich conversations about design, whilst others are more critical and appeal for caution here (Boys, Chapter 4). There is also a need for evaluation and design processes to be documented (or to be *self-documenting*) (Radcliffe, 2008, p. 14), to ensure that principles remain explicit through multiple evaluation-design iterations. Also important is student and staff involvement in evaluation and design (Thomas, 2010, p. 503; Neary et al., 2010, p. 22), which can act to ground and enrich both processes.

The Identity of the Evaluators

LS·e activities have often been conducted by Estates teams (Roberts and Weaver, 2006, p. 102; Van Note Chism, 2002, p. 7), which allows work to be informed by institutional reality and outputs to be related to policy. But LS·e is an activity which involves making judgements about many factors, such as pedagogy and technology, which fall outside Estates' traditional areas of expertise. Thus, many LS·e programmes need to be carried out by interdisciplinary teams, which could involve technical support staff, academics, students, architects and Estates departments and others; crucially, these groups are themselves not internally uniform in outlook or specialism. Such problems of collaboration around LS·e have been addressed from various angles within the literature: Jamieson (2003, p. 123) considers it crucial that academic developers (trainers) are involved; Neary et al. (2010, p. 7) consider that the central issue is how academics, from disparate disciplines, communicate with Estates; Bligh and Lorenz (2010, p. 12) consider the situation to be a 'superset' of the collaboration which happens around educational technology roll-out; and Roberts and Weaver (2006, p. 104) consider the formation of new academic teams to address such issues. Crucially, LS·e programmes must involve sufficient personnel to influence policy. Therefore we would emphasise the need for dialogue between those concerned with policy (senior management), design (architects, estates professionals), pedagogy (academics, learning technologists) and experience (students, teachers, support staff), critically engaging with others in ways which acknowledge areas of relative expertise, including taking account of ecological considerations.

Data Gathering

Though many evaluators tend to distinguish between projects according to their data gathering techniques, above we have suggested that such techniques are secondary to the *values* of evaluation programmes (and to some extent, need to be derived from these values). Rather than attempting to provide a catalogue of data collection methods, here we content ourselves with a few key points:
- Evaluators should choose data collection and analysis techniques based upon *what they want to know* – rather than deciding which data is easy to collect, and then reverse engineering *what they claim to have wanted to know* (Pearshouse et al., 2009, p. 11);
- It is sensible to use pre-collected or automatically generated data if these genuinely relate to an evaluation's terms of reference;
- Evaluations need to be co-ordinated with wider institutional evaluation programmes – to avoid 'evaluation fatigue' (Roberts and Weaver, 2006, pp. 102–103) and to foment the notion, if possible, that LS·e is an important component of institutional evaluation strategies;
- It is worth considering immersive (interactive) modes of evaluation in addition to the 'harvesting' of data, for example, by using innovative spaces for workshops, enrolling Estates staff on academic modules to experience space from a different perspective, etc.

CONCLUSION

We have argued that the *model* of evaluation used, and the *values* which underpin it, define an evaluation programme better than surface-level features such as data collection mechanisms. Furthermore, since LS·e inevitably takes place within an institutional context, the skill of the evaluators is crucial in *balancing* an evaluation's core values against contextual constraints, in *relating* evaluation outputs to institutional contexts so that they can be used, and in rendering context *explicit* throughout the process (including in outputs) so as to minimise the risk of the learning space design being transferred to other locations in inappropriate, conservative or simply misunderstood ways. LS·e critiques the ways in which space affects learning and is a crucial site where non-academic staff (estates managers, technical and information professionals) can engage with issues outside their usual remit – pedagogy, student experience, and academic voice. The involvement of academics in such processes forces a focus on the physicality of their pedagogic and research practice, and the involvement of students can be empowering and enable ongoing processes of dialogue.

Since it is possible to read our JELS report (Pearshouse et al., 2009) as lamenting the lack of what we have here called Activity Support LS·e, it is important to state that we do not wish to privilege certain models of LS·e over others, though we do view the Outcomes Model as unhelpful in many practical contexts, and we argue that some Scenario Provision evaluations might better meet their own stated objectives if they were constructed differently. Generally though, as a result of programmatic triangulation or as a reaction to other evaluations, these models often co-exist. This ecosystem of LS·e models accurately reflects the fact that learning spaces are valuable in different ways, to different people, and can be interpreted at a variety of levels.

We would like to end by arguing for better *reporting* and dissemination of LS·e outcomes to other interested practitioners. There are still comparatively few in depth reports of evaluations, and fewer still which found significant problems with spaces or which highlight adoption obstacles. Furthermore, those commendable reports that do exist are often not widely disseminated in ways that mirror the distribution of research outputs (such as publication in peer-reviewed periodicals, or presentations at relevant conferences). Institutions do not relish embarrassment, yet progress in other investigative fields occurs because reports emphasise the *insights* that are gained rather than a specific project's success. Rigorously reported and properly disseminated LS·e outputs can provide experience of how spaces affect learning across a wide variety of contexts; also fuelling learning spaces itself as an important field of interdisciplinary enquiry which can explore the spatial implications of learning theories and, on that basis, go on to challenge those theories as evidence is accumulated and meta-analysed. Simultaneously, LS·e provides an opportunity to investigate the ways in which institutional context constrains learning activities and (under certain conditions) can contribute to a process of challenging those constraints politically by reporting problems upwards within institutional hierarchies and outwards to the post-compulsory education sector more widely. Were such a step change to be achieved for LS·e, then the resultant discussion around LS·e programmes might truly allow them to achieve their aim of incrementally improving learning space design, drawing more generalisable conclusions, and enabling suitable cross-transfer to other contexts, thereby impacting more usefully on learning.

REFERENCES

Astin, A. W. (1984/1999). Student involvement: A developmental theory for higher education. *Journal of College Student Development, 40*(5), 518–529.

Bielaczyc, K. (2006). Designing social infrastructure: Critical issues in creating learning environments with technology. *The Journal of the Learning Sciences, 15*(3), 301–329.

Bligh, B., & Lorenz, K. (2010). The rhetoric of multi-display learning spaces: Exploratory experiences in visual art disciplines. *Seminar.net: International Journal of Media, Technology and Lifelong Learning, 6*(1), 7–27.

Brooks, D. C. (in press). Space matters: The impact of formal learning environments on student learning. *British Journal of Educational Technology.*

Crook, C., & Mitchell, G. (submitted). Ambience in social learning: Student engagement with new designs for learning spaces. *Cambridge Journal of Education.*

Fraser, K. (2009). *Investigating how the theory of change approach can inform the evaluation of a learning space: Sheffield University's information commons.* Unpublished MA dissertation, The University of Sheffield, Sheffield.

Graetz, K. A., & Goliber, M. J. (2002). Designing collaborative learning places: Psychological foundations and new frontiers. *New Directions for Teaching and Learning, 92*, 13–22.

Hillier, B. (1996/2007). *Space is the machine.* London: Space Syntax.

Hunley, S., & Schaller, M. (2006). Assessing learning spaces. In D. G. Oblinger (Ed.), *Learning spaces.* Boulder, CO: Educause.

Hunley, S., & Schaller, M. (2009). Assessment: The key to creating spaces that promote learning. *Educause Review, 44*(2), 26–34.

Jamieson, P. (2003). Designing more effective on-campus teaching and learning spaces: A role for academic developers. *International Journal for Academic Development, 8*(1/2), 119–133.

Kaynar, I. (2005). Visibility, movement paths and preferences in open plan museums: An observational and descriptive study of the Ann Arbor Hands-on Museum. In A. Van Nes (Ed.), *5th International Space Syntax Symposium Proceedings* (Vol. II). Amsterdam: Techne Press.

NAO. (1996). *Space management in higher education: A good practice guide.* London: National Audit Office.

Neary, M., Harrison, A., Crellin, G., Parekh, N., Saunders, G., Duggan, F., et al. (2010). *Learning landscapes in higher education: Clearing pathways, making spaces, involving academics in the leadership, governance and management of academic spaces in higher education.* Lincoln: Centre for Educational Research and Development.

Pearshouse, I., Bligh, B., Brown, E., Lewthwaite, S., Graber, R., Hartnell-Young, E., et al. (2009). *A study of effective models and practices for technology supported physical learning spaces (JELS): Final report.* Bristol: Joint Information Systems Committee.

Powell, D. (2008). Evaluation and the pedagogy-space-technology framework. In D. Radcliffe, H. Wilson, D. Powell, & B. Tibbetts (Eds.), *Learning spaces in higher education: Positive outcomes by design.* St. Lucia: The University of Queensland.

Radcliffe, D. (2008). A pedagogy-space-technology (PST) framework for designing and evaluating learning places. In D. Radcliffe, H. Wilson, D. Powell, & B. Tibbetts (Eds.), *Learning spaces in higher education: Positive outcomes by design.* St. Lucia: The University of Queensland.

Roberts, S., & Weaver, M. (2006). Spaces for learners and learning: Evaluating the impact of technology-rich learning spaces. *New Review of Academic Librarianship, 12*(2), 95–107.

Sandoval, W. A. (2004). Developing learning theory by refining conjectures embodied in educational designs. *Educational Psychologist, 39*(4), 213–223.

SMG. (2006). *Space utilisation: Practice, performance and guidelines.* Lincoln: Space Management Group.

Temple, P. (2008). Learning spaces in higher education: An under-researched topic. *London Review of Education, 6*(3), 229–241.

Thomas, H. (2010). Learning spaces, learning environments and the dis'placement'of learning. *British Journal of Educational Technology, 41*(3), 502–511.

Van Note Chism, N. (2002). A tale of two classrooms. *New directions for teaching and learning, 92,* 5–12.

Warger, T., & Dobbin, G. (2009). *Learning environments: Where space, technology and culture converge.* ELI Paper 1. Boulder, CO: Educause.

Watson, L. (2007). Building the future of learning. *European Journal of Education, 42*(2), 255–263.

Wilson, H. (2008). The process of creating learning space. In D. Radcliffe, H. Wilson, D. Powell, & B. Tibbetts (Eds.), *Learning spaces in higher education: Positive outcomes by design.* St. Lucia: The University of Queensland.

CLARE MELHUISH

2. METHODS FOR UNDERSTANDING
THE RELATIONSHIPS BETWEEN LEARNING
AND SPACE

INTRODUCTION

The increasing impact of computer technology and other media on educational processes has stimulated a wave of recent research initiatives. These are directed at evaluating the benefits or otherwise of technological interventions in post-compulsory educational settings. This material, much of which is readily available online, provides a starting-point for an exploration of methods for understanding relationships between learning and space. However, whilst studies of the impact of new technologies on learning are adding to our knowledge of contemporary learning experiences, this paper will argue that - in order to understand how designed settings affect teaching and learning - research studies need to make space and its occupation central. It therefore explores the potential of using ethnographic research methods drawn from the disciplines of social anthropology and environmental psychology.

EVALUATING THE IMPACT OF TECHNOLOGY

Since 2005 the Joint Information Systems Committee (JISC) has commissioned a number of studies focussed on the impact of new learning technologies. The Lex study – research into learner experiences of e-learning (Mayes, 2006; Creanor et al., 2006) – was prompted by an awareness that although 'e-Learning is widely perceived as a learner-friendly mode of learning, offering alternative, self-paced and personalised ways of studying' (O'Brien and Beetham, 2008 p. 1), little was known at that time about learners' own perception of e-learning. The research was based on a sample of 55 mainly skilled digital learners (71% of whom were in employment) 'to avoid undue emphasis on the anxiety and frustration that frequently characterise those in the throes of learning new skills' (ibid., p. 5). The data was collected through face-to-face interviews, and Interview Plus (recall enhanced by reference to a blog or resources in an e-portfolio), using an Interpretative Phenomenology Approach (IPA), as popularised in healthcare research, a method I will return to later in this chapter. The key findings were that today's learners lead complex lives, requiring sophisticated time-management skills; that the boundaries between learning and other aspects of learners' lives are increasingly blurred; and that e-learning helps to negotiate those boundaries.

A. Boddington and J. Boys (eds.), Re-Shaping Learning: A Critical Reader: The Future of Learning Spaces in Post-Compulsory Education, 19–31.

Control and choice are of great importance – for example, being able to personalise the learning environment by selecting technologies meaningful to the learner – and, although learners value tutors who are fully engaged with e-learning, they also rely heavily on informal support networks. While older learners feel the young have an advantage, as a group, effective e-learners of all ages are flexible, resourceful, self-aware and highly motivated.

This study was followed by *LXP: Student Experiences of Technologies* (Conole, Darby et al., 2005–06), which explored disciplinary differences in uses of technology by university students through a variety of quantitative and qualitative methodologies, including an online survey, interviews and audio logs. This sample was much larger, involving some 400 learners across medicine, dentistry and veterinary medicine; economics; information and computer sciences, and languages and linguistics. The findings in this case were that e-learning resources are widely supplemented by personal technologies – mobile phones, laptops and PDAs – and that learners also make use of standard software to create, manipulate and present content. Internet search engines are preferred to libraries for information retrieval and, again, peer support provided by informal networks of friends and family, using email, texting, MSN® Messenger, chat or Skype™, provides an underworld of communication and information-sharing invisible to tutors, and one that comple-ments the work of tutors themselves. Learning is here approached as another form of consumer practice, where personal choice is of central importance.

In 2007, JISC funded a further study entitled the *Design and Management of Open Plan Technology-Rich Learning and Teaching Spaces* (Watson et al., 2007), which was more spatially focussed. It comprised 24 case studies of large, open-plan spaces, mostly on a library scale, within a variety of study environments. However, it did not include any evaluation of student responses to the new spaces. It did highlight the fact that the spatial setting hosts learning practices, which, in general, have become more social in nature, and that this can often cause problems, such as disruptive noise levels, mobile phone use, and food and drink consumption; another consistent problem was temperature control. One of the institutions included in the study (Glasgow Caledonian University) had carried out its own survey evaluation, which found its resource to be popular with users, but probably too lively for study at graduate level.

In 2008, JISC put out a podcast on 'student learning experiences' accompanied by a publication and CD-Rom, *In Their Own Words* (O'Brien and Beetham, 2008), which gave a platform to the 'voices' recorded in the earlier LEX and LXP studies. The conclusion was that, although the new communications technologies, including e-mail, instant messaging, message boards, and wikis were very useful in promoting flexible, open and personalised learning networks, characterised by both increased autonomy and increased social interaction, there were also some concerns. These were that there was a lack of training in the skills required to operate programmes such as PowerPoint, and that a minority of learners without their own equipment faced problems and were quickly disadvantaged and marginalised in an e-learning environment. This was followed in 2009 by a suite of tools and checklists for learner-centred evaluation based on this and further research into learners' perceptions of blended learning, the distinctive experiences of learners with disabilities and – in an important longitudinal study – how learners use technology differently as they progress from one stage of education to another' (O'Brien and Beetham, 2008 p. 4). In addition, Pearshouse et al. (2009) produced *A study of effective evaluation models and practices for technology-supported physical learning spaces*. This was undertaken on the basis that

> new spaces and technologies disrupt the old modes of teaching and learning as they are often based on a shift from a transmission model to a deliberately flexible, student-centred approach... the role space plays in creating productive higher education communities is not well understood.(p. 4)

The study looked further at the spatial implications of new technologies, and specifically investigated 'good practice' in methods of evaluation that have been and might be used to assess what design features of the new, technology-supported spaces contribute to learning (Bligh and Pearshouse, Chapter 1).

The UK government also commissioned a Committee of Inquiry into the Changing Learner Experience, headed by Professor Sir David Melville CBE, to consider the impact of the newest technologies such as social networking and mobile devices on the behaviour and attitudes of students coming up to and just entering higher education, and the issues they raise for universities and colleges. Published in 2009 under the title, *Higher education in a Web 2.0 world: report of an independent Committee of Inquiry into the impact on higher education of students' widespread use of Web 2.0 technologies*, it concluded that higher education has a key role, in partnership with students, to develop approaches to learning and teaching informed by the impact of ICT, but not only focusing on ICT-based teaching and learning:

> Rather it means adapting to and capitalising on evolving and intensifying behaviours that are being shaped by the experience of the newest technologies. In practice it means building on and steering the positive aspects of those behaviours such as experimentation, collaboration and teamwork, while addressing the negatives such as a casual and insufficiently critical attitude to information. The means to these ends should be the best tools for the job, whatever they may be. (Pearshouse et al 2009, p. 40)

RE-CENTRING PHYSICAL SPACE

Although JISC has commissioned some research into the implications of technology for the design of the physical setting of learning within the educational institution, there is a danger that the emphasis on technology *per se* and its implications for learning may lead to a neglect of spatial quality in the learning environment. As Paechter et al. (2001) point out, the advantages of 'virtual space' are that it effectively 'disembodies' learners, allowing 'alternative identities' to be developed, 'which are powerful and empowering' (2001, p. 3). However, where learning still takes place within the territory of the educational institution 'the localised contextual nature of learning' needs to be recognised; in other words, 'how we as embodied individuals are changed by our experiences in these spaces' (p. 1). Czordas, in his discussion of cultural phenomenology, draws attention to the fact that embodiment is a condition – that of being a 'bodily being', interacting with the world through the senses, not just the mind – that humans cannot escape, a fundamental dimension of experience (Czordas, 1999). Similarly, Paechter et al. (2001) stress that learning takes place not only in the mind, but 'embodied learners occupying particular spaces.' 'We have learned that ... the environmental conditions for learning (objects, people, symbols, and their relationships) are much more influential than we've previously thought...', write Trilling and Hood (Paechter et al., 2001, p. 14). In their 10-point challenge list (pp. 26–27), they underline the need to balance the 'virtual and the visceral' in the learning environment, to incorporate 'places for constructive tinkering', and for students to 'forget about technology once a day'. As Scott affirms later in the same volume, the 'situated' and 'socially embedded' (p. 40) dimensions of learning are fundamental to the experience of the process. And indeed, as Hirsch and Silverstone have shown in the domestic context, the experience of using technology must itself be understood as a situated and socially embedded experience which needs to be analysed with some care (Hirsch and Silverstone 1992).

The power of physical space to affect learning processes has been recognized by architects and educationalists since the end of the 19th century, resulting in many interesting European experiments in the design of schools and universities – see for example the work of Duiker, Teragni, Beaudoin and Lods, Dudok, Candilis Josic Woods (Berlin Free University), Lasdun (Hallfield School, London), Aalto, van Eyck, Scharoun (Geschwister-Scholl-Gymnasium, Lünen) and Hertzberger. In the main, the trend has been away from tight, regularised, hierarchical learning spaces, where the emphasis is on discipline and transmitted learning, and towards free-flowing, 'loose-fit', multi-purpose environments, which encourage individual creativity, social interaction and the confidence to shake off mental straightjackets and develop exploratory thought processes. As Dudek (2000) points out, designers working in these fields have drawn considerably in recent years on the emerging discipline of environmental psychology, including the work of authors such as Hall (cf. Hall in Proshansky et al., 1976), Lofland (1976), Lofland and Lofland (1995), Rapoport (1969), Goffman (1956, 1963) and others on the social use of space. Dudek's survey of new school architecture describes a renewed movement towards the

> encouragement of spaces which themselves further the development and learning of the child through his or her comprehension of space.... A consideration of more esoteric factors such as the effects on behaviour of colour, light and texture will be woven into the more practical aspects of designing for comfort, health and education (Dudek, 2000, p. xiv).

In addition, designers are paying increased attention to the relationship between interior and exterior, private and communal space, through the treatment of thresholds and boundaries; to the incorporation of specific cultural references where appropriate, the achievement of multivalent, non-hierarchical, and non-segregating spatial structures; and making integrated relationships between material and virtual space, focussing on how technology is installed and operated in learning spaces to balance the two.

Dudek makes a point of highlighting the drawbacks of computer technology, specifically at school-age level, but also in terms of the possible implications for human environmental awareness generally. As Paechter et al. (2001) acknowledge, virtual space can provide a valuable alternative to, and escape from, the restrictions and restraints potentially imposed by contested physical space. Dudek notes, in the context of children's interest in computer games, that 'part of the attraction lies in the visual and aural representation of three-dimensional spaces, which can be manipulated and effected by the operator'(Dudek 2000, p. 39). But the fact that most popular computer games are based on interactions which are essentially destructive in character is potentially problematic: 'a generation of children is developing a relationship with space, through their computers, which is obsessive and violent'. While this may sound extreme, Dudek's more general observation that 'their ability to develop an environmental awareness is limited, since the spaces of their computer are at best engaging only three of the senses' underlines a valid concern about the implications of this for the production and inhabitation of real space in future generations. These observations, in line with those of Paechter et al. (2001), suggest that, even as technology takes on an increasingly significant role within the learning environment, the quality of the physical setting, in terms of spatial form, colour, light and materiality becomes ever more important, in order to compensate for the potentially negative impacts of virtual space and interactions on embodied environmental awareness.

INVESTIGATING EMBODIED SPACE

Crucially though, physical qualities cannot be considered in absolute terms. Different individuals' experience of embodiment within particular settings, and their perception and response of the same settings may differ considerably, reflecting differences in age, gender, personality, physical characteristics and cultural and social experience. Gibson clearly states that 'perception of the environment is inseparable from perception of one's own body' (Gibson, 1977, p. 67). His key concept is of *affordances* - the physical properties (including other people) which a particular environment 'offers animals, what it provides or furnishes, for good or ill' (1977, p. 68) – both in terms of basic needs and a further 'astonishing variety of behaviours' (p. 75). This, however, does not address the significance of human temperamental, social and cultural diversity. Although certain qualities in an environment may be widely understood as beneficial or pleasurable, it cannot be assumed there will be a consensus over what makes a good or bad, successful or unsuccessful space. The wide variability in the conditions of human embodiment, cultural and social experience entails a level of complexity in evaluating the process of human interaction with spatial environments. Here, I want to next look at how this has been addressed through ethnographic research methods by some social anthropologists working in this area.

The anthropology of education - such as it exists - focuses on the social, political and moral aspects of educational processes in different cultural contexts. It has not examined the immediate spatial settings in which teaching and learning processes take place, or the impacts of spatial and material form (understood as a representation of particular social and cultural values) on those processes. According to Frederick Erickson, 'cognitive learning that has been deliberately taught' has been neglected altogether in anthropological studies, and he underlines the need for ethnographic inquiry into 'taught' cognitive learning. 'The literature of general ethnography contains few narrative accounts of taught cognitive learning... this might be because taught cognitive learning is seen by many anthropologists as school learning, a topic that has been avoided by anthropology...' (Erickson, 1982 p.149). In the field of social anthropology the most relevant literature to this discussion is that which specifically addresses spatial issues in the analysis of social relations and behavioural patterns, including literature which crosses the boundaries of social anthropology, geography and environmental psychology (e.g. Low & Lawrence-Zuniga, 2003; Katz, Mitchell & Marston, 2003). On the one hand, there is a danger in over-emphasising, or 'fetishising', the role of physical space in directing or determining human behaviours (Rogers & Vertovec, 1995) while neglecting to address underlying social issues, which may, in fact, be more significant. Social anthropologists such as Gans, for example, have underlined the fact that the effects of particular spatial and environmental conditions are not predictable, but contingent on the differences in lifestyles and socialisation of different social groups – they may be successful in one social context, but not in another (Gans, 1962). But others stress the importance of recognizing the role that physical space has to play in shaping behaviours and social rituals mapped onto space, and giving physical form to social structures and cultural dynamics. Space is not, then, neutral, pure or abstract, but has a significant role to play in terms of representing and, significantly, perpetuating social relations (Laguerre, 1990) – a fact which has been recognized by utopian urban thinkers and designers for centuries, with particularly dramatic results in the 20th century, as cities were radically redesigned in the services of new models of social organisation and bureaucracy (Pinder, 2005).

This understanding of the social and political potency of physical space lay at the heart of the urban and social theory propounded by French Marxist urbanists and sociologists during the 1960s and 1970s, notably Henri Lefebvre, who railed against the functionalist, rationalist reorganisation of urban social space in Europe (and its former colonies) during the post-war period as a manifestation of state-sponsored capitalism run by a technocratic elite (Lefebvre, 1991; Pinder, 2005). Anthropologists such as Chombart de Lauwe and Maurice Halbwachs engaged with planners and architects in a dialogue based on a structuralist analysis of urban and domestic space, reflecting the powerful influence of Levi-Strauss at the time, in order to reveal how it worked as a hierarchical, ordered system of potent symbolic elements. Bourdieu coined the term 'habitus' to describe the mesh of cultural, social, and physical elements, which makes up the specific environmental context of people's lives (Bourdieu, 1970, 1979). The effects of this debate were eventually to lead the French government to sponsor the first sociological investigations into the impact of the new urban housing and planning initiatives on people's lives and experience at the end of the 1960s and early 1970s, with a view to understanding the problems that they seemed to have created.

Although this might seem remote from the university environments and culture of higher education teaching and learning in the UK in the early 21st century, the ethnographic methods which were employed are of considerable relevance to the study in hand and others which seek to explore the implications of spatial form and layout for social experience and, specifically, processes of institutional teaching and learning from one site to another.

ETHNOGRAPHIC METHODS AND ANALYSIS

Augoyard's study of one of the new state housing projects at Grenoble (Augoyard, 1979/2007), which subsequently influenced de Certeau (de Certeau, 1979/1984), was a detailed phenomenological enquiry into the act of walking as a form of inhabitation of any particular environment. He calls it 'ambulatory practice', explaining that: 'daily strolls persistently confer value upon certain elements, spatial particularities that overflow the rightful functional partitions and shake up the territorial sequences' (Augoyard, 1979/2003, p. 73). He stressed the difference between the static, planned spaces designed by architects and planners, and 'lived space' as experienced phenomenologically, through the senses, through physical movement, and through the imagination, by inhabitants. Walking, move- ment, and the associated process of verbally naming, or describing, different elements of the environment, reveals much about the way different individuals relate to spaces and environments, and embodies the social dimension which activates and often also deconstructs the original formal intentions mapped out on the drawing board. In other words, design intentions may end up being derailed by the subsequent process of inhabitation in specific socio-spatial contexts, underlining the need for analysts to be cautious in attributing deterministic qualities to space itself.

Augoyard's analysis was based on detailed observation, mapping, photographic documentation, interviews, and a quasi-scientific notation of individuals moving around the housing project in the course of their daily business – the basic research methods of the ethnographer/anthropologist (Hammersley & Atkinson, 1983), but tempered by an aspiration towards objectivity, which was rejected by anthropologists of the hermeneutic, Geertzian school, who stressed the essentially personal and subjective character of interpretation. The phrase 'thick description' was coined by Geertz to refer to a process of cultural observation and interpretation, which drew inspiration from literary theory rather than the scientific-objective approach of French structuralism, and which presented culture in the form of a fiction written by the ethnographer (Geertz, 1973). Geertz's work was not specifically concerned with the intersection of culture and space, but his subjective, interpretative approach parallels that of the environmental and architectural phenomenologists who have promoted an understanding of space as subjectively perceived, through the senses and the imagination, by the individual – such that the same space may be experienced and described by different individuals in quite different ways (cf Seamon 2005).

Following this rubric, research into the relationship between people and their environment should be entered into free of any 'a priori' theory and concepts or predetermined methodological procedures. It is essentially an empirical method of study, wherein the researcher must remain fundamentally open-minded as to s/he observes in the field, what responses s/he may elicit from respondents, and what those responses may signify. These are the accepted fundamental principles of any ethnographic research, where the ethnographer, as 'author', must aim to set aside any preconceptions and personal bias when entering the field so as to draw out rather than prompt responses from participants; whilst ultimately acknowledging, through the process of interpreting the data, the ways in which the final analysis is shaped by the inescapable conditions of the author's own background and prior experience. This is very clearly set out by Clifford, who underlines the centrality of the process of writing or making texts itself to what anthropologists do (Clifford & Marcus, 1986), and the fact that the cultural accounts which ethnographers/ anthropologists produce should be understood as 'true fictions' – constructed, artificial and invented – rather than as a set of objective, scientific truths. Ethnographic writing, he argues, is essentially an art form, which, as he demonstrates (Clifford, 1988), has been closely linked historically to literature and fine art practices, especially French Surrealism in the 1920s, with which it shared an interest in the techniques of collage and juxtaposition and the cultural valorisation of impurity and syncretism over and above rationalism and order.

LEARNING FROM HEALTHCARE STUDIES?

Ethnographic methodology has, however, gained currency in recent healthcare research (in a somewhat limited form based heavily on the collection of verbal data). Here it is largely known as Interpretative Phenomenology Approach or IPA. It was initially seen as a radical approach, in contrast to the behaviourist paradigmatic methods of traditional psychology, because it premised the participant's view rather than that of the researcher. This required the establishment of a rapport between participant and researcher in order to draw out insights that could not be achieved through the old, objectifying methods. Smith and Osborn state that 'the main currency for an IPA study is the meanings particular experiences, events, states hold for participants ... it involves detailed examination of the participant's lifeworld ... personal experience ... personal perception...' (Smith & Osborn, 2003, p. 51). The researcher must make sense of that personal world through the process of empathetic, interpretative activity – in other words it is a 'double hermeneutic'. They point out that it owes a debt to the school of symbolic interactionism (with ref to Denzin, 1995), which set out to explore how meanings are constructed and communicated by individuals interacting in a social and personal world.

IPA emphasises the need for in-depth, qualitative research, as opposed to quantitative and experimental methodology. It favours small samples of respondents,

and painstaking, detailed analysis on a case-by-case basis, rather than the construction of generalizations through the use of large-scale survey techniques and
questionnaires associated with conventional sociological research. Semi-structured
interviews are regarded as the best way to collect data, rather than written personal
accounts, diaries, etc., since they allow researcher and participant to engage in a
dialogue, and provide the researcher with the flexibility to probe any interesting
areas that may arise during the course of the conversation. As Clifford points out,
'verbal structures ... determine all representations of reality' (Clifford and Marcus,
1986, p. 10), emphasising the importance of the spoken word to our understanding
of cultural behaviours. However, in ethnographic practice, verbal accounts form
only one part of the cultural data to be collected, along with visual and textual
evidence and detailed observation of behavioural patterns - all of which is
subjected to a process of decoding and recoding in the effort to understand the
complex social forms, conventions and institutions which humans engage in and
construct around themselves. In IPA, by contrast, it is the recorded and transcribed
interview that constitutes the primary raw material for interpretation, directed
towards the identification of significant themes ('coding') and comparative analysis
of those themes across the sample.

Smith, Jarman and Osborn (1999) clearly distinguish IPA from Discourse
Analysis, which, following trends in linguistics and semiotics, emphasises the
importance of language itself as a clear and objective measure of human intention
and perception, capable of scientific de-coding:

> DA regards verbal reports as behaviours in their own right which should be
> the focus of functional analyses. IPA by contrast is concerned with cognitions,
> that is, with understanding what the particular respondent thinks or believes
> about the topic under discussion. Thus IPA, while recognizing that a person's
> thoughts are not transparently available from, for example, interview transcripts,
> engages in the analytic process in order, hopefully to be able to say some-
> thing about that thinking. (Smith, Jarman & Osborn, 1999, p. 219)

The process of 'coding' in IPA involves identifying, from the raw material (and not
a priori) relevant themes that can be used to describe specific aspects of individual
and shared experience. Smith, Jarman and Osborn cite some examples – e.g. 'types
of relationship' (within a medical setting), specifically 'types of nurse-patient
relationship', might be defined as either parental/ partnership/ supervisory, or
friendship – or different combinations of those. The 'nursing role' theme might
be defined as: caring-loving/ responsibility/ human-nursing/ demanding-tiring/
and or wanting to help. And the 'features of relationship' might include: trust/
resistance/ involvement/ distance/ emotions/ anger, etc. They stress that the
process of analysis in IPA is essentially personal and interpretative. As in the
ethnography practiced by anthropologists, the creative, speculative, and intuitive
approach means that one person's interpretation of the raw data may be quite
different from another's. There can be no objective 'truth' as such. But, on the
other hand, there will be unique, qualitative insights that could not have been
delivered by any other route.

ILLUMINATING RELATIONSHIPS BETWEEN LEARNING AND SPACE

This chapter has explored methods for better understanding relationships between learning and the physical space in which it takes place. In Chapter 6 in this volume I will develop this approach through a case study (see also Boys, 2010). Finally, it should be noted that the methods recommended here are not intended to result in either design 'solutions' or guidance on how to design new physical spaces for post-compulsory education. This follows Parlett and Hamilton (1972) who argue that the primary concern of evaluative research 'is description and interpretation rather than measurement and prediction' (pp. 10–11) so as 'to contribute to decision-making'. As they go on to write:

> Each group or constituency will look to the [research] report for help in making different decisions. [...] A decision based on one group's evaluative criteria would, almost certainly, be disputed by other groups with different priorities. A 'mastery of fundamentals' for one group is, for another, a 'stifling of creativity. [...]

> Illuminative evaluation thus concentrates on the information-gathering rather than the decision-making component of evaluation. The task is to provide a comprehensive understanding of the complex reality (or realities) surrounding the program: in short, to illuminate. In [their research], therefore, the evaluator aims to sharpen discussion, disentangle complexities, isolate the significant from the trivial, and to raise the sophistication of the debate. (Parlett & Hamilton, 1972, pp. 31–32)

REFERENCES

a. Technology Focus

Ari, R. (2006). Expanding the boundaries through the use of technology in informal learning spaces. In *TenCate SIGUCCS '06: Proceedings of the 34th annual ACM SIGUCCS conference on user services*.
Barker, L. J., Garvin-Doxas, K., & Roberts, E. (2005). 'What can computer science learn from a fine arts approach to teaching?' SESSION: The first year: Studies of student performance. *ACM SIGCSE Bulletin, 37*(1), 421–425.
Carbone, A., & Sheard, J. (2002). A studio-based teaching and learning model in IT: What do first year students think? In *Annual joint conference integrating technology into computer science education. Proceedings of the 7th annual conference on innovation and technology in computer science education* (pp. 213–217).
Conole, G., Laat, M. de, Dillon, T., & Darby, J. (2005–2006). *LXP: Student experiences of technologies*. JISC.
Creanor, L., Gowan, D., Trinder, K., & Howells, C. (2006). *LEX: The learner experience of e-Learning – Final project report*. JISC.
Denk, J., & Fox, L. (2008). The evolution of learning spaces. In *Proceedings of the 36th annual ACM SIGUCCS conference on user services* (pp. 199–202).
Dodero, J. M., Camino F., & Sanz, D. (2003). An experience of students' participation in blended vs. online styles of learning. In *ACM SIGCSE bulletin* (Vol. 35, p. 4). New York.
Ertl, H., Hayward, G., Wright, S., Edwards, A., Lunt, I., Mills, D., et al. (2007). *The student learning experience in higher education: Literature review report for the Higher Education Academy*. HEA. Retrieved from http://www.heacademy.ac.uk/projects/detail/lr_2007_hayward

Evaluating Learning Spaces, Flashlight Tools, TLT Group (Teaching, Learning and Technology). Retrieved from http://www.tltgroup.org/Flashlight/Handbook/Learning_Spaces_Eval.htm

Janz, K. D., & Moore, M. (2007). Envisioning new learning spaces: Creating a center for visualization at Indiana State University. In *SIGUCCS '07: Proceedings of the 35th annual ACM SIGUCCS conference on user services.*

Holley, D. L. (2008). *Spaces and places: Negotiating learning in the context of new technology.* PhD thesis, University of London: London.

Jeffers, D. (2008). Is there a second life in your future? In *Proceedings of the 36th annual ACM SIGUCCS conference on user services* (pp. 187–190).

Kerr, S. T. (1996). Technology and the future of schooling. In S. T. Kerr (Ed.), *Yearbook of the national society for the study of education.* Chicago: NSSE.

King, A. (1993). From sage on the stage to guide on the side. *College Teaching, 41*(1), 30–35.

Laurillard, D. M. (1993). *Rethinking university teaching: A framework for the effective use of educational technology.* London: Routledge.

Learners' Experience of e-Learning programme, JISC (suite of tools, final versions avail from Mar '09: checklists for practitioners and a learner-centered evaluation toolkit). Retrieved from http://www.jisc.ac.uk/whatwedo/campaigns/studentexperiences/studentperspective.aspx

Lex project (learner experiences of e-learning). (2005). JISC.

Mayes, T. (2006). *LEX: Methodology report.* JISC. Retrieved from www.jisc.ac.uk/elp_learneroutcomes

O'Brien, R., & Beetham, H. (2008). *Student learning experience*, podcast for JISC (Joint Information Systems Committee) & 'In their own words – investigating the learners' experience of e-learning' (associated publication).

Pearshouse, I., Bligh, B., Brown, E., Lewthwaite, S., Graber, R., Hartnell-Young, E., et al. (2009). *A study of effective evaluation models and practices for technology supported physical learning spaces.* JISC (see associated learning study plan). Retrieved from http://www.jisc.ac.uk/whatwedo/projects/learningspaces08.aspx

Razavi, M. N., & Iverson, L. (2006). A grounded theory of information sharing behavior in a personal learning space. In *CSCW '06: Proceedings of the 2006 20th anniversary conference on computer supported cooperative work.*

Report of an independent Committee of Inquiry into the impact on higher education of students' widespread use of Web 2.0 technologies. (2009). *Higher education in a Web 2.0 world.* JISC. Retrieved from http://www.jisc.ac.uk/publications/generalpublications/2009/heweb2.aspx

Watson, L., Anderson, H., & Strachan, K. (2007). *Design and management of open plan technology-rich learning and teaching spaces study.* JISC. Retrieved from http://www.jiscinfonet.ac.uk/themes/tele

Webster, L. D., & Mirielli, E. J. (2007). Student reflections on an academic service learning experience in a computer science classroom. In *Conference on Information Technology Education (formerly CITC). Proceedings of the 8th ACM SIGITE conference on information technology education, Destin, FL. SESSION: Ethics and service learning* (pp. 207–212).

b. Ethnography, Space and Learning

Augoyard, J.-F. (1979/2007). *Step by step: Everyday walks in a French urban housing project.* Minneapolis, MN/London: University of Minnesota Press.

Bourdieu, P. (1970). The Kabyle house or the world reversed. In *The logic of practice* (pp. 271–283). Cambridge: Polity Press.

Bourdieu, P. (1979/1984). *Distinction: A social critique of the judgement of taste.* London: Routledge.

Bourdieu, P., & Passeron, J.-C. (1990). *Reproduction in education, society, and culture* (T. Bottomore (Foreword) & R. Nice, Trans.). London; Newbury Park, CA: Sage, in association with *Theory, Culture & Society*, Dept. of Administrative and Social Studies, Teesside Polytechnic.

Boys, J. (2010). *Towards creative learning spaces: Re-thinking the architecture of post-compulsory education.* London and New York: Routledge.

De Certeau, M. (1979/1984). *The practice of everyday life*. Berkeley, CA; London: University of California Press.

Denzin, N. (1995). *The cinematic society: The voyeur's gaze*. London: Sage.

Dudek, M. (2000/2002). *Architecture of schools: The new learning environments*. Oxford: Architectural Press.

Clifford, J., & Marcus, G. (Eds.). (1986). *Writing culture: The poetics and politics of ethnography*. Berkeley, CA: University of California Press.

Clifford, J. (1988). *The predicament of culture: Twentieth-century ethnography, literature and art*. Cambridge, MA; London: Harvard University Press.

Cole, M., et al. (1971). *The cultural context of learning and thinking: An exploration in experimental anthropology*. London: Methuen.

Colomina, B. (1992). Domestic Voyeurism. In B. Colomina (Ed.), *Sexuality and space* (pp. 73–128). Princeton Papers on Architecture. New York: Princeton Architectural Press.

Czordas, T. (1999). Embodiment and cultural phenomenology. In G. Weiss & H. Haber (Eds.), *Perspectives on embodiment: The intersections of nature and culture* (pp. 143–162). London: Routledge.

Denzin, N. K. & Lincoln, Y. S. (Eds.). (1998). *Collecting and interpreting qualitative materials*. London: Sage.

Erickson, F. (1982). Taught cognitive learning in its immediate environments: A neglected topic in the anthropology of education. *Anthropology and Education Quarterly, 13*(2), 149–180.

Gans, H. (1962). *The urban villagers: Group and class in the life of Italian-Americans*. New York: Free Press of Glencoe.

Gaver, W. H., Dunne, A., & Pcenti, E. (1999a). Cultural probes. In *Interactions: The Journal of Mental Health Nursing, 6*(1), 21–29.

Geertz, C. (1973). Thick description: Toward an interpretive theory of culture. In *The interpretation of cultures: Selected essays* (pp. 3–30). New York: Basic Books.

Gibson, J. J. (1977). The theory of affordances. In R. Shaw & J. Bransford (Eds.), *Perceiving, acting and knowing: Toward an ecological psychology*. Hillsdale; New York; London: Erlbaum.

Goffman, E. (1956). *The presentation of self in everyday life*. Edinburgh: University of Edinburgh, Social Sciences Research Centre.

Goffman, E. (1963). *Behaviour in public places*. New York: Glencoe Free Press.

Hall, E. T. (1976). The anthropology of space. In Prohansky, Ittelson, & Rivlin (Eds.), *Environmental psychology: People and their physical settings* (p. 158). New York: Holt Rinehart and Winston.

Hammersley, M., & Atkinson, P. (1983). *Ethnography: Principles in practice*. London: Tavistock Publications.

Hirsch, E., & Silverstone, R. (1992). *Consuming technologies: Media and information in domestic spaces*. London: Routledge.

Katz, C. (Ed.), with Mitchell, K., & Marston, S. A. (2003). *Life's work: Geographies of social reproduction*. Oxford: Blackwell.

Laguerre, M. (1990). *Urban poverty in the urban Caribbean: French Martinique as a social laboratory*. Basingstoke: Macmillan.

Lefebvre, H. (1991). *The production of space*. Oxford: Blackwell.

Lock, M., & Farquhar, J. (2007). *Beyond the body proper: Reading the anthropology of material life*. Durham, NC: Duke University Press.

Lofland, J., & Lyn, H. (1995). *Analyzing social settings: A guide to qualitative observation and analysis*. Belmont, CA: Wadsworth Publishing.

Lofland, L. (1976). The modern city: spatial ordering. In H. M. Proshansky, W. H. Ittelson, & L. G. Rivlin (Eds.), *Environmental psychology: People and their physical settings*. New York: Holt, Rinehard and Winston.

Low, S. M., & Lawrence-Zuniga, D. (2003). *Anthropology of space and place: Locating culture*. Oxford: Blackwell.

McCleod, M. (2000). Everyday and "Other" spaces. In Rendell, Borden, & Penner (Eds.), *Gender space architecture: An interdisciplinary discussion* (pp. 182–202). London: Routledge.

Melhuish, C. (1996). *Architecture and anthropology*. Architectural Design Profile 124. London: Academy Editions.

Norman, D. (1988). *The design of everyday things*. New York: Doubleday.

Paechter, C. F., Harrison, R., & Edwards, R. (2001). *Learning, space and identity*. London: Sage.

Paillard, J. (Ed.). (1991). *Brain and space*. Oxford: Oxford University Press.

Pallasmaa, J. (1994, July). An architecture of the seven senses. In *A+U special issue: questions of perception: Phenomenology of architecture* (pp. 27–38).

Parlett, M. R., & Hamilton, D. (1972). *Evaluation as illumination: A new approach to the study of innovatory programmes*. Workshop at Cambridge, and unpublished report Occasional paper 9, Centre for research in the educational sciences, University of Edinburgh.

Pinder, D., (2005). *Visions of the city: Utopianism, power and politics in 20th-century urbanism*. Edinburgh: Edinburgh University Press.

Rapoport, A. (1969). *House form and culture*. Englewood Cliffs, NJ: Prentice-Hall.

Rogers, A., & Vertovec, S. (1995). *The urban context: Ethnicity, social networks, and situational analysis*. Oxford: Berg.

Ryave, A. L., & Schenkein, J. N. (1974). Notes on the art of walking. In R. Turner (Ed.), *Ethnomethodology* (pp. 65–274). Harmondsworth: Penguin.

Sacks, H. (1984). On doing being ordinary. In J. M. Atkinson & J. C. Heritage (Eds.), *Structures of social action* (pp. 413–429). Cambridge: Cambridge University Press.

Seamon, D. (n.d.). Phenomenology, place, environment and architecture: A review. *Environmental and Architectural Phenomenology Newsletter*. Retrieved from http://www.arch.ksu.edu/seamon/Seamon

Smith, L., Jarman, M., & Osborne, M. (1999). Doing interpretative phenomenological analysis. In M. Murray & K. Chamberlain (Eds.), *Qualitative health psychology*. London: Sage.

Smith, J. A., & Osborn, M. (2003). Interpretative phenomenological analysis. In J. A. Smith (Ed.), *Qualitative psychology: A practical guide to methods*. London: Sage.

Swales, J. M. (1998). *Other floors, other voices: A textography of a small university building*. Mahway, NJ; London: Lawrence Erlbaum.

Smith, P. (1974). *The design of learning spaces: A report on a one-year pilot investigation, carried out in 1973 for the former National Council for Educational Technology*. London: Council for Educational Technology for the United Kingdom.

Spencer, C., & Blades, M. (2006). *Children and their environments: Learning, using, and designing spaces*. Cambridge, UK; New York: Cambridge University Press.

Tilley, C. (Ed.). (1994). Space, place, landscape and perception: Phenomenological perspectives. *A phenomenology of landscape* (pp. 7–34). Oxford: Berg.

JOS BOYS AND HILARY SMITH

3. WHAT DO WE KNOW ABOUT WHAT IS BEING BUILT?

New Typologies of Learning Spaces

INTRODUCTION

Over the last decade there have been many arguments in favour of new types of 'informal' learning spaces for post-compulsory education (Joint Information Systems Committee (JISC), 2006; Tertiary Education Facilities Management Association (TEFMA), 2006; Oblinger, 2006; Scottish Funding Council, 2006; Jamieson, 2008; Neary et al., 2010). These typically emphasise student-centred, playful, interactive and technology-rich environments. Just as importantly, such spaces are almost always set in opposition to a perceived norm of dull lecture halls, populated by dry pontificating professors lecturing to large groups of bored and passive students. Debate, then, is often framed around a simple binary and self-justifying good-bad division between such informal and formal learning spaces. In this chapter we want instead to first explore what learning spaces are actually being designed for post-compulsory education in the current period (concentrating on the UK), and then examine the interrelationships between specific built examples and the dominant ideas and debates circulating around and between educational, architectural and estates planning experts. We will suggest that:

– Whilst many good examples of innovative learning spaces are being built, a specific subset of these tends to circulate widely, leading to potential problems with both citation distortion and the developing evidence base of 'good' examples.
– There are an increasing number of innovative learning environments that incorporate ideas of informal rather than formal learning, suggesting that the new typology is already becoming part of the mainstream
– The focus on informal learning environments in many current educational debates has made invisible other kinds of new learning environments, which can also help inform our understanding of appropriate learning spaces for post-compulsory education in the 21st century.
– We urgently need more research on the spatial and design implications of different forms of post-compulsory learning; both new 'informal' environments and other ways of designing learning spaces

As with Bligh and Pearshouse (Chapter 1) we believe that learning space design remains under-researched and poorly evaluated. So, rather than merely providing some contemporary examples of 'good' learning design this chapter will instead question how and why certain kinds of physical learning environment are offered

A. Boddington and J. Boys (eds.), Re-Shaping Learning: A Critical Reader: The Future of Learning Spaces in Post-Compulsory Education, 33–47.

up as exemplary and critically examine some of the gaps and complications in such framings – what ideas are being reinforced and what left out. In particular, we suggest that the complexities of relationships between learning and the space in which it takes place are being avoided here, through a tendency to resort to simplistic spatial and aesthetic metaphors. Whilst metaphor or analogy can be a creative generator of ideas about different kinds of learning spaces (Table 3.1) it is

Table 3.1. Examples of informal learning design in the UK
(reprinted from Boys, 2010 pp. 20–21)

Learning space	Environment	Design attributes
Saltire Centre, Glasgow Caledonian University http://www.gcu.ac.uk/thesaltirecentre/ (2006, BDP architects) Library, atrium, internet café, informal learning, flexible study spaces, technology-rich environment, landmark building, art commission		"Using the idea that learning begins with a conversation, we created a wide range of environments to stimulate thought or discussion. These included group areas, cafés, incidental places on circulation routes, silent 'monk cells' and terraced south-facing garden areas." (http://www.bdp.com/Projects/By-Name/P-Z/Saltire-Centre/ accessed 16/05/10)
Telford College, Edinburgh www.ed-coll.ac.uk/ (2006, HOK Architects) Social hub, atrium, internet café, learning streets, open-access computer labs, flexible study spaces, technology-rich environment		"The college includes a wide variety of learning environments equipped with 'touchdown' desks for students to freely use the internet and to work on assignments. Providing natural light and ventilation to the classrooms on either side, the Learning Streets avoids the 'corridor' effect typical of large education establishments." (.http://www.hok.com/ accessed 16/05/10)
Learning Grid, University of Warwick www2.warwick.ac.uk/ (2004, MJP Architects) Library, atrium, student resource centre, informal learning, technology-rich environment, flexible study spaces, artwork commission		"MJP used a range of screens and furniture to create a loose arrangement of working areas that the students can reconfigure to suit their changing needs. Curves, colours and textured materials are used to create a lively environment - and as a reaction against other facilities which provide dreary rows of computer desks." (http://www.mjparchitects.co.uk/Learning_Grid.php accessed 16/05/10)
Centre for Inquiry-based Learning in the Arts and Social Sciences (CILASS), and Information Commons, University of Sheffield. www.shef.ac.uk/cilass/ (2007, RMJM architects) Information Commons, open-access computer labs, informal learning, flexible study spaces, technology-rich environment		"Provides a 24/7 integrated learning environment for undergraduate and postgraduate students. It provides 1,350 new study spaces where students can study individually or in groups, using print and electronic materials. It has been designed to accommodate current and future learning methods and technologies." (http://www.rmjm.com/projects/information-commons-university-of-sheffield-england accessed 16/05/10)
Techno-café, Department of Computer Science, University of Durham http://www.dur.ac.uk/alic/technocafe/ (2006, P H Partnership) internet café, informal learning, flexible study space, technology rich environment		"The client required an innovative computer lab which offered interactive space for people to socialise during group work sessions. Work Pods encapsulating state of the art AV technology and interactive tablet PCs were developed within a modern interior and functional space to offer a hint of techno chic. Pods clad in translucent polycarbonate material, were backlit to provide a soft-lit environment." (http://www.phparchitects.co.uk/?section=technocafe.php accessed 16/05/10)
InQbate Creativity Zone, University of Sussex http://www.inqbate.co.uk/ (2006, University of Sussex) Immersive environment, new technologies, flexible teaching and learning space, teaching creativity		"Fully technology-enabled, but not technology-driven, the Sussex creativity zone provides teaching staff with personal, pedagogic and technical support, along with resources that can be used in a variety of configurations. It is hoped that this will support more innovative and effective teaching and learning in both the InQbate creativity zone itself as well as other teaching spaces on campus." (http://www.inqbate.co.uk/content/view/33/97/ accessed 16/05/10)

often used to enable a kind of slippage, which can make invisible other ways of thinking (Boys, chapter 4). The reliance on metaphor means that innovative design intentions and concepts come to be seen as transparently and obviously the same as their intended realisation and impact, such that for example, the appearance of a playful environment automatically means students will both have fun and learn informally. One is naturally 'like' the other. Here we will argue that we need to be much more careful in separating out design intentions from both their translation into actual form, and from the lived experiences of different occupants; and in developing methods for evaluating the impact of different kinds of designed spaces on learning.

CURRENT EXAMPLES AND TERMINOLOGIES

We began our study by exploring which examples of new learning spaces – and the design languages associated with them – were being used in key texts. These examples have influenced debates over the last 2 years, as evidenced by their repeated citation across sources, as well as mentions at conferences, etc. (Table 3.2). It should be noted that we need to be wary of merely repeating examples from previous literature as 'obvious' good practice, where there is a lack of explicit supporting evaluation evidence that the space has had a successful impact on learning.

Table 3.2. Example pattern of citations of UK learning space examples

	Joint Info Systems Committee (JISC) 2006	*Watson, L. et al, 2007*	*Birming- ham uni LDU, 2005*	*Scottish Funding Council, 2006*	*Harrison, A. & Cairns, A, 2008*	*Neary et al, 2010*
Learning Gateway, St Martin's College, Uni of. Cumbria	x	x				2
Telford FE College, Edinburgh	x			x	x	3
The Saltire Centre, Glasgow Caledonian University	x	x	x	x		4
Civic Quarter Library, Leeds Met University	x		x			2
South East Essex FE College	x		x			2

Table 3.2. (Continued)

InterActive Classroom, Uni. of Strathclyde	x	x		2
The Learning Grid, University of Warwick	x	x	x	3
CETL in Creativity, University of Sussex	x			1
The Hive, Queen Mary, University of London			x	1
White Space, University of Abertay				0

As already noted, in the UK the focus has been on informal and social learning spaces; with some work also on shared research areas and on academic workplaces. The new kinds of learning spaces in these reports offer a range of design metaphors and physical arrangements, all of which tend to centre on a certain set of associated ideas. Spaces are envisaged as enabling collaboration and interaction (both educational and social), articulated, for example, as 'atrium', 'street', 'hub', 'drop-in centre' and 'learning café'; particular spatial layouts for enabling a range of group and individual study combinations in space, such as learning 'nooks', 'pods', 'nexus' and 'clusters'; a tendency to informal, 'softer' furniture such as beanbags, asymmetric furniture layouts, bright colours and 'landmark' elements such as special features or artist commissions; and finally, an emphasis on what are usually called technology-rich environments. A good example of this kind of design vocabulary is Telford College in Edinburgh, designed by HOK Architects in 2006. Here, the central student social area is combined with the main entrance and reception to make a space that integrates the public and students, with the explicit intention of 'making the whole campus accessible and welcoming to the wider community'. Café-style tables are laid out beneath a double-height top-lit and arched space known as the 'Hub', lined on each side by a range of services in single-height wings, like shops. Student Services, a hairdressing salon, a beauty therapy salon, food stalls and a college restaurant are thus intermixed. In addition, the college provides a series of 'learning streets' as each level. These are wide corridors that contain open access computing facilities, as well as a series of study alcoves, and act as 'spines' to rows of classrooms and workshop facilities.

Similarly, the Saltire Centre, Glasgow Caledonian University – another frequently referenced example – is based on a large, shared space. The Saltire library centres around glass atrium and exhibition space, five storeys high, which 'in addition to providing maximum natural lighting [...] will aid natural ventilation and environmental control within the building', and is here linked to one 'street' – a student services mall – this time offering 'a one- stop- shop for our students, enabling them to access all of the services that they might need in a single location' (http://www.gcu.ac.uk/thesaltirecentre/building/index.html). There is a 'learning café' for 'relaxed group study space', outdoor terraces, and a variety of seating arrangements and types, as well as two 'landmark' artists' commissions. But whilst Telford uses the key elements (hub + learning streets) as a means to structure the layout of the whole building, Saltire is designed to provide a variety of different spaces, from noisy social interaction areas for group work, to places for silent study. It was also intended that this flexibility would enable staff 'to experiment further with student-centred, active learning approaches'.

From these and other examples, it seems that a series of new design types are already coming into such common usage as to potentially be the new norm, around this language of 'hubs' 'streets', 'clusters' and 'beanbags'. This is not to suggest that such spaces are 'wrong' or not well designed. Rather it is to raise several important questions that are not often asked. How are these new typologies being developed and justified and what forms of evidence and evaluation support them? Has there been any 'citation distortion', that is, concentration on, and repetition of, certain examples rather than others? Are these new kinds of environment enhancing learning as predicted, and if so, where is the evaluation evidence? Are there other useful design examples that tend to be ignored in the literature and if so, why? How do these particular design concepts, framed at the level of learning encounters, connect to other terminologies more prevalent at the level of the educational institution such as 'sense of place' (Dober, 1992; Temple, Chapter 10). Does this recent addition of new types of learning space provide for the full range of learning in post-compulsory education, or are there important gaps and alternatives which are not being considered?

To investigate what other examples of learning spaces in post-compulsory education were *not* being cited in theses debates, we looked at the listings in architectural magazines for a randomly selected period. As expected, there are many, many examples of buildings being designed for universities, colleges and other institutions, especially given that in the UK there had been (until recently) a major capital building programme in both the post-compulsory education and schools sectors. Even the most desultory search of some online UK architectural journals from January to July 2010 showed newly designed examples of learning spaces in post-compulsory education that ranged from a banquet created out of cardboard by architecture students at the University of Cambridge (http://www.arplus.com/9298/cardboard-banquet-cambridge-uk-by/); via Thomas Heatherwick's latest project – eight units for artists/craftspeople/creative industry types on the campus of Aberystwyth University - and a waterfront building at the University Campus Suffolk, Ipswich; to more fully fledged architectural projects at Downing College Cambridge, Nottingham University (Bioscience Building), University of Liverpool (Library), Edinburgh University (School of Informatics), Trinity University College, Carmarthen, Wales (new teaching block), University of East London (Cass School of Education), Fitzwilliam College Cambridge (Library and IT Centre), University of Essex, (new Business School and Library extension) and Kings

College London (Neuroscience Institute). Of course, it is obvious – when we think about it – that the range of potentially good examples of learning spaces for post-compulsory education is enormous. The more crucial point here, then, is the problem of just how we can engage with such a large number of already built examples; and how we can begin to understand from all of these what does and doesn't work for different learning contexts and requirements.

LOOKING BEYOND 'INFORMAL' LEARNING SPACES

In order to do this, we need to do (at least) two things. As already mentioned, we need to be more critical of the learning spaces examples currently in general circulation by, for example, demanding proper evaluative evidence of impact on learning - or other explicit performance measures - rather than merely repeating existing citations. And we need to more rigorously compare and contrast the various spatial and design languages and arrangements being used to articulate different aspects of post-compulsory learning. This is not necessarily about moving beyond the 'hub, cluster and beanbag'– which we suggest are already on their way to forming the *normal* typology of contemporary learning spaces – but about developing a deeper understanding of this typology's implications for learning and of how and where its language might be extended, challenged or transformed. Fiona Duggan in this volume, for example, offers a case study where students at a further education college wanted learning spaces that reflected professional and employment-related relationships, rather than informal learning per se (Chapter 11). It is also worthwhile to look beyond the university or college, by extending into adult education in museums, galleries and libraries; and to critically examine other building types such as offices (Thody, Chapter 9). Elsewhere, Boys (2010) has discussed a few examples of these other types. Here, we will just outline some of the arguments she makes there, by drawing out differences in the various architectural means being offered for shaping learning. Importantly, these few examples are not just about expressing informal learning through space design, but rather aim for something deeper; they want to *re-categorise* the assumed relationships in educational activities between teacher, learner, researcher, citizen and employee, that is, where and how learning occurs. It should also be noted that these examples are not offered as *substitutes* for the learning space designs already mentioned, or assumed as 'better' versions of practice. Rather it is through the examination of other spaces such as these – as *comparative* forms of arrangement – that we can better inform and open up to more rigorous enquiry, current ideas about when and how design can help enhance the learning spaces of post-compulsory education.

Idea Store, Whitechapel, London

The five-storey Idea Store in Whitechapel was designed by architects Adjaye Associates in 2005, as one of six in Tower Hamlets; part of a local authority strategy to re-think and re-energise its library provision in the area (Figure 3.1). It combines traditional library and information services, with classrooms for adult education

Figure 3.1. Interior of Idea Store, Whitechapel, London. Photograph: Jos Boys.

(supported by courses supplied on site by Tower Hamlets FE College), a local history archive and a variety of reading and study spaces.

As the architects describe it:

> The building is conceived as a simple stack of flexible floor plates wrapped in a unified facade that combines transparency with colour. A curtain wall consisting of a repeating pattern of coloured glass, clear glass, and glass faced aluminium panels encloses all four facades. Each floor is arranged like a promenade that reveals the services and facilities being offered while affording arresting views of the surrounding area. [...] The café is placed on the top floor to draw people past the various facilities and rewards them with panoramic views of the city of London. (http://www.adjaye.com/)

This project, then, reverses the Telford College model of offering community facilities within a campus setting. Instead it brings more formal educational spaces out into the public realm of the library, already a setting for voluntary, informal learning. Here the classrooms act in at least two ways. They offer a potential transition zone – a bridge – between the learning here and more structured further education study at the college itself. And they provide flexible additional learning spaces, which are densely occupied all the time in many ways, including being taken over for general study by individuals and groups when no organised sessions are on. In this process the architectural planning is also reversed from the current informal and social learning university typologies we have been considering. Rather than a central atrium, which makes the experience mainly one of looking *inwards*, at the Idea Store Whitechapel, the relatively simple device of 'wrapping' library shelves around the central staircase core and then surrounding it with a 'fat' band of circulation with windows to one side means that almost all the various study spaces look *outwards*. A variety of seating and desks in individual, group and moveable arrangements arrayed along the perimeter of this outside wall can then form nooks and corners, with varying degrees of privacy, separation and view.

British Library, London

In a similar vein, but aimed at a different constituency, the British Library in London (designed by Colin St John Wilson and completed in 1997) has opened itself up to wider audiences compared with its previous relatively exclusive incarnation as the British Museum Reading Room. Again a series of study spaces are offered, from a canteen and café, to various 'corners' and corridors, as well as the main reading room itself, supported by a range of different furniture and settings, and giving access to a variety of exhibitions, collections and archives. What is most relevant to the arguments here is that, although very different in design to the Whitechapel building, the British Library also offers an environment of relaxed studious calm. It is undoubtedly about learning, visually expressed through the central, transparent book-stack rising through each storey in the public zone; and mediated via a design language of soft lighting, crafted materials and clean, white surfaces, framed by the architect's interest in the inter-relationships between human presence, proportion and detail. The building's layout and atmosphere articulate places for a variety of modes of learning, simultaneously offering up spaces for distraction, relaxation and absorption as well as for activities that may be collaborative and/or solitary, concentrated and/or informal. As such, in different ways both buildings offer at least a dialogue with, if not a critique of, those learning spaces in universities that rely on beanbags, bright colours and the expression of playfulness and 'fun' to indicate that social and informal learning is taking place.

White Space, University of Abertay

Within the university sector in the UK, there has been a range of initiatives at the intersections between post-compulsory education, business and local communities. What makes White Space stand out is not its 'architectural' quality (unlike the previous two examples) because it is a relatively basic conversion of an existing warehouse. Rather, the project is exceptional in its creative re-thinking of the potentially multi-layered intersections between and across students, teachers, researchers and practitioners; that is, it goes beyond the simple student-teacher dyad. Developed within the University's School of Computing and Creative Techno-logies, the space combines open tutorial and seminar areas with lecturers' work-spaces, provision for local businesses, high-quality digital facilities and relaxation areas:

> The White Space concept surrounds our students with the buzz of a real working environment, allowing them to share real-world knowledge and experience. Tutorials and lectures also take place here, which encourages lively discussions in the relaxation area with fellow students and staff afterwards. [...] White Space is about creating a set of essential, personalised assets and

including their development in all of our programmes (http://www.abertay.
ac.uk/studying/schools/amg/, assessed 10/02/09)

Thus, for example, a Masters course combines a business start-up unit for each
student at mezzanine level, together with shared facilities, all organised around a
central seminar space (Figure 3.2).

*Figure 3.2. Masters course facilities, White Space, University of Abertay.
Photograph: Jos Boys.*

Each of these examples would need to be analysed in much greater depth (see
Pearhouse and Bligh, Chapter 1, Melhuish, Chapter 2) to enable us to draw out any
useful conclusions about the intersections between the design of space and its
impact on learning. Here though, as with Duggan's three alternative 'models'
(Chapter 11), what these examples aim to offer are alternative ways of thinking
about learning which open it up for critical comparisons and debates; rather than
closing things down through the assumption of an 'obvious' informal design typology
(obvious only through its binary opposition to the 'appearance' of formality.)

THE VALUE AND PROBLEM OF USING METAPHOR
FOR DESIGNING LEARNING SPACES

As I mentioned at the beginning of this chapter, metaphor is a central, though not
always explicit, aspect of architectural design. As Peter Jamieson writes about his
approach to working collaboratively on learning space design:

The use of 'metaphor' can provide a basis for individuals and teams (especially
when they have little formal design expertise) to engage in the design process
and establish a common language. I have used the metaphor of the 'classroom
as nightclub or cabaret' as the basis for a recent and extremely effective
refurbishment of a traditional classroom into a multi- level collaborative

learning environment. Other metaphors I have used include 'classroom as empty space' – a room with little furniture and which conjures up various thoughts of what a student would do and how they would do it; 'classroom as a sandpit' – a space for play and discovery (words that are seldom used when describing learning in higher education); 'classroom as café' – a casual lounge setting with no obvious 'front' of class location. (Jamieson, 2008, p. 32)

In the new typologies for learning spaces, concepts such as atrium, street or hub do two things simultaneously. They act metaphorically to represent through analogy the idea of inter-mixing, sharing and unexpected encounters; and they are used to literally articulate the space as an organisational form with these assumed characteristics[1]. So, the 'drop-in centre', learning 'café', 'learning nook' or study 'pod' offer a metaphorical image of different kinds of informal grouping as well as intending to offer the various locations in which peer-to-peer and informal teacher–student interaction can easily occur. The tendency to informal, 'softer' furniture such as beanbags, asymmetric furniture layouts, bright colours and 'landmark' elements such as special features or artist commissions also speaks of these new socially oriented and informal 'identities'; as does the associative resonance between new technologies (with their focus on social networking, anytime access and interactivity) and new attitudes to learning.

But, in fact, such a use of metaphor – not only as a useful generative device but also literally mapped into actual design realisations – raises many questions. First, to what extent are such metaphors shared? While beanbags may well express informal, comfortable, playful and relaxed ways of working to some students, others see them as childish and inappropriate (Melhuish, Chapter 6). Second, are there other metaphors (besides the ones currently in vogue) that might usefully add to our repertoire for post-compulsory education, as indicated by Jamieson[2]? Softroom, the architects of the Sackler Centre for Arts Education at the Victoria and Albert Museum in London, for example, reference artists' studios as a key metaphor in support of their design (http://www.vimeo.com/5858785, accessed 26/03/10). How many and how far might metaphors go before they cease to 'work' in relationship to our current ideas about learning? More generally, how does the underlying associational process work such that a metaphor has particular resonance in specific situations? And perhaps most importantly, what is the relationship between the expressive, representational aspects of such metaphors and their lived experience? In relation to this last question there remains surprisingly little research. Where work exists it tends to stem from anthropology and ethnography rather than education or architecture. And it is deeply critical of the mismatches, particularly in modernist design, between original metaphorical intentions and the experiences of everyday life (Boudon, 1979; Holston, 1989). This underlying tendency for particular problems, where the metaphorical intention is taken as evidence of what actually happens, can be illustrated again and again. For example, the idea of the 'street' (which has been a staple of post-war secondary school design in the UK (Saint, 1987)) has had many criticisms there, but has been re-articulated again, for example, in new post-compulsory research institutes, particularly in emerging areas such as biotechnology. This is not to say that some street-type spaces do not work in educational environments, only that they are often based on the simplistic notion that mere adjacency will, of itself, enable constructive inter-action. For, as Nigel Thrift writes, 'these buildings are clearly meant to manipulate time and space in order to produce intensified social interaction so that all manner of crossovers of ideas can be achieved' (Thrift, 2008, p. 44). He lists several buildings in the UK and the USA designed on this basis and goes on to outline their common features:

> First, they will often include an explicit attempt to represent 'life', whether that be swooping architecture, some form of public display of science, or similar devices. Second, they are meant to be highly interdisciplinary. [...] Very often, they will place apparently unlike activities (such as computer laboratories and wet laboratories) side by side, or have unorthodox office allocation schedules, all intended to stimulate interdisciplinarity. Third, they are porous. Personnel [...] and information constantly flow through them. [...] Fourth, in keeping with an architectural rhetoric about changing ways of working which arose in the mid-1980s and is now an established convention, they are meant to encourage creative sociability, arising out of and fuelling further unpredictable interactions. From cafes to temporary dens, to informal meeting rooms, to walkways that force their denizens to interact (Duffy & Powell, 1997), the idea is clearly to encourage a 'buzz' of continuous conversation oriented to 'transactional knowledge' and, it is assumed, inno-vation. Fifth, they are meant to be transparent: there are numerous vantage points from which to spot and track activity, both to add to the general ambience and to point to the values/value of the scientific activity that is going on. (Thrift, 2008, p. 45)

But Thrift also goes on to note that 'although these buildings place a clear premium on interdisciplinary discovery, it is often not clear how that process of discovery is being maximised'. He suggests that in addition to the representational/functional/ facilitative elements of the architecture itself, the managers of these buildings have also had to implement new *processes* – the designation of explicit 'brokers' and 'pathfinders' to enable cross- disciplinary collaboration, mechanisms to keep people 'on the move so as to avoid group decay and organisational inertia' (2008, p. 46).

Metaphor then is a useful but dangerous tool for designers, their clients and users. It can represent a social-spatial idea and give it the appearance of 'obvious' and 'commonly agreed' reality, especially where it becomes a well-recognised convention through time. But this does not mean that the resulting space is inter-preted by all its occupiers in the same way; that other ways of expressing spatial and social relationships are not possible which are not generated from metaphor; and – most crucially – that the representational image necessarily or transparently translates into an equivalent everyday lived experience. In many ways this is a counter- intuitive idea; we are so used to taking design metaphors as powerful expressions of social reality, linking high-rise housing, for example, to poverty and social deprivation, and suburban estates to middle-class conformity, that we are surprised (and consider it newsworthy) when reality fails to match the metaphor – for example, where a violent crime happens in a suburban area. But at the same time, we often experience the inconsistencies and tensions between the representational qualities of a space and its lived engagement. In the above example of 'street' designs for new research institutes, for example, many of us would remain unconvinced that merely being put together with a variety of people in close proximity is likely to 'automatically' enhance our relationships with them, unless there is already a commitment to this end by all the individuals involved. Even more problematically, the use of metaphor can constrain other, more rigorous and theoretical, engagements with space and learning. The commonsense analysis of space, where designs that look informal are somehow assumed to generate informal learning is tautological (with each 'proving' the other in a closed loop). It seems so obvious that a more informal setting will generate informal learning that we fail to ask deeper questions. For example, if our aim is to help students to learn *how to learn* in this way (that learning is about being collaborative, creative, interactive and lateral) then we may in fact need to develop a highly structured series of development activities[3]. Whether these are considered formal or informal is actually of little consequence. What matters is whether the teaching and learning is of value, and has an effective impact.

This problem with the use of metaphor as a design method is not new to architecture and interior design. Along with cultural and critical theorists more generally, designers and critics have long been arguing against exactly this emphasis on representation (where space is articulated as a setting) and towards practices (where space is a process), an issue Boys will explore further in Chapter 4. She will suggest how some current ideas about learning from both architectural and educational theory, centring on learning as a liminal and transitional journey are valuable to this debate about learning spaces, because whilst being deeply 'spatial' they do not offer obvious design metaphors, and therefore demand a different kind of thinking. Interestingly, none of the three built examples outlined above needed to make obvious metaphorical references, focussing instead, as we have said, on articulating social and spatial relationships. In addition, whilst Adjaye and Wilson are from different architectural generations and approaches, they each bring their own recognisable design attitude to bear and, with it, a tendency to a particular language of form which is not specific to post-compulsory learning, but rather has been adapted to a specific situation. And White Space is a simple and relatively 'non-designed' space (except in as much as creative groupings enjoy the imagery of re-using industrial buildings.)

CONCLUSIONS: ENGAGING WITH THE COMPLEXITY
OF LEARNING SPACES

In one emerging educational theory, post-compulsory learning is seen as an engagement with what Meyer and Land (2003) call 'threshold concepts' that is the specific knowledge and practices of a subject specialism which sit beyond everyday commonsense and are in fact, often counter-intuitive, and therefore hard to understand. This is a kind of 'troublesome knowledge' as described by Perkins - 'that which appears counter-intuitive, alien (emanating from another culture or discourse), or seemingly incoherent' (in Meyer & Land, 2003, p. 7). As Cousin puts it:

[F]rom this view, mastery of a threshold concept can be inhibited by the prevalence of a "common sense" or intuitive understanding of it. Getting students to reverse their intuitive understandings is also troublesome because the reversal can involve an uncomfortable, emotional repositioning. (Cousin, 2006, p. 1)

The assumption in many discussions about learning spaces that informal and formal learning are in some simple binary opposition to each other, which can be literally and transparently translated into architectural form through designs that *appear* either 'playful' or 'boring' is just such an example of pre-liminal unthought-through 'commonsense'. And the inter-relationships between an activity and the space in which it takes place can feel counter-intuitive. This is in spite of that fact that we know that *both* learning and architectural design are complicated processes of transition and translation. In each case participants bring with them different knowledge, beliefs and attitudes to the problem in hand; and engage with and negotiate their position through time, based on partial knowledge of complex variables (Sherringham and Stewart, Chapter 8). To add to our difficulties, these various understandings and compromises must somehow then be translated into *another* language besides talk and text, the vocabulary of three-dimensional material form and space. Whether new-build or a conversion, possible design choices are also constrained by the material parameters of the existing site, and can only be produced through another sequence of processes – procurement, building, cons-truction and management. Finally, the resulting spaces are occupied by many different people and adapted and transformed through time as requirements and attitudes change. How little like the assumed metaphorical, transparent and direct connection between design intention and reality is this!

In this chapter, we have suggested that a new typology for learning spaces is already becoming the norm, in the UK at least, as particular built environments become increasingly commonly cited as examples of what universities and colleges *should* be doing. We are not suggesting that this vocabulary is wrong, only that whilst simplistic metaphors may be useful for generating ideas about form, they do not work as an 'obvious' mode of evaluation and, in fact, can often *stop* us thinking rigorously about space and learning. In addition, by accepting the language of streets, clusters, hubs and beanbags as the 'obvious' commonsense, other potentially valuable modes for articulating the spaces of post-compulsory learning (from across architectural, educational and estates management perspectives) can become invisible, ineffectively articulated or remain under-researched. Here we have begun to indicate that deliberately problematicising the relationship between space and the learning that goes on in it has a very important potential for future debates about improving educational spaces. This is not just about being more creatively critical of existing assumptions. It can also set us on the path to an equally difficult but more rich and deep engagement with learning, not just as a shift from formal to informal modes but as an opportunity to completely re-think and re-categorise what post-compulsory learning *is*, where it should take place, and the extent to which space (in all its various meanings and interpretations) *matters* in this process.

NOTES

[1] Boddington (personal correspondence) notes that these kinds of metaphors often align the university, the city and urbanism in interesting ways that need more unpacking; both to see why this connection currently appears so potent, and to explore when and if these metaphors run out of their usefulness and currency. We should be asking, for example, why learning (particularly social learning) is so often associated with the spaces of the street and of crowds. See also Temple, Chapter 10.

[2] There are many potential alternative metaphors not considered here, for example, the idea of a 'learning home', which suggests a sense of rootedness and familiarity, a domestic space that offers more in the way of dialogue with other contemporary educational concerns such as academic 'health' and well-being, rather than the focus offered by ideas of collaborative streets and hubs. See also Sagan, chapter 5, for a discussion of 'holding' environments.

[3] The dangers of the metaphor and of the misrepresentations and misalignments of image and representation that it can engender are important issues not just for architects and designers, but have similarly counter-intuitive effects in the management and construction of *learning* itself. Rigour and structure in the design of learning activities may well be needed within an informal setting in order to properly support students' educational development. In art and design disciplines, for example, learning to be creative is often seen simply as a 'freeing up' of the imagination. This relaxed seeming image belies the importance of providing a very tight safety net that both 'holds' learners and enables them to take creative risks confidently and effectively. We also need to find frameworks for evaluation that reveal these underlying anomalies and do not conflate different conditions of spatiality.

REFERENCES

Birmingham University Learning Development Unit. (2005). *Study on how innovative technologies are influencing the design of physical learning spaces in the post-16 sector (JISC eSpaces Study)*. Retrieved February 27, 2011, from http://www.ldu.bham.ac.uk/other/espaces.shtml

Boudon, P. (1979). *Lived in architecture: Le Corbusier's Pessac revisited*. Cambridge, MA: MIT Press.

Boys, J. (2010). *Towards creative learning spaces; Re-thinking the architecture of post-compulsory education*. London: Routledge.

Cousin, G. (2006, December 17). An introduction to threshold concepts. *Planet*. Retrieved January 29, 2011 from http://www.gees.ac.uk/planet/p17/gc.pdf

Duffy, F., & Powell, K. (1997). *The new office*. London: Conran Octopus.

Harrison, A., & Cairns, A. (2008). *The changing academic workplace*. DEGW UK Ltd.

Holston, J. (1989). *The modernist city: An anthropological critique of Brasilia*. Chicago: University of Chicago Press.

Jamieson, P. (2008). *Creating new generation learning environments on the University Campus*.

Woods Bagot Research Press. Retrieved February 07, 2009, from http://www.woodsbagot.com/en/Documents/Public_Research/WB5307_U21_FA-7_final.pdf

Joint Information Systems Committee (JISC). (2006). *Designing spaces for effective learning*. Retrieved February 07, 2009, from http://www.jisc.ac.uk/eli_learningspaces.html

Joint Information Systems Committee (JISC). (2009). *A study of effective evaluation models and practices for technology supported physical learning spaces*. Retrieved March 26, 2010, from http://www.jisc.ac.uk/media/documents/projects/jels_final_report_30.06.09.doc

Meyer, J. H. F., & Land, R. (2003). Threshold concepts and troublesome knowledge (1): Linkages to ways of thinking and practicing. In C. Rust (Ed.), *Improving student learning – equality and diversity*. Oxford: OCSLD.

Neary, M., Harrison, A., Crelin, G., Parekh, N., Saunders, G., Duggan, F., et al. (2010). *Learning landscapes in higher education*. Centre for Educational Research and Development, University of Lincoln. Retrieved May 02, 2010, from http://learninglandscapes.blogs.lincoln.ac.uk/files/2010/04/FinalReport.pdf

Oblinger, D. G. (Ed.). (2006). *Learning spaces*. Educause. Retrieved February 07, 2009, from http://www.educause.edu/LearningSpaces/10569

Saint, A. (1987). *Towards a social architecture: The role of school-building in post-war England*. London: Yale University Press.

Scottish Funding Council. (2006). *Spaces for learning: A review of learning spaces in further and higher education*. Retrieved February 07, 2009, from http://aleximarmot.com/research/

Tertiary Education Facilities Management Association (TEFMA). (2006). *Learning environments in tertiary education*. Retrieved February 07, 2009, from http://www.tefma.com/infoservices/publications/learning.jsp

Thrift, N. (2008). *Non-Representational theory: Space, politics, affect*. London: Routledge.

Watson, L., et al. (2007). *The design and management of open plan technology rich learning and teaching spaces in further and higher education in the UK - Case studies*. Retrieved February 27, 2011, from http://www.jisc.ac.uk/whatwedo/projects/managinglearningspaces.aspx

JOS BOYS

4. WHERE IS THE THEORY?

INTRODUCTION

Over recent years a considerable number of new learning spaces have been built for post-compulsory education. It has already been suggested (Chapter 3) that in the UK and elsewhere a main focus has been the perceived need to shift from formal to informal learning and from single-function to more hybrid and interactive spaces. However, as the last chapter also showed, whilst many of these developments have been both innovative and interesting, the arguments behind them have too often been built on simplistic commonsense binary oppositions. As the diagram (Figure 4.1) illustrates, these are usually structured via chains of associative metaphors, which are then set against an oppositional - and therefore assumed negative - grouping. In addition the relationship between the social and the spatial is visualised as a kind of vertical line, like a mirror where each reflects the other. Space is thus assumed to act primarily as a *representation* of the social in its appearance and layout.

In this chapter I start from the position that such a common (and unthought through) framing of the problem often makes invisible the need for more complex

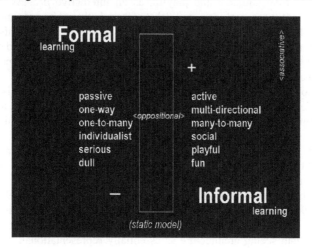

Figure 4.1. Learning space framed through the patterning of binary associations and oppositions (re-printed from Boys, 2010, p. 5).

A. Boddington and J. Boys (eds.), Re-Shaping Learning: A Critical Reader: The Future of Learning Spaces in Post-Compulsory Education, 49–66.

debates, or for a more rigorous conceptual framework which explicitly articulates relationships between space and the activities that go on in it. And I will begin to investigate what conceptual frameworks and research methods are available to help us better understand such socio-spatial relationships, by suggesting that both architecture and education already have more sophisticated ways of envisaging the complexity, dynamism, hybridity and partiality of learning, space and the inter-sections between them. Many contemporary theories in these subject areas have shifted from (or attempted to shift from) arguments based on what is diagrammed above. They have shown the gaps and inadequacies in a binary patterning which links the social and the spatial mainly through representation and instead try to conceptualise space and the activities that go on in it in a much more dynamic, integrated yet non-congruent way. This has considerable implications for learning space design; and for re-thinking the architecture of post-compulsory education more generally.

LEARNING SPACES AND THE INVISIBLITY OF CONTEMPORARY THEORY

One of the most interesting things for me when I began to research learning spaces in the 1990s was the odd gap between the assumptions experts in the field made about how architecture 'worked', compared to how they thought about education. Material space was usually seen as providing the *setting* in which behaviours could be changed in a relatively mechanical, proscriptive (determinist) and straightforward way – very much within a modernist idiom[1]. Learning, on the other hand, was being articulated through a much more contemporary (post-modernist) paradigm as something informal, situated and playful, as an interactive *process*. Even more strangely, current theoretical ideas and debates from both architecture and education were only infrequently referred to in the learning spaces literature. This set a two-part research agenda: to explore whether and how recent architectural and educational theories and approaches could inform our engagement with learning spaces; and to see how we could expand and enhance learning space debates beyond the artificiality of the informal/formal learning divide. This has meant also engaging with the variety of different perspectives on what matters about learning, and opening up the complexity of, and difficulties in conceptualising relationships between learning and space adequately (Boys, 2010).

The first important point for this chapter is to recognise that much current architectural theory and practice is actually based on a thorough *critique* of modernist and behaviourist assumptions about how designed space 'works', a paradigm shift which has been happening since at least the 1980s (Tschumi, 1994a, 1994b; Koolhaas, 1997). Through this period there has been a re- conceptualisation of the relationships between space and the activities it contains in three important ways. First, rather than seeing architecture as essentially representational, symbolic and metaphorical (where meaning-making occurs through what space 'expresses') it is increasingly understood as non-representational or events-based; that is, meaning-making occurs through the activation of space by our multiple, diverse and embodied experiences. As part of this framing, space and its uses are not different aspects that reflect each other - as the binary oppositions model assumes - but are inseparable and interlocked, dynamically informing and influencing each other. At the same time, space and its occupation are only partially related. Space is not so much the means whereby specific behavioural effects occur through reactions to specific stimuli 'so that one can both expect and predict a close correspondence between what is learnt and what is taught' (Hooper-Greenhill, 2000, p. 133), but as a folded (and folding) terrain across which socio-spatial events are unevenly enacted (Deleuze and Guattari, 2000). Embodied experiences are not behaviours, but *social and spatial practices*, deeply informed both by their situated context and what the individual and/or group brings to a space. Unlike the previous diagram, here the relationship between space and the activities that go on in it can be visualised, not as a vertical but as a horizontal line; making dynamic and fluid but also partial and often non-transparent, counter-intuitive connections (Figure 4.2). The links are not through associative/ oppositional analogies, but through over-lapping/gap-producing processes across both space and time. Such an approach is often referred to as not the 'either/or' of thinking through binary oppositions but the 'and/and' of uneven and complex inter-relationships, that is, paying attention to what Derrida calls supplementaries (2001).

This, leads to the second important point. Because space and its occupation are always dynamic, non-congruent, partial and situated, they *cannot* operate as transparent, coherent and obvious reflections of each other. There cannot be a literal 'reading' off either the activity or the space. Instead, different social and spatial practices have to be unravelled through analyses of specific intersecting spaces, activities and contexts. This is always about encounters *between* space and its occupation. The 'space' to be explored is not so much the external, physical environment itself, as the spaces *in-between* what we bring to a situation, and the material context in which we find ourselves (Sagan, Chapter 5). And, as I have

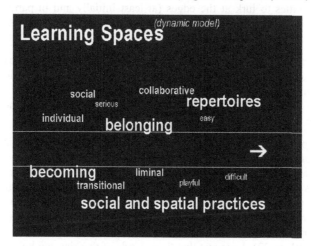

Figure 4.2. Learning space framed as the patterning of socio-spatial practices (re-printed from Boys 2010, p. 7).

already suggested, such encounters are not simply functional or behavioural. Rather than involving either the mind (intellectual, abstract, visual) or the body (immediate, experiential, sensual) these are *affective*, that is, they impact across body, mind and feelings simultaneously. Affect, then, is not just about emotions but 'understood as a form of thinking, often indirect and non- reflective, true, but thinking all the same' (Thrift, 2008, p. 175). Space is therefore one of our means of thinking about the world and of embodying thought into action. We change space through our affective encounters, just as space changes us, through a process of continual, embodied *negotiations* (Sherringham and Stewart, Chapter 8).

Crucially for the argument here, contemporary educational theory also increasingly envisages learning as just such a series of affective encounters. We are beginning to better understand that the explicit and outward learning and teaching relationships between students and tutors cannot be separated from their unspoken interactions (Austerlitz, 2008). These are the embodied, emotional, sensory interactions between individuals and across groups; and the transitional and liminal (ambiguous, seemingly undefined and potentially disorienting) learning journeys that students undertake. So educational theory is exploring, for instance, the difficulties of engaging with 'troublesome knowledge' and the possibilities of getting 'stuck' (Meyer & Land, 2003, 2006); as well as the collaborative and contested social meaning-making that flows through a whole community of 'knowers' - what Lave and Wenger call communities of practice (1991). In these kinds of articulation learning is about the 'increasing access of learners to participating roles in expert performances' (p. 17), that is, a lengthy and centrally social process through which students do not just learn physics or design, for example, but are also learning to be physicists or designers. Interestingly, such framing uses rich spatial analogies to try and capture the learning process. Thus, Lave and Wenger, for example, articulate learning as mainly a centripetal and transitional movement from periphery to centre. And it is the opportunities to lurk at the edges (at least initially and in particular ways) – what they call legitimate peripheral participation or LLP – that is viewed as a deeply valuable method of learning:

> Peripherality suggests that there are multiple, varied, more- or- less engaged and inclusive ways of being located in the fields of participation defined by a community. [...] *Changing* locations and perspectives are part of actors' learning trajectories, development of identities, and forms of membership. (Lave & Wenger, 1991, pp. 35–36 emphasis in original)

The concept of LPP, then, tries to capture learning as this developing process of ongoing and embodied engagements with knowledgeable experts (old timers) through increasing degrees of responsibility, understanding and control. Ultimately the authors argue that this is not just one form of learning; rather it is a general theoretical perspective 'about the relational character of knowledge and learning, about the negotiated character of meaning, and about the concerned (engaged, dilemma-driven) nature of learning activity for the people involved' (Lave & Wenger, 1991, p. 33). I suggest that these kinds of theories can help us understand more about the socio-spatial practices of post-compulsory education. However, it is also crucial to note both the value of this work, and the need for care in its application 'back' to actual learning space design. We have recently witnessed what has been called a spatial turn (Warf and Arias, 2008) in the articulation of ideas and theories which is having a considerable effect on how learning is conceptualised. As mentioned in the previous chapter, these newer understandings go beyond metaphor and association, framing learning in ways that are intensely spatial, but nevertheless do not lead easily to direct design analogies or 'obvious' representations. There is no obvious or immediate aesthetic or organisational layout that can express concepts such as legitimate peripheral participation or of liminal and transitional spaces (unlike the way 'informal', for example, translates so directly into soft furniture and warm colours). This is a valuable way of aiding debate, because it prevents any 'commonsense' slippage between social idea/intention and spatial form/appearance. Examples of such conceptualisations of learning in this volume include Savin-Baden's 'boundary crossings' (chapter 7), Sagan's 'holding environments' (chapter 5) and Barnett's ideas of 'widening out' and 'air' (chapter 13). Importantly, though, we still need to make explicit just what kinds of *translation* processes (Bhabha, 1994) are necessary to inter-relate such abstract spatial conceptualisations with both the design of actual material spaces and the everyday learning encounters that go on in them.

TOWARDS LEARNING AS A SOCIO-SPATIAL PRACTICE

How, then, can such contemporary theories from both architecture and education better open up our understandings of, and debates about, learning spaces? It has already been suggested that we need to understand relationships between space and occupation as a horizontal one of intersecting, complex and partially related processes. This leaves us different kinds of conceptual and methodological problems to those posed by the commonsense 'reflective' framework. First, it means opening up for detailed investigation just how spatial and social processes intersect as integrated but also uneven, dynamic and non-congruent relationships. If architectural space is no longer predominantly understood as either an expressive representation of what goes on in it or seen as a device for changing behaviours, how can we examine it 'differently'? As with other authors (Augoyard, 1979: Savin-Baden, 2008) I will look to Lefebvre's seminal work *The Production of Space* (1991) as a means of proposing new methodologies.

Second, we need to unravel more precisely what is distinctive about the socio-spatial practices of learning in post-compulsory education. This, I suggest, requires an engagement with space at a number of different 'levels' (Boys, 2009). There are the spaces of learning *encounters* themselves, that is, the everyday situated negotiations between learners, teachers and other participants in the educational process across a variety of contexts. At the next level up there is the space of the educational institution. This space is about the dynamic patterning and re-patterning of the socio-spatial *relationships*. It (unevenly) articulates contested understandings of what should go together and what should be kept apart in providing 'learning' in a particular context. Then, at what might be called a societal level there are *conceptual* spaces of learning. These are the ideas – often contested – about what education is for, how it should be divided up, and who studies what, where and when. Of course, conceptual ideas about learning can engage at the level of every-day encounters or institutional relationships, just as individual learning encounters are informed, for example, by how a specific educational agenda is enacted institutionally. Each level interweaves with others. And, as before, these different levels are not static or comprehensive entities but uneven and endlessly changing socio-spatial practices; their 'shape' will always be ambiguous, and they do not seamlessly cohere together, but have between them many gaps, contradictions, overlaps, and unexpected consequences. Whilst other authors in this volume have proposed other ways of 'slicing' learning processes (Sagan, Chapter 5; Barnett, Chapter 13) here I will conclude by attempting to show how such artificial divisions into 'levels' can nonetheless be useful in helping us think more rigorously and creatively about learning spaces.

RELATING SPACE AND ITS OCCUPATION

As I have already noted, from the 1980s and 1990s avant-garde and radical architecture developed a new paradigm of how design 'worked', influenced by theories and approaches particularly from linguistic theory. For writers such as Jean Baudrillard (1994) and Jacques Derrida (2001) there was no direct connection between what the author intended and how a book's narrative was interpreted by its many readers. Rather than a direct match between idea and result that could be straightforwardly analysed and revealed as coherent and complete, there are both 'gaps' and extras in the space in-between the 'thing' and its realisation/ interpretation/ experience. Analysis becomes, in this case, not so much the construction of a recognisable self-contained and stable totality as the 'deconstruction' of several irreconcilable, contradictory and unstable meanings, which are inherent to any act of production and consumption. As Boddington (Chapter 14) also notes, this informed the development of architectural theories and practices that refused the modernist dictum of form following function (that building design should reflect its contents) in favour of a more partial and hybrid architecture that questions, enables and animates rather than attempts to 'fix' particular social relationships.

Yet, the aim of building design is still almost invariably seen as attempting to make a best 'match' or fit with the activities that it contains. This appears such obvious commonsense that it is hardly ever questioned. As we look at, and participate in, built space we often note how it does 'not work'; that is, where it fails to perform appropriately in support of the things that we are doing or want to do. But as soon as we begin to unpick the many, partial, complex and often contested processes through which buildings and spaces are achieved, managed, adapted, removed or replaced, we begin to see that designed space is much more ambiguous. It does not –and cannot – make a direct and perfect 'fit' between activities and material, spatial and/or aesthetic arrangements; nor is it a direct, transparently obvious correlation between function and form. It is much more about problematic compromises, collisions and unexpected outcomes. The ideas of both event-based design and non-congruence between design intention and its interpretation/experience try to capture some of this ambiguity and to admit to the impossibility of any specific architectural design working at all times, for every-one. How, then, can we re-think the relationships between learning and space from this perspective?

The articulation of a more complex and partial relationship between space and its occupation has been explored by Henri Lefebvre through what he famously called a 'spatial triad'. In his book *The Production of Space* (1991) Lefebvre proposed that a better method for analysing the messy complexity of space was to consider it through three aspects, rather than use the two-part associative/ oppositional framework already criticised here. Lefebvre called the first thread of this three-part division the *spatial practices* of a society. By this he means our daily routines, articulated as the inter-relationships of bodies, objects, space and time. These are the ordinary, unconsidered experiences and practices, the 'making concrete' of what is the obvious thing to do, and where. Second, these everyday social and spatial practices are intersected by what Lefebvre calls *representations of space*, meaning the conceptualisations of space used by planners, scientists and other experts, through, for example, maps, plans, models and designs. For Lefebvre (following his Marxist leanings) architects and other built environment professionals are pre-dominantly concerned with legitimising an existing societal ideology and structure by making representations of society in a particular shape - "through built form that that tends towards a system of verbal signs" (Lefebvre, 1991, p. 39). Thus his concept of representations of space describes design as essentially the imposition of a dominant model of social relationships through the making of particular material landscapes rather than others.

Finally, the third part of the triad is what Lefebvre calls *representational space*, that is, the spaces where we attempt to intervene in, and adapt existing material spaces to our own requirements. For him this is articulated most strongly as a grassroots political act, where ordinary people seek to appropriate and/or transform the nor-mative representations of space made by architects and others. That these two latter threads are seen as oppositional attempts to inscribe different meanings on the built environment (mainly through representation) locates Lefebvre very specifically in both the time and context in which he was writing. Here I want to open up each of these to more complex understandings of process and agency. Rather than seeing decision-makers and designers as automatically inscribing space with societal norms, and 'ordinary' people as always aiming to challenge those patterns, I will envisage all of us, whatever our roles, as aiming to 'make sense' of, and survive in the world; where space - whether conceptual, material, social, personal- is one of the mechanisms through which we attempt this. What is important and relevant about Lebfevre's insights is in his envisaging of material space as the (uneven and complex) result of competing attempts over meaning-making; his argument that this should be explored through everyday social routines and designed spaces simul-taneously; and his understanding that such explorations centrally include a recog-nition of the unequal relationships between those who have power and control over the design of space (and over social processes more generally) and those who don't.

So - with apologies to Lefebvre - I propose an outline framework for linking material space and its occupation as learning based on his spatial triad, but adapted to a more contemporary, i.e. non-Marxist and post-structuralist, framing. In this articulation there are three partial, non-comprehensive and overlapping threads, which often have gaps, unintended consequences, or contradictory elements both within and between them. These are:

- the 'ordinary' routines (everyday social and spatial practices) of existing educational provision
- attempts at specific designed transformations of these 'ordinary' routines of learning
- participant perceptions of, relationships to and negotiations with both the 'ordinary' routines of learning and of specific designed transformations

Instead of a closed oppositional 'backwards-and-forwards' of learning between either it's assumed formal/bad and informal/good locations – or even a circular movement from outside to centre, as described by the communities of practice model – perhaps we can envisage such a patterning more as three parallel lines which overlap sometimes, or stretch far apart; sometimes running very closely together for long periods of time, or moving jerkily; sometimes thick in their intensity, sometimes petering out. Intersections between lines are always dynamic, with changing relationships towards and away from seeming coherence and stability (Figure 4.3). Where threads drift too far apart, then the pattern is likely to be lost and a new pattern begins to form as new viewpoints are offered and begin to resonate more widely. In this visualisation, intensity and overlapping might signify both powerfully valued socio-spatial practices and places where contradictions are multiplying, with new alternatives being generated. Threads which are weak and thinly spaced might suggest socio-spatial practices that have become so routinised as to be little considered, or where space is merely anonymous and perceived as without meaning. This, then, is a means of, for example, investigating the current 'place' of the formal/informal learning debate within educational practices more generally.

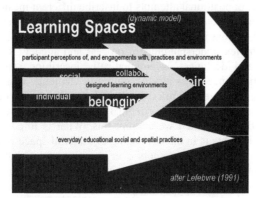

Figure 4. 3. Analysing socio-spatial practices (adapted from Lefebvre, 1991 and re-printed from Boys 2010, p. 81).

The value of the kind of method offered here is that it opens up arguments about learning spaces to the gaps, tensions and unintended consequences inherent in the everyday socio-spatial practices of post-compulsory education. It enables us to visualise the spaces in-between the ordinary routines and conventional social and spatial practices of learning, our different interpretations of those social and spatial practices, and actual attempts at manipulating form and space towards particular learning 'ends'. As I have said, these patterns never settle, nor can they be explained in totality. Importantly, each of these aspects is always situated in relationship to both particular places and people; and no aspect is obvious, congruent or complete, either on its own terms, or with others. These never align (or do so only momentarily) so that the resulting pattern is what Geertz (1973) famously called a 'thick description' (Melhuish, chapters 2 and 7); that is, it is a rich and layered account that does not result in a 'solution' or conclusion, but can *illuminate* (Parlett & Hamilton, 1972) our decision- making.

THE ENCOUNTERS, RELATIONSHIPS AND CONCEPTUALISATIONS OF LEARNING

Whilst this rather simplistic adaptation of Lefebvre offers the outline of a conceptual framework for thinking about the relationships between learning and space, there is still much to be done in better articulating the nature of each of these threads and their intersections. For the rest of this chapter, I want to concentrate on how we can begin to unravel the distinctive 'ordinary' routines of learning - its existing socio-spatial practices - within post-compulsory education. I suggest that educators are still poor (for a variety of reasons) at being able to explain precisely what it is that we do in teaching, learning and research at the advanced levels - and that this not only affects our understanding of how learning spaces 'work' (and how to improve them), but also the authority and relative power of post-compulsory educational institutions in promoting their value to others. To do this I will look first at learning encounters, by critically interrogating some of the work of Scott-Webber (2004); then at ways of articulating learning space at the level of the educational institution through both Wenger's use of the concept of the repertoire and a critical engagement with the communities of practice model. Finally, I will briefly consider how learning is 'located' at the level of society and how this, too, impacts on learning spaces.

Learning Encounters

In her book *In Sync* (2004) on learning space design, Leonie Scott-Webber begins by suggesting that building and interior designers are not very good at making use of existing research, mainly because of the differences in vocabularies used by various specialists involved in the built environment. She therefore offers her work as a 'translation' of her subject area – environmental behaviour research – particularly focusing on the form and manipulation of material space concerning 'the situations we find ourselves in when we need to share information (knowledge sharing)'

(Scott- Webber, 2004, p. 1). What is interesting here is both her articulation of knowledge exchange as central to learning space design at a post-compulsory level, and her attempts to articulate different levels of knowledge- sharing, development and creation. Whilst these are initially framed as a fixed set of archetypical behaviours (pp. 42–44) they are also articulated in considerable detail as particular social and spatial activities and practices. To take one example, the 'knowledge creation' space is outlined as requiring five types of embodied – thinking through doing - experiences:

– Research to become knowledgeable about the problem under study;
– Define the innovation opportunity or problem;
– Generate options and recognise the need for a new solution;
– Incubate – let the job rest and distil over time in order to process and digest information; and
– Select an option and interpret into a product idea. (Scott-Webber, 2004, p. 59)

Scott-Webber suggests that this involves two distinct areas which 'must be included and yet interrelated: (1) a place of refuge to think and incubate, and (2) a place to collaborate and share information' (2004, p. 59). This kind of learning then, needs to enable individual and group activities; to support personal and interactive engagement; to provide a variety of degrees of privacy/protection and proximity/collaboration/ social engagement, together with information sharing, that is, exposure to 'parts, pieces, artefacts ... and for the group to use, remember, and stay stimulated (information persistence)'; and - what is often forgotten - 'thoughtful reflection or mindless activity (e.g., a ping- pong table area)' (2004, p. 59).

Whether we agree with this particular list or not, such a close and careful mapping can help us to both articulate and debate learning as the practice of particular and distinctive learning encounters with spaces, objects and others. As a behavioural and environmental psychologist, Scott-Webber offers such sets of relationships as archetypes, that is, as somehow delineating an absolute 'essence' of learning. I suggest that such observations in fact reveal aspects of detailed everyday – routinised but culturally generated – social and spatial practices of learning in post-compulsory education, here particularly as inscribed in the creative disciplines. In this reading, the activities listed above are an example of Lefebvre's *spatial practices* in relationship to one type of learning. These are not so much 'inherent' in our psyches as negotiated personally, socially and culturally as part of the making and re- making of both individual learners and various educational and professional communities of practice. As Hooper-Greenhill says, our relationships to both space and learning are active processes; where as individuals we bring what we already know (through previous experience) to each new engagement with a situation, activity or space, so as to both make sense of it and to *learn* from it. Here, she suggests the implications for such learning in a museum context:

The task ... is to provide experiences that invite visitors to make meaning through deploying and extending their existing interpretative strategies and repertoires, using their prior knowledge and their preferred learning styles, and testing their hypotheses against those of others, including experts. (Hooper-Greenhill, 2000, pp. 139–140)

Thus, the movement towards expertise will (or should) occur both as an overall trajectory from periphery to centre, as Lave and Wenger suggest, and as a continuing (re)locating of oneself in the *spaces-in-between* one's individual understandings and beliefs and the knowledge, skills and attitudes of the community of practice. What we need to add, then, is an examination of how best to critically *intersect* the particular teaching and learning practices Scott-Webber describes with, first, other competing and/or differently framed ones; second, the affective engagements (and therefore perceptions and interpretations) of these practices by their various participants; and, third how design works as an act of translation in between the practices described and their material realisations.

Socio-Spatial Relationships in Learning Institutions

For Wenger communities of practice do not just provide a trajectory towards expertise, but are also one of the means of making particular rules and conventions appear obvious, ordinary and invisible. 'Inward' movement is thus a process of both increasing absorption, and *normalising*, of the knowledge and attitudes that defines a specific community of practice as opposed to another. Here space and objects are heavily implicated. One of the ways in which specific social practices become ordinary routines is through their endless repetition and re-making, as actions, concepts, objects and architecture. This is 'reification', defined as:

> [T]he process of giving form to our experience by producing objects that congeal that experience into 'thingness'. In so doing, we create points of focus around which the negotiation of meaning becomes organized [...] any community of this kind produces abstractions, tools, symbols, terms and concepts that reify something of that practice in a congealed form. (Wenger, 1998, pp. 58–59)

Each community of practice thus has what he calls its own *repertoire* and reification can happen through everything from abstract ideas to bus tickets:

> A wide range of processes that include making, designing, representing, naming, encoding and describing, as well as perceiving, interpreting, using, reusing, decoding and recasting [...] from entries in a journal to historical records, from poems to encyclopaedias, from names to classification systems, from dolmens to space probes, from the Constitution to a signature on a credit card slip, from gourmet recipes to medical procedures, from flashy advertisements to census data, from single concepts to entire theories, from the evening news to national archives, from lesson plans to the compilation of text-books, from private address lists to sophisticated credit-reporting databases, from tortuous political speeches to the yellow pages. In all these cases aspects of human experience and practice are congealed into fixed form and given the status of object. (Wenger, 1998, p. 60)

For Wenger reification is a useful and constructive mechanism that helps glue together communities of practice; for many other authors it is a problematic and inequitable process. They ask instead whose 'ordinary' is being congealed and in whose interests. Theorists such as Michel Foucault, (1970, 1977) Pierre Bourdieu, (1987) and Homi Bhabha (1994), have analysed how the congealing of a particular 'ordinary' is perpetuated through the material fabric of society. Reification here becomes the attempt to make transparent and obvious (by locating it externally in the 'concrete' world) what is actually a specific articulation of ideas and practices; and a particular translation of these ideas and practices into things and spaces. Other theorists, for example in ethnomethodology, have explored how to open up to critical investigation the fact that a crucial part of such routine practices is precisely their very invisibility (Garfinkel, 1967: Ryave and Schenkein, 1974: Payne, 1976, Sacks, 1984). This, they argue, obscures what is actually going on, so as to make invisible and unquestioned who is left in or out and what is recognised as acceptable behaviour (see also Sagan, Chapter 5; Boys, 2008). Learning spaces research urgently needs to develop ways of describing and critically engaging with such underlying mechanisms From this viewpoint, a particular educational repertoire can obscure both other alternatives and actual contestations over what learning is and how it should take place. As Soja writes:

> We must be insistently aware of how space can be made to hide consequences from us, how relations of power and discipline are inscribed into the apparently innocent spatiality of social life, how human geographies become filled with politics and ideology. (Soja, 1989, p. 6)

I suggest, then, that material space should not be understood as directly reflecting the social life it contains, but as the uneven patterning between/across various attempts to 'make concrete' specific social practices rather than others; that is, as the terrain of (and resource for) competing repertoires. The ongoing debates over what learning spaces should be like in post-compulsory education, and the range of innovative built examples produced as a result, only highlights these endless struggles as different individuals and groups *consciously and deliberately* challenge existing arrangements, with the aim of moving towards a new 'normalisation', where alternative understandings of, for example, informal/social learning - together with their associated repertoires - become absorbed into ordinary and no longer thought about commonsense (Boys and Smith, Chapter 3). This means that we should not only list the repertoire of a given community of practice at any one time – for example its typical building types – but we must also open up what is being challenged and how, and the processes through which such 'campaigns' are, or are not, successful.

I have already suggested that we remain quite poor at articulating the 'ordinary' social and spatial practices of learning in universities and colleges in the kind of language Scott-Webber indicates - and some of the reasons why, given the inbuilt tendency of everyday socio-spatial practices to be invisible in precisely this ordinary use. How, then, can we begin to unravel what constitutes the distinctive repertoire(s) of post-compulsory education? In one way this is quite straightforward. Most further and higher education in the UK, for example, is made up of similar components; or, following Wenger, has become reified into a particular repertoire.

Besides furnishings such as seminar tables and chairs, this includes rooms such as lecture theatres, seminar rooms, design studios and computer laboratories; the lecture, tutorial, experiment, essay and presentation; the learning 'module' with its associated learning outcome and assessment criteria; the curriculum and academic timetable; the academic year cycle; patterns of taught and self-directed study; sequenced levels of achievement with controlled entry and progression points across a number of years; methods of research funding, development and assessment; regulatory relationships with stakeholders and associated services such as library, student support, staff offices, administrative support facilities, canteens and cafés, students' union, sports facilities and rental accommodation. What we need to do, then, is to find ways of analysing these repertoires, not as functional patterns of space and equipment usage, but as partial maps of particular socio-spatial relationships - of what is prioritised and valued, of what is kept apart and what together.

Of course such repertoires can also be examined to reveal their differences in various contexts, dependent on the specific characteristics of particular institutions (for example, campus, town-based, university/ex- polytechnic, further education college, elite/research-based/teaching-based) and/or on the socio-spatial practices of various academic disciplines. This means better understanding both the similarities and distinctive variations across different educational 'granularities' and the dynamic processes through which post-compulsory learning, teaching and research repertoires are more or less settled or contested through time and in different situations. This is not just a matter of tracing competing perspectives, and coming to a view about their relative value or effectiveness - for example different ways of articulating an institutional identity and its representation in the design of university campuses (Temple, chapter 10). Rather it needs an examination of how and why particular social meanings and practices come to be articulated and negotiated; how these come to be recognised more generally (and by whom); and how they are translated into specific repertoires, for example, through a particular design approach and vocabulary used to convert specific ideas about learning into an actual material environment.

Competing Socio-spatial Conceptualisations of Learning

If the repertoires of post-compulsory education - of which space is a part - are unstable and contested, so too are the underlying conceptualisations of learning out of which these different repertoires come to be crafted. Here, again, the communities of practice model offers an interesting starting point. In their book Lave and Wenger set out to criticise learning within the academy/ formal learning sector by juxtaposing it to situated - that is, workplace-based learning - offered up as a better, because socially engaged, form of learning. They argue that rather than students attending lectures and writing exams, they learn better through participation in an ongoing specialist activity with others who have varying degrees of expertise. But what Lave and Wenger miss is that within post- compulsory education just such a *'on-the-job'* process is taking place – in bringing new entrants into not just the community of a specialist subject area, but also into an *educational* community of practice which has historically had knowledge creation and development at its core. This is (or should be) an explicit process in post-compulsory education that has had a major role historically precisely in its continuing development of knowledge for its own sake. For this activity the educational institution *is* the 'situated' location, not just some substitute for a more 'real' place. Learning, in this context, is precisely the kind of activity Lave and Wenger prefer; it is a form of doing. This, I suggest, results in inherent tensions in higher education that separate it from education at primary and secondary levels. This is because post-compulsory education brings learning as a means to develop expertise in a subject discipline which will be used outside the academy, together with learning as a means of enabling the growth and change of the academy (both disciplinary and institutional) as a *centre of knowledge itself.* The practice- based and situated learning methods favoured by Lave and Wenger assume learning as an outward- oriented activity, aimed at increasing application in the real world.[2] However, in setting such processes against 'formal' learning, they ignore the parallel (rather than oppositional) concept of learning for its own sake, for the development of knowledge itself – what could be called 'inward- oriented learning'. This is not to suggest that it has no 'real world' basis or application, only that the motivating force is learning and knowledge development rather than professional or commercial practice. Thus, just as there are spaces-in-between individual learning and the subject knowledge that constitutes a community of practice, so too there are spaces-in-between the outward and inward- oriented trajectories taken by students and staff as they locate themselves in relation to the various spaces in and around professional/subject and educational/research oriented directions. These, tensions and the lack of their explicit articulation *within* the institution makes post-compulsory education vulnerable to other 'readings' from *beyond* the academy. As many authors have shown (Barnett 2000, 2005: Savin-Baden, 2008) it is precisely competing struggles at the social, cultural and political level over the relative visibility and value of these different tendencies that are currently affecting the 'shape' of post-compulsory education nationally and internationally. This, too, is an important aspect of the learning spaces debate.

CONCLUSION

The key underlying argument in this chapter has been that it is precisely the ideas that are affecting attitudes to learning – emphasising the personal, situated, hybrid, informal, interactive – which are also affecting how contemporary architecture is being *thought*. Yet, most of the current debate around innovative forms of learning spaces is still being articulated through older modernist ideas and assumptions about how architecture works, which believe that design can provide a direct fit between space and its occupation, and can be designed as a functional and representational response to human behaviour. These ideas are not wrong, but they do tend to frame possibilities in particular ways rather than others. This 'other' way of looking at architecture suggested here is important for three main reasons. First, it enables us to bring to bear a different kind of examination on the intersections of architectural approaches and designs with educational theories and practices, so as to begin to build a richer and more conceptually rigorous conceptual framework. This can help us better articulate the social and spatial practices of learning; and more clearly see what matters about the design of space for learning, particularly in the post-compulsory sector. This is not about creating a design 'guide' or arguing for particular 'solutions'. It is about accepting partiality, conflict and contradictions, working out what are the relevant questions to ask, and exploring what sorts of 'illuminating' methods and techniques can support learning space design decision-making. Most crucially, it involves building some kind of model of how learning and space are inter-related that enables a degree of comparative examination, whilst not avoiding or over-simplifying the complexities and multiple levels of socio-spatial practices, or the effects of specific contexts. Here, starting from Lefebvre, I have suggested that we can open up both analysis and debate by exploring learning spaces through the three part, complex and non-aligned inter-sections between ordinary routines (socio-spatial practices), specific designed environments, and participant perceptions of and engagements with (that is, how they locate themselves in-between) both socio-spatial learning practices and specific learning environments. I have also proposed that there are competing attempts to define these 'ordinary' routines of learning, operating at three inter-penetrative levels; direct learning encounters, the socio-spatial relationships and practices of an educational institution and at the society-wide conceptions of what education is or should be.

Second, then, this 'other' way of looking is concerned to consider the design of material space, and the extent to which it matters in learning. Here I have only begun to suggest how it is possible to locate architectural space differently, beyond representation or stimuli-response behavioural change. Rather, building design can be seen as having a complex and uneven relationship with the activities that go on within it, an attitude that opens up the potential for alternative ways of thinking about the architectural spaces of post-compulsory education beyond the formal/ informal learning divide. This is about how we might re-articulate learning spaces as a bundling of distinctive but contested and potentially contradictory social and spatial practices and about unravelling and examining the different repertoires connected to learning, teaching and research at post-compulsory levels[33]. In this understanding,

> architecture is just one mechanism – a part of the repertoire –through which attempts are undertaken to make concrete various (and often competing or ambiguous) understandings of learning, teaching and research. When space is articulated in this way – as integral to, but not central or singular in the challenges and arguments around the future of the university – the role of the architect and of design practices and processes subtly changes, requiring perhaps most crucially, that we begin to ask new and different kinds of questions about learning, space and design. (Boys, 2010 p. 175)

Thirdly, and very importantly, this chapter shows just how little we know about the problem of learning spaces. We have hardly begun to scratch the surface. The field remains seriously under-theorised and under-researched. A better, more rigorous and more creative conceptual framework for understanding the relationships between built space and its occupation is of relevance to both educational and architectural theory, where intersections across these disciplines remain poorly articulated. Developing tools for understanding the everyday social and spatial practices of learning – and of how these change – are of value to those who may have previously thought little about the relationships between space and activities, to those who find themselves involved in actual building projects, to those for whom the practice of architecture and design is central, and to those who are concerned with understanding more about what makes a good educational environment. It also suggests that we need to explore more explicitly our different socio-spatial conceptualisations of learning, and to have ways for debating contested notions of value around post-compulsory education. Whilst the conceptual frameworks and methods outlined here manage to be both over-structured and diagrammatically vague, the underlying aim is neither about defining rigid categorisations or relationships, nor making comprehensive and coherent descriptions of the various threads and levels described. Rather, it is to accept the ambiguities and impossibilities of such attempts at categorisation, and to instead focus on understanding something of the underlying complexities, contradictions and supplementaries that give shape to, and activate, learning spaces.

NOTES

[1]   Here the term modernism is used as shorthand to describe an intellectual and design movement which saw as itself as socially progressive, with the ability to improve environments through scientific rationalism, functionalism and technology. This was underpinned by what Lyotard (1984) has called the 'grand narrative', that is, a misplaced belief in universalist claims that the world can be understood accurately and completely. See also Harvey (1989).

[2]   Importantly, Lave and Wenger do not articulate this form of workplace-based studies mechanically as merely training, but are assiduous in underlining the value of meaning- making to learning – 'practice is about meaning as an experience of everyday life' (1991, p. 52).

[3]   It should be noted that such an articulation of the architecture of learning spaces also needs to incorporate issues about physical (and virtual) spaces that *go beyond* the activities of learning itself, for example, management and resource sustainability. This requires the integration (rather than merely 'adding' in parallel) of an understanding of space as a scarce resource with particular – often limiting – properties; an issue I have dealt with at greater length elsewhere (Boys 2010).

REFERENCES

Augoyard, J.-F. (1979/2007). *Step by step: Everyday walks in a French Urban Housing Project.* Minneapolis/London: University of Minnesota Press.

Austerlitz, N. (Ed.). (2008). *Unspoken interactions: Exploring the unspoken dimension of learning and teaching in creative subject.* London: Clip Cetl; Edinburgh: Word Power Books.

Barnett, R. (2000). *Realising the university in an age of supercomplexity.* Buckingham: Open University Press.

Barnett, R. (Ed.). (2005). *Re-Shaping the university: New relationships between research, scholarship and teaching.* Maidenhead: Open University Press.

Baudrillard, J. (1994). *Simulcra and simulation.* Michigan, MI: University of Michigan Press.

Bhabha, H. K. (1994). *The location of culture*. London: Routledge.

Bourdieu, P. (1987). *Distinction: A social critique of the judgement of taste*. Cambridge: Harvard University Press.

Boys, J. (2008). *Between unsafe spaces and the comfort zone? Exploring the impact of learning environments on "doing" learning*, conference paper presented at *e-Learning and Learning Environments for the Future*, Solstice 2008, 5 June, Edge Hill University, UK.

Boys, J. (2009). Beyond the beanbag? Towards new ways of thinking about learning spaces. *Networks*, 8(Autumn). Retrieved March 28, 2010, from http://www.adm.heacademy.ac.uk/resources/features/beyond- the- beanbag- towards- new- ways- ofthinking-about- learning- spaces

Boys, J. (2010). *Towards creative learning spaces: Re-thinking the architecture of post-compulsory education*. London and New York: Routledge.

Deleuze, G., & Guattari, F. (2000). *A thousand plateaus*. London: Athlone Press.

Derrida, J. (2001). *Writing and difference*. London: Routledge Classics.

Foucault, M. (1970). *The order of things: An archaeology of the human sciences*. New York: Pantheon Books.

Foucault, M. 1995 (1977). *Discipline and punish: The birth of the prison*. New York: Vintage.

Garfinkel, H. (1967). *Studies in ethnomethodology*. Cambridge: Polity Press.

Geertz, C. (1973). Thick description: Toward an interpretive theory of culture. In *The interpretation of cultures: Selected essays* (pp. 3–30). New York: Basic Books.

Harvey, D. (1989). *The condition of postmodernity: An enquiry into the origins of cultural change*. Oxford: Wiley- Blackwell.

Hooper-Greenhill, E. (2000). *Museums and visual culture*. London: Routledge.

Koolhaas, R. (1997). *Delirious New York: A retroactive manifesto for Manhattan*. New York: Monacelli Press.

Lave, J., & Wenger, E. (1991). *Situated learning: Legitimate peripheral participation*. Cambridge: Cambridge University Press.

Lefebvre, H. (1991). *The production of space*. Oxford: Blackwell.

Lyotard, J.-F. (1984). *The postmodern condition: A report on knowledge*. Minneapolis, MN: University of Minnesota Press.

Meyer, J. H. F., & Land, R. (2003). Threshold concepts and troublesome knowledge (1): Linkages to ways of thinking and practicing. In C. Rust (Ed.), *Improving student learning – equality and diversity*. Oxford: OCSLD.

Meyer, J. H. F., & Land, R. (Eds.). (2006). *Overcoming barriers to student understanding: Threshold concepts and troublesome knowledge*. London: Routledge.

Parlett, M., & Hamilton, D. (1972). *Evaluation as illumination: A new approach to the study of innovative programs*, occasional paper, Edinburgh University Centre for Research in the Educational Sciences/ Nuffield Foundation. Retrieved April 02, 2010, from http://www.eric.ed.gov:80/ERICWebPortal/custom/portlets/recordDetails/detailmini.jsp?_nfpb=true&_&ERICExtSearch_SearchValue_0=ED1 67634&ERICExtSearch_SearchType_0=no&accno=ED167634

Payne G, C. (1976). Making a lesson happen: An ethnomethodolgical analysis. In M. Hammersley & P. Woods (Eds.), *The process of schooling*. London: Routledge.

Ryave, A. L., & Schenkein, J. N. (1974). Notes on the art of walking. In R. Turner (Ed.), *Ethnomethodoloy*. Harmondsworth: Penguin.

Sacks, H. (1984). On doing 'being ordinary'. In J. M. Atkinson & J. Heritage (Eds.), *Structures of social action. Studies in conversation analysis*. Cambridge: Cambridge University Press.

Savin-Baden, M. (2008). *Learning spaces: Creating opportunities for knowledge creation in academic life*. Buckingham: Open University Press.

Scott-Webber, L. (2004). *In Sync: Environmental behaviour research and the design of learning spaces*. Ann Arbour, MI: Society for College and University Planning (SCUP).

Soja, E. W. (1989). *Postmodern geographies: The reassertion of space in critical social theory*. London: Verso.

Thrift, N. (2008). *Non-Representational theory: Space, politics, affect*. London: Routledge.

Tschumi, B. (1994a). *The Manhattan transcripts* (2nd ed.). New York: John Wiley & Sons.
Tschumi, B. (1994b). *Architecture and disjunction*. Cambridge, MA: MIT Press.
Warf, B., & Arias, S. (Eds.). (2008). *The spatial turn: Interdisciplinary perspectives*. London: Routledge.
Wenger, E. (1998). *Communities of practice: Learning, meaning and identity*. Cambridge: Cambridge University Press.

PART 2: WHAT KIND OF SPACE IS LEARNING?

OLIVIA SAGAN

5. BETWEEN THE LINES

The Transitional Space of Learning

Educational discourse is saturated with descriptors of space. We know all too well the spatial notions of top and bottom grades, of 'under' graduate, 'foundation' level, and 'higher' education. We assess in different *fields* and have learned about the 'spiral' curriculum', 'scaffolded' learning and 'zones' of proximal development (Vygotsky, 1962). There is 'open' learning and 'distance' learning, 'threshold' concepts, 'core' subjects, and 'peripheral' learning (Lave & Wenger, 1991). Students engage in both 'vertical' and 'horizontal' learning (Shulman, 1987) and we strive for 'breadth' of understanding, 'depth' of knowledge and 'deep' learning to counter-act 'surface' learning. Sometimes the language betrays the very social structures we are trying to eradicate: 'inclusive' learning suggests the persistence of 'exclusive' learning, an 'in' to be included into and an'out' to which others are relegated. Indeed the hierarchical, height-privileged notions of 'upper' class, 'higher' degrees and 'foundation' degrees or 'bridging' courses reveal how spatial language 'can capture us, almost unthinking, in particular, pernicious discourses…' (Paechter, 2004, p. 458). But what actually is the space of *learning*?

This chapter brings an understanding of transitional space (Winnicott, 1971) to the question of where learning takes place, suggesting it happens in the space between the taught and the learned, through a joining or collision of the learner's internal space with the external. In this space 'aspects of the self are created and transformed in relationships with others and with the matrices of culture' (Day-Sclater, 2003, p. 326), a relational process both fraught and gifted with emotional investment and risk. In this space, inward and outward foci converge (Spitz, 1991) bringing object and subject into play, creating a third temporarily, before being subsumed. In this convergence, learner meets knowledge (or subject, or teacher) and the moment commands a bringing forth of that learner with all her history, experience, knowledge, hopes, phantasies, and fears to meet with the other and meld. After this moment of play and melding, the learner retreats from the object, having taken of that moment, and thus becoming other.

This chapter explores the constituent elements of such a space, and questions how they might be provided for within an educational environment increasingly cramped, a curriculum increasingly crowded, and a thinking space - for both learners and teachers - increasingly small.

A. Boddington and J. Boys (eds.), Re-Shaping Learning: A Critical Reader: The Future of Learning Spaces in Post-Compulsory Education, 69–79.

OPENING UP THE TRANSITIONAL

'To find a form that accommodates the mess, that is the task of the artist now.' Samuel Beckett[1]

Let me précis three vignettes, which I have written about in more detail elsewhere (Sagan, 2008), as a way in to discussing the transitional.

First: Abdi, a pre-school, Somali refugee child is wreaking general havoc at an easel with some thick black paint. He is kindly but firmly given the message that this 'picture' is not quite nice. The mess he is making is not quite what we'd like to show Mum when she comes to collect him. On turning away from Abdi, Emma, merrily painting colourful, flower-like shapes, is praised.

Second: Phillip, a mentally ill adult learner of basic literacy appears to make no noticeable progress over three years. Apparently entrenched in patterns of self-sabotage, Phillip defies the best intentions, let alone assessment criteria, individual learning plans and notions of progression. The teacher struggles to provide more learner-centred activity that will encourage engagement with the content of the writing; each activity is adeptly reconstructed by Phillip, in the image of his own failure.

Third: Carol, a Fine Art student with bipolar disorder, intrepidly portrays her abusive and traumatic upbringing through collage. The group and their tutor, in the crit, are open to the content, empathic; listening. At her tutorial, however, Carol is told that while the autobiographic content is encouraged in a liberal arts environment, could she perhaps temper the way in which she *talks* about it, which is, quite frankly, *scary*?

Now, what's going on here? In each learning situation the educator is, quite naturally, concerned with a certain type of output, one which evidences learning and 'progress'. But each also struggles to compensate, through the output, for the unbearable weight of *mess*. Messy lives, messy feelings, messy learning. My first point is that the messy *is* the human, and that our drive to tidy, along with our tidy drives, says much about our distance from that human. Such distance also tells of a feared messiness of our selves, and of how by tidying, we may be foreclosing on learning. In each situation, certain negative noises, albeit from very well-meaning practitioners, are being made to the learner. And in each situation, the triangle of learner, teacher, object (painting, written product, collage) is not pliable enough, not sufficiently nuanced, to offer a space wherein each learner may feel more seen – *warts and all*. This is not a criticism of the teacher; it is an observation of what is, in part, an inevitable result of an erosion of focus on the being of teaching, and a heightened focus on its doing. It is also a reminder that, simultaneous with the challenge experienced by the learner in confronting the new and the possibly painful, is the inherent difficulty experienced by teachers confronting difficult knowledge (Pitt & Britzman, 2003), knowledge which disrupts.

The substance of this chapter is to explore what kind of space can hold such difficulty sufficiently for it to move from unthought, to thought of, and to be incorporated into a moment of transformative learning. In order to do this, we need to first consider what kind of a self we are talking about, and how that self comes to thought, and is able thereafter to insert itself into a given learning space.

BECOMING 'I'

What provokes us to think is always a traumatic encounter with some external Real which brutally imposes itself on us, shattering our established ways of thinking. (Zizek, 2000. p. 213)

Who we are, or who we become, as learners in relation to an 'other', be it teacher or object or phantasy, depends on whether we accept an idea of a shifting, contingent self (more than likely as a 21st century educationalist) or whether we are still charmed by notions of a 19th century Romantic, essential self (Thody, Chapter 9). For Winnicott himself, on whose theory of the transitional this paper is based, this was an unresolved question (Richards, 2002), despite him being commonly regarded as an adherent to a concept of a 'true' self, in relation to a 'false self' (Winnicott, 1960). The very word transitional, while applied to a range of phenomena, always conjures movement and change, and Winnicott's preoccupation with what might healthily facilitate that change suggests in itself an acceptance of a work in progress; the self as unfinished, as malleable. This image is more consonant with post-modern depictions of self than those of his contemporaries and may explain Winnicott's enduring appeal to educationalists, artists, therapists and social workers all of whom believe, with varying degrees of passion, in the beyondness of self – the co-creation of self *vis-à-vis* others; environment; relationship; culture. However, this understanding also entails a recognition that factors such as environment, culture, gender and class play a significant part not only in making us who we are, but also in *re*making how we thereafter interconnect further with such factors. Psychosocially, both unconscious and conscious factors contribute to the (re)building of self, the psychosocial subject '…possessing an unconscious dimension of subjectivity' (Frost & Hoggett, 2008, p. 440). However, this subject also inhabits 'a world of power relations and status hierarchies' (Frost & Hogget, 2008, p. 440) to which we respond in (un)conscious ways. Such responses are premised upon a need to defend against anxiety, experienced when threats to the self are perceived. These responses replicate patterns of behaviour based on early experiences when, as an infant, we negotiated the difficult and primary learning task of separation from primary caregiver, and explored the boundaries of me/not me. It is through this difficult separation that the machinery of thought is built.

MIRRORING, SPACE AND VALIDATION

How we become a *thinking* self, one capable of imagining other and able to join in the transitional spaces of learning, needs a consideration of the constituent elements of a primary experience. One of the vital elements of a good-enough early experience is that it offers the infant the play and security of *mirroring* (Winnicott 1990). Through mirroring, the infant sees, in the face of the primary caregiver, an image of itself, or, rather, *itself* – 'the mother is looking at the baby and *what she looks like is related to what she sees there*' (Winnicott, 1990, p. 112). As Richards (2002, p. 194) notes, 'The child's early learning is thus situated squarely in an interpersonal process, and is totally dependent on the reflection of the other'. Our lifelong and lifewide (Jackson, 2008) learning experiences are coloured by this early experience and a primary need to be *seen*. I will henceforth use the term 'validated' as it is more easily transferable to thinking about adult educational experience. Validation, then, suggests the positive mirroring of an individual in the 'face' of the teacher, the learning institution, the subject itself, one's peers and so on; and transcends a purely visual and facial mirroring, by moving towards a more metaphorical validation, through sign, symbol, space and the 'face' of learning. All institutions emit visual and textual messages about which 'stories' are culturally sanctioned within its walls and these messages are more likely to be 'decoded' by those in possession of the cultural capital which provides the 'bank' from which such symbols and text have been drawn (Temple, Chapter 10). Here is a replication of the 'benign' circle – only less benign to some learners than others, those without the requisite vocabulary. Public and social spaces are the means by which different forms of capital (Bourdieu, 1989) come to have currency and, as Skeggs observes, 'when one enters a physical space such as a bar, school or home, one brings with one, embodied, certain quantities of different capitals' (1999, p. 214).

Post-structuralists have argued forcefully that the subject is constructed through language; subject positions being constituted through the larger discourses of society. In being so constructed, we embody and reproduce the very discourses which have constructed us. Certain 'knowledge' is enscripted onto our bodies, and this is the mechanism for the self-regulation (Foucault, 1977) which we undertake. This also helps to explain the comfort or discomfort we feel in particular public spaces. One enters such spaces with both (I would argue) the constraints placed on one through the discourses which have moulded us, and a more or less satisfactory trace memory of early mirroring. We carry a greater or lesser anxiety about our potential for validation. The nagging question about belonging: 'Will I fit in here?' is loaded. This now gives us something to work with when thinking about learning and enables us to think more usefully about transitional space.

In the primary experience, it is precisely through a fluid mirroring within a safe environment that the ability to *play* is born. In the play of reciprocity the infant begins to form a sense of me and not me and the work of separation/dependence begins, with its tensions of inner/outer; illusion/reality; concrete/symbolic. Enter the role of the transitional object, the first object onto which the infant transfers the feelings for the primary caregiver, constituting 'an intermediate place between internal and external, easing the process of separation between the baby and the mother' (Gosso, 2004, p. 12). In this scenario of play are laid the seeds of learning and creativity. Psychoanalytically, play, learning and creativity are counter-implicated, and in educational theory a comprehensive study of their intersections has yet to be attempted, in part, perhaps because of the useful trouble and troubling use of both post-structural and psychoanalytic theory. Suffice to say at this point that we are confident (and psychoanalysis is resolute) there is a connection between the three, and that the ability to play is integral to both learning and creativity. The infant, held, (physically and psychically) is able to join in a game of mirroring, through which experiments with separation can take place. None of this is un-tinged with aggression and hate - the work of separation and dependence, on the part of both the infant and the caregiver, being rich with ambivalence. It is the first and greatest lesson, to let go of what you love and to tolerate the hate of the loved object which is perceived to be causing the 'pain'. As adults, our learning is predicated upon 'transforming the early work of learning to love to the belated work of loving to learn' (Britzman, 1999, p. 2). Safety is crucial, as separation and its attendant experiments with me/not me constitutes a fight, literally, to be, to resist the seduction of returning to the amorphousness of the non-defined. Such developmental work is a task, such confrontations with a changing me in relation to other is difficult. This echoes Barnett's (2007) notion of a space-for-being, a pedagogical space which engages the student in pedagogic challenges and ontological risk (see also Barnett, Chapter 13 in this volume). Such *learning* requires, indeed, a catalyst and the surfacing and working through of hate; aggression; ambivalence; fear – the shedding of comfortable skins. The need to manage such separation, ambivalence and affect is met through experimentation with a third (object) and the stage on which this drama unfolds is the potential space. The experience of this deep shift in our condition, and later, yet still formative, experiences, are replicated in adult learning:

> Learning is uncannily organized by repetitions of past investments and conflicts – or, in short, new editions of old conflicts. (Pitt & Britzman, 2003, p. 761)

Before we go on, I'd like to bring Abdi back in to begin to apply some of this to a learning instance. Despite Abdi's background of trauma, his pre-school classroom was offering a situation in which he could work through some of his pain. In the vignette above, we see it offering a holding environment, good-enough for him to begin to explore, through a transitional object (the painting) some of his internal conflict, the pain and darkness nestled there. This was a brave act, reflecting the resilience of children and the strength of the psyche to attempt to repair itself despite the damage. But in this transitional space, in this instance, a third element was desperately needed; a caregiver (in this case the teacher) who could recognise, in the hustle and bustle of a busy pre-school setting amidst her daily burden of learning targets, objectives and tick boxes, the salience of this moment. It needed her to work with the mess of the painting, the feelings expressed and the soiling of his shirt, the mess of having to show mummy something '*un*-pleasant' and the mess of the comparison with Emma's delightful flowers. It needed her to stay with Abdi, holding and de-toxifying some of the toxic elements experienced by him, and reciprocating by showing in her face, words and mannerisms, that she recognises this pain, and this is a safe place to show it, a space that can contain:

> Emotional holding is the holding and containment of disturbed feelings which are inhibiting the capacity for relationship, emotional growth and learning; it involves demonstrating that distressing feelings can be tolerated... (Greenhalgh, 1994, p. 107)

The transitional object evidences the ability to symbolise, presenting a medium through which the tension and dialectic of inner/outer, illusion and reality are played out.

> That space between the symbol and the symbolized, mediated by the interpreting self, is the space in which we are alive as human beings…This is Winnicott's potential space. (Ogden, 1992, p. 213)

This illusion, and the play with and on it, is a necessary part of development, learning and creativity. It offers a relief from *'the strain of relating inner and outer reality'* (Winnicott, 1971, p. 13) by 'allowing' a space where the two merge. This ability to symbolise is fundamental to mental health. An inability to have an 'as-if' experience or object, or having a perception of a symbol as the thing itself, as in symbolic equation (Segal, 1957) is a distinguishing characteristic of disturbed mental states, discussion of which is beyond the scope of this chapter. Suffice to say here that play (the 'belief' of pouring tea out for teddy) and creativity (the poem, for example, as an area of illusion and phantasy) are fundamental demonstrations of the ability to symbolise. Through such symbols, we dream, work through internal conflict, phantasise and develop as a human being. This 'work' – of play and creativity enacted in a potential space, is a primary experience of which we demand replication, in some way, in our lifelong learning.

The environment in which we can play, create, believe in the 'reality' of the knowledge and enact aggression towards the shock of the new, this potential space, is not dependent on a particular physical space, although of course warmth, colour, light and air are important. But it is dependent on a psychical space, a space for thinking and holding, a space for allowing individuals to be human *beings* rather than human doings. This requires of the institution a particular capacity:

> In secure organizations social influence is exercised in a framework dominated by an awareness of mental states, concerns, thoughts, and feelings of individuals within the system – that is, a capacity for mentalization. (Fonagy, 2003, p. 223)

What would the cost actually have been, of showing Abdi's mum a picture of dense black lines and soggy paint? What would the cost have been of helping her to recognise that play is sometimes ugly and messy, and the ugly and the messy are *vital*? Or, in Carol's example, what was the threat to us, in the crit, of the shock of the 'brutal imposition' of the stream of unadulterated, manically fast, free-associative, raw verbal expression which was Carol, speaking about her work, when on an upward cycle? What is the threat of the uncomfortable story to individuals and institutions – and what kind of space can hold, can mediate this discomfort? In both situations, there was *already* an aware and tolerant pedagogic space. One can infer from here that the lack of containment or tolerance for difficult learning in even more orthodox learning situations may well result in foreclosure on expression and a stridently limited validation of selves that do not conform.

UNSETTLNG AND UNSETTLED SPACES

So now, we can begin here to think about learning at university or college as transitional space, having laid down a few thoughts. These thoughts, in summary, are that the encounter with the new - in this context new knowledge - is necessarily *unsettling* in that it unseats our image of who we are; imagine, for example, the shock of the confrontation with knowledge that the world is round after the certainty and 'sense' that it is flat. Think not only of the intellectual challenge of this, but of the vertigo that the body would have experienced as it momentarily felt the risk of fall off a sphere.

This encounter carries with it the traces and shadows of earlier encounters. Most markedly, the encounter with learning carries residue of the encounter of separation, with its loss and aggression, but, in the event of good-enough holding, mirroring, and the enabling of play and creativity, it also carries the flush of love and growth too; we fear learning but yearn for it too. The space of this encounter also carries, and reconstructs, the discourses which both bind and license us, and define 'what can be said, which is based on what cannot be said, and what is marginalised, silenced and repressed' (Edwards & Usher, 1994, p. 8). The space of learning is no neutral zone. Learning, in which you, I and the object, form a triangle evocative of the Oedipal, with its couple and child, is discursive and relational; and, as such, takes place in time and space. Space, according to McGregor, is 'literally *made* through our interactions' (McGregor, 2003, p. 354, emphasis in the original). It is constructed through the beings in it, and through the messages, signs, symbols, texts, images and discourse which pervade it - from and between these subjects with their attendant positions. Now we can begin to think about the thinking and learning that occurs in potential space – and to understand a bit more the power and potential that resides, otherwise bafflingly, in *in-between* space. Space which is neither yours nor mine – constituted of both the internal world and the external, hybrid, *transitional:*

> ... there are potential spaces. These are gaps that do not exist in or of themselves but are deliberately created for diverse aesthetic or communicative purposes. These are also intervals that are imbued with meanings of their own simply because they represent a missed beat of the heart's communion with the Other. The line break in poetry and a fumbling pause in free association constitute spaces of this sort. (Hooke & Akhtar, 2007, p. 3)

Disjunctive space (Savin-Baden, 2008), heterotopic (Foucault, 1984) contested space, appropriated space, liminal space, and smooth (as opposed to striated) space (Deleuze & Guattari, 1988), all enjoy an in-betweeness, a fluidity, a becoming. They also each threaten to generate, through their edginess, an encounter that unsettles but also holds out an allure; the gossip arena in corridors (Hurdley, 2010) the cyber space of dissident activity; the student occupation. Consider too the almost accidental and extra-curricular activities in educational institutions, activities which magically lose their punch as soon as they become gathered into the mainstream, subjected to 'the sequestration and institutionalisation of a radical idea into a position where it can do no harm' (Bell,1995, p. 72). Such spaces, like that created by the flash mob, are powerful because they defy allocated space, and re-engineer for us an original encounter with taboo, the defying of the status quo. They also allow a space for becoming other in some as yet unimagined form; they are potential spaces. They are not, through beanbags, *created*.

THE SOFT SUBSTANCE IN A HARD SPACE

So where do some of these thoughts lead us to, in terms of pedagogic practice? Firstly, to some light debunking. The in-between space, the smooth within the striated, the liminal, will, indeed *must* always, like dissidents, create themselves. As mentioned above, the allocation of a few primary colours and matching beanbags do not necessarily make 'an interactive student space' – any more than a reflective elective necessarily reflects much more than an image of the institution in its own mirror. Indeed Barnett, (Chapter 13) cautions us that 'learning spaces may just be a device for bringing about a new order of student domestication'. Neither, does a Virtual Learning Environment (VLE) provide alternative pedagogical practice. The VLE is, rather, 'heavily coded for stability, authority and convention' as argued by Bayne (2008, p. 398) in her analysis, and 'limits the information space as a domain where new and potentially radical other pedagogic practices might emerge'. Following Rose (2001), then, a space, like an image, crammed as it is with messages, symbols and metaphor, is never innocent, but rather enables particular ways of seeing (and being) while occluding others, situating and constituting subjects in specific ways. As Lefebvre argued in his now classic *The Production of Space* (1991), space acts as both construct and replicator of social relations and power structures, a vital detail to bear in mind as we continue our work to widen participation and to finesse our concept of inclusive learning environments.

My argument has meandered rather, in space, and I am aware that I have spoken or alluded to a variety of spaces within education. So now I bring these together under three main area concerns, in order to make at least some observation of practicalities. I have spoken of the institutional space, and the need for a capacity for mentalization, in other words, a thinking institution, one which broadly contains ambivalence and anxiety, and allows for digression, dissent, mess. Leadership styles are heavily implicated here, testing the capacity of current leadership modes for tolerating uncertainty (French, 2001), and thinking through challenge and mess rather than immediately reacting. Intertwined here is the curriculum space thus envisaged, and the space within the structure of pedagogic practice, visualized as ladder, scaffold or...other? Sennett (2008) favours an exploration of 'incomplete form' – buildings that are not 'over -determined' but which can be altered over time. Such 'incomplete form' in our spaces, and the courage to refrain from over-determining our practices would seem a useful message. Chapman (2006, p. xxiii) argues that the institutional story is told through the campus, 'an unalloyed account of what the institution is all about', and incomplete form, once again, may hold a key to how we emit a message of becoming; a message of allowing space for stories alternative to the culturally sanctioned.

Secondly, this chapter has had at its heart, the space of the encounter with learning; the moment in between the taught and the learned, in which, *relationship* carries the weight of having enabled play and creativity, validation and safety, or, conversely, having foreclosed on them. On my wish list, then, of how to create a learning space which acts transitionally, which provides a space conducive to thought, and which has air enough to breathe validation of the learner, I would focus again on the teacher/student relationship and what the teacher can facilitate:

Pedagogical space itself deserves to be dissected. It is clear, is it not, that it includes not only epistemological space (the space to think the impossible), but ontological space, in which the student can bring herself into a new state of being. The inspiring teacher, accordingly, gives the student space in which she can become more fully herself, to gain her own air, to become in an authentic way. (Barnett, 2007, p. 116)

Finally, and directly related, I want to return to Abdi, Phillip and Carol, and the triangular, transitional space, an encounter altogether more private and nuanced that that of the institutional space or the broad pedagogic space. It is in this quiet, small encounter with difficult knowledge, knowledge difficult both for the learner and the teacher, and with the encounter with the mess of that knowledge, the mess of lives, of aspiration, of expression, that lessons for life are learned. As with any 'brutal imposition' we have at that moment a choice - to disavow, to relegate, to tidy or to find a form that accommodates the mess. And it is precisely at this moment, when the profession, the institution, the curriculum, the content and the hour of the day, combined with that teacher's own history of holding and containment, all press down on her and squeeze her into one response rather than another. The inexorable drive in higher education towards less physical contact and more virtual, with students 'having no place in the building to call their own,' rendering them 'for the majority of the time, absent presences' (Hurdley, 2010, p. 57) means that the quality of contact and the transitional space of learning, minimized as it increasingly is, needs more attention rather than less.

NOTES

[1]   Quoted in Deirdre Bair, Samuel Beckett, a Biography, chapter. 21 (1978). New York, Simon & Schuster; Revised edition (April 15, 1990)

REFERENCES

Barnett, R. (2007). *A will to learn, being a student in an age of uncertainty.* Maidenhead: Open University Press.

Bayne, S. (2008). Higher education as a visual practice: Seeing through the virtual learning environment. *Teaching in Higher Education, 13*(4), 395–410.

Bell, D. L. (1995). Knowledge and its pretenders: Bion's contribution to knowledge and thought. In J. Ellwood (Ed.). *Psychosis: Understanding and treatment* (pp. 70–82). London: Jessica Kingsley Publishers.

Bourdieu, P. (1989). Social space and symbolic power. *Sociological Theory, 7,* 14–25.

Britzman, D. (1999). Between 'living' and 'accepting': Observations on the work of angst in learning. In S. Appel (Ed.), *Psychoanalysis and pedagogy* (pp. 1–16). London: Bergin and Garvey.

Chapman, M. (2006). *American places: In search of the twenty-first century campus.* Westport, CT: American Council on Education/Praeger.

Day-Sclater, S. (2003). What is the subject? *Narrative Inquiry, 13,* 317–330.

Deleuze, G., & Guattari, F. (1988). *A thousand plateaus: Capitalism and schizophrenia*. London: Continuum.

Edwards, R., & Usher, R. (1994). Disciplining the subject: The power of competence. *Studies in the Education of Adults, 26*(1), 1–14.

Fonagy, P. (2003). The violence in our schools: What can a psychoanalytically informed approach contribute? *Journal of Applied Psychoanalytic Studies, 5*(2), 223–237.

Foucault, M. (1977). *Discipline and punish: The birth of the prison*. London: Allen Lane.

Foucault, M. (1984). *Of other spaces (1967) Heterotopias*. Retrieved from http://foucault.info/documents/heteroTopia/foucault.heteroTopia.en.html

French, R. (2001). *Negative capability, dispersal and the containment of emotion*. Paper presented at The International Society for the Psychoanalytic Study of Organizations Symposium, 2000, Emotions in Organizations, The Contribution of Psychoanalytic Approaches, London.

Frost, L., & Hoggett, P. (2008). Human agency and social suffering. *Critical Social Policy, 28*, 438–460.

Greenhalgh, P. (1994). *Emotional growth and learning*. London: Routledge.

Gosso, S. (Ed.). (2004). *Psychoanalysis and art: Kleinian perspectives*. London: Karnac.

Hooke, M. T., & Akhtar, S. (2007). *The geography of meanings: Psychoanalytic perspectives on place, space, land and dislocation*. London: The International Psychoanalysis Library.

Hurdley, R. (2010). The power of corridors: Connecting doors, mobilising materials, plotting openness. *The Sociological Review, 58*(1), 45–64.

Jackson, N. J. (2008). *A life-wide curriculum: enriching a traditional WIL scheme through new approaches to experience-based learning*. Proceedings of the WACE Symposium Sydney 2008. Retrieved from http://www.acen.edu.au/images/resources/conferences/wace_conference_08/e-proceedings.pdf

Lave, J., & Wenger, E. (1991). *Situated learning: Legitimate peripheral participation*. Cambridge: University of Cambridge Press.

Lefebvre, H. (1991). *The production of space* (D. Nicholson-Smith, Trans.). Oxford: Blackwell.

McGregor, J. (2003). Making spaces: Teacher workplace topologies. *Pedagogy, Culture, Society, 11*(3), 353–375.

Ogden, T. H. (1992). *The matrix of the mind: Object relations and the psychoanalytic dialogue*. London, Maresfield Library.

Paechter, C. (2004). Metaphors of space in educational theory and practice. *Pedagogy, Culture and Society, 12*(3), 449–465.

Pitt, A., & Britzman, D. (2003). Speculations on qualities of difficult knowledge in teaching and learning: An experiment in psychoanalytic research. *Qualitative Studies in Education, 16*(6), 755–776.

Richards, V. (2002). 'Winnicott and education'. In D. Barford (Ed.), *The ship of thought: Essays on psychoanalysis and learning* (chap. 10, pp. 192–211). London: Karnac.

Rose, G. (2001). *Visual methodologies*. London: Sage.

Sagan, O. (2008). *Creative considerations and difficult designs: What next in pedagogic research in art & design education?* 4th International CLTAD Conference, 3–4 April, Lycée Francais, NY.

Savin-Baden, M. (2008). *Learning spaces: Creating opportunities for knowledge creation in academic life*. Maidenhead: Open University Press.

Segal, H. (1957). Notes on symbol formation. *International Journal of Psychoanalysis, 38*, 391–397.

Shulman, L. (1987). Knowledge and teaching: Foundations of the New Reform. *Harvard Educational Review of Educational Research, 57*, 1–22.

Sennett, R. (2008). *The public realm*. Retrieved from http://www.richardsennett.com/site/SENN/Templates/General2.aspx?pageid=16

Skeggs, B. (1999). Matter out of place: Visibility and sexualities in leisure spaces. *Leisure Studies, 18*(3), 213–232.

Spitz, E. H. (1991). *Image and insight: Essays in psychoanalysis and the arts*. New York: Columbia University Press.

Vygotsky, L. S. (1962). *Thought and language*. Cambridge, MA: Harvard University Press.

Winnicott, D. W. (1960). Ego distortion in terms of true and false self, in the maturational process and the facilitating environment. In *Studies in the theory of emotional development* (pp. 140–152). New York: International UP Inc. 1965.

Winnicott, D. W. (1971). *Playing and reality*. London: Tavistock/Routledge.

Zizek, S. (2000). 'Da Capo senza fine'. In J. Butler, E. Laclau, & S. Zizek (Eds.), *Contingency, hegemony, universality*. London: Verso.

CLARE MELHUISH

6. WHAT MATTERS ABOUT SPACE FOR LEARNING

Exploring Perceptions and Experiences

This ethnographic case study investigates staff and student experiences of undergraduate teaching and learning in three new, specially designed spaces at two UK universities. On a small scale, it explores the themes, and applies some of the methodologies of research and data analysis, set out in Chapter 2. The findings highlight some valuable points for further study and consideration in this field of inquiry, and constitute a significant counterpoint to the recent emphasis on the role and significance of technological innovation in shaping new models of teaching and learning in post-compulsory education. Instead, this study shifts the emphasis to a consideration of the role and significance of physical space itself - combined with social and cultural factors in the learning environment - in the process of re-shaping pedagogical paradigms. It looked specifically at spatial, material and sensory qualities (furniture and spatial layout, lighting, smells, colour and sound), at technological infrastructure, and at perceived status and image. The overall aim was to explore student and staff *perceptions* of the impact of such spaces on their own personal and collective experiences of learning and teaching.

The sites in question were the three new, technology-supported teaching spaces created by and for the two Centres for Excellence in Teaching and Learning (CETL) which ran for 5 years to 2010[1]: InQbate Creativity Zone at the University of Sussex; the associated Creativity Centre at the University of Brighton; and the CETLD (CETL through Design) room, office and café, also at the University of Brighton but on a different campus. The research project began with detailed observational descriptions of the physical space of each centre, together with observations of learning and teaching activities. The second component of the research comprised interviews and focus groups with a small number of students and staff which explored their perceptions of the spatial, material and sensory qualities of each facility and how this was seen to have an impact on their learning and teaching. This paper presents some of the ethnographic material generated in relation to two areas of enquiry[2] - firstly, perceptions of status and image conveyed by the spaces concerned, and secondly, the effects of informal furniture and settings on teaching and learning processes. It also outlines a set of overall findings. These suggest that new learning spaces perform and have agency at both a symbolic and a functional level within their educational institutions and specific contexts; and that participants' understanding of these issues can both be articulated explicitly and are perceived by them as important to the experiencing of space.

A. Boddington and J. Boys (eds.), Re-Shaping Learning: A Critical Reader: The Future of Learning Spaces in Post-Compulsory Education, 81–91.

THE SYMBOLIC ROLE OF SPACE: VISIBILITY, EXCLUSIVITY, AND INTERFACE

'They said, oh there's this amazing room… you know, the really white, white room'[3] (Figure 6.1). The student focus group at InQbate Creativity Zone (University of Sussex) described the new learning resource as, 'the main sort of draw to the university now'. The sheer whiteness of the room (both floor and walls) sets it apart, and makes it stand out from its surroundings, both physically and institutionally. But on open day 'it was locked and so no-one got to see it. A lot of people were like, oh, we heard about this amazing space that you spent loads of money on and we can't see it'. This new learning space is thus identified as a high-value, even precious space, which must be protected at all costs – to the point of excluding the very students it is intended to attract. At the same time, this sense of its exclusivity helps to perpetuate its image as something special and out of the ordinary which gives the university a special advantage over the others. One of the implications of this is that the space is being increasingly hired out to outside companies – 'because they [the university] can't afford to have it apparently'. There is a general perception that the expense of running the place may jeopardise students' and staff access to it, which is regarded as a serious drawback because, as one tutor says it is 'an excellent resource'. This sense of uncertainty and mild resentment seems quite pervasive. 'We're not timetabled in there', comments one student about the Creativity Zone: 'it's a booking thing. Because when we go in there, they don't get any money'.

At the same time, its attractiveness to outside users is one of the key virtues of the space. It acts as a magnet and a destination for industry representatives from the outside world and the students greatly enjoy this interaction and opportunity to engage with professionals within their university and course context. As a physical space, it can be reconfigured in various ways to accommodate different kinds of events, and has a professional, ordered ambience. Yet, as with the Creativity Centre, these new learning spaces are deeply embedded within existing buildings, making them difficult to find and without a strong exterior profile. In both cases

Figure 6.1. InQbate Creativity Zone, University of Sussex. Photograph: Clare Melhuish.

physical access is via an undistinguished and poorly signposted sequence of institutional corridor spaces.

Students from the Creativity Centre, University of Brighton echo the comments of their counterparts at Sussex when they describe the way in which the space was used as a selling-point to attract them as prospective students, but had subsequently been withheld from them: 'We got shown all the plans when we came to look round, it was like this is it, it's going to be amazing, this is going to be here'. But, 'it's quite a different sort of story when you get there'. There is a sense that it is 'people outside the uni, rather than us users' who are privileged in terms of its use, and that, essentially, 'it's more for show'. As one student says, 'Initially I was very impressed. I thought it was something new, I have never seen this before... but because you're not going to get to use it, only once in a while or twice in the whole of the year ... it defeats the purpose of all that money going into these fancy bits and bobs'. While these comments reflect a basic level of frustration regarding the availability of the space, they also imply a more general sense of mistrust on the part of students towards the institutional hierarchy and the way it is set up to promote itself within the free market of higher education. These sentiments are also echoed by tutors: 'we get people trying to do prestigious meetings in here... something that's got external people in it and you go, oh, fair enough...'; and, 'I can see that we need prestigious things as well' (i.e. expensive technology). To an extent this is accepted while, at the same time, the fact that it reduces access to the resources for themselves as tutors is frustrating, since there is a huge demand for 'useful teaching space' that 'you can use when you need it'.

Students' comments thus reveal a level of awareness and acceptance of the conditions governing the delivery of higher education, and the all-important cost factor, even while they may resent the impact of those conditions on their own educational experience. At the same time, the perceived exclusivity of the space does also add to an understanding of its value, and so the very exclusivity which teachers find frustrating is also carefully controlled and perpetuated. For example, Creativity Centre staff operate an elaborate and carefully vetted booking system, which not only requires a written justification for the proposed use of the space beforehand, but also submission of an evaluation of the experience afterwards. This process is supported by a Good Practice Guide which sets out conditions and expectations for use of the space. Whilst this system is aimed at helping tutors improve their teaching and learning methods, it also effectively keeps casual users at bay, including students lacking the requisite commitment and motivation to engage with the resources properly, or 'meaningfully', as one of the staff member put it. Students perceive the learning facilities as a closely-guarded space: 'all of the time it's locked so you can't get in there anyway'; you can only book it'; 'you have to pay to book it out'; 'or you've got other bookings in there, people'. However it is not impossible for students to take the initiative and book it for themselves, as one group did, holding a computer games event in the space to raise money and feed into their professional practice. In other words, it may be that it is not necessarily a question of closed access, but also one of motivation to engage with a different institutional framework to the 'normal' ones for room allocation and booking.

While designed as an informal space, the Creativity Centre space is in fact heavily used for formal presentations and receptions in this role as an interface between academia and the industry – the real world of applied knowledge. Again, the space is perceived as being more professional than academic in ambience and functionality: 'you get to see what maybe you can use in the future... it'll benefit our future enormously, when it comes to design work.' And again, 'it's trying to push you into the real world'. As with the Creativity Zone, the fact that students value the possibility of new interactions beyond their academic peer group is expressed not only in the context of the opportunities the learning space provides for engaging with professionals and professional practice – 'they love it when people can come in from outside', comments one tutor – but also through the sentiments they voice regarding the possibility of increased interaction across year groups on their course. 'It would be quite useful actually for first years, second years, third years, all to be taught in this block, and all be here, because you only meet another year once'; 'the crossover would be a lot more'. Comments such as these emphasise the importance that spaces such as InQbate and the Creativity Centre play within universities both symbolically and functionally, as focal points for an emerging educational practice which is becoming increasingly fluid in terms of its internal and external disciplinary boundaries, and increasingly focussed on the necessity of teaching employability skills as much as imparting subject knowledge.

In common with spaces described above, CETLD is widely regarded as a facility that represents a bridge between the university and the outside world of professional practice. In this case, however, there is a conscious use of a specific language of design to communicate an identity for the space, through its furniture and fittings, which is recognizably modern, professional, and sophisticated. It is quite a 'controlled' space explains one tutor, which does not allow for more messy activities, but enables students to feel more equal with the staff who teach them, and more connected with the professional world beyond academia in which many staff also operate. The room therefore provides a fitting setting for students' engagement with what staff bring in from outside: 'you want to learn... this person's opinion can be trusted because they're actually doing it... somebody that's doing it and taking a little bit of time out to then talk to you about it'. There is a perception that this may be the only appropriate space in the university to accommodate this exchange. As one student says,

> the first time I saw this room I didn't know that we were going to have classes in here. People were sitting in groups and it seemed very project-based. Almost like a consultant office or something where you sit in a group and you brainstorm and have all these ideas and intellectual discussion. So I was quite excited to get in here. It seems as if it was a slightly more advanced level where you'd have your own ideas and discussion and develop your take on things – learning rather than education.

Like InQbate and the Creativity Centre, the CETLD room is thus perceived as a high-status venue, which has 'got a purpose', is 'serious... challenging', and in which users themselves become elevated to a higher status or level of engagement.

This effect is not just limited to the time spent in the space, but also endures beyond that: 'this is the only class I've ever done where every week I will go home and I will write up my sketchbook', comments one student. In contrast to the Creativity Centre the experience is less about play and loosening up; rather, to quote one tutor, it is a 'civilised space', which almost approaches her fantasy of 'a space where you go in for a civilised academic chat'. Another tutor describes it as 'a bit like a front parlour' – an appropriate setting in which 'you can welcome a [high-profile] visitor'. This status is reinforced by the fact that it is easily accessible, on the ground floor, from the main entrance to the campus. It is also easily visible through its glazed display cabinet, giving a view onto red, white and black items of furniture inside, which are 'obviously meant to be examples of good and innovative design' (Figure 6.2).

But, at the same time, and paradoxically, it does not have a high level of visibility within the institution. One tutor maintains that the name means nothing to most students, and many of them don't know what its purpose is or whether they are permitted access to it or not. The display of magazines inside suggests free access and browsing, and a notice on the door indicates free access on Mondays on Fridays. But there is a perception that it can only be booked for use, and you cannot just wander in and out: 'you couldn't do that'. The booking system establishes clear boundaries around its use, which effectively gives the facility invisibility except to those 'in the know' about how the system works. The problem, as perceived by one tutor, is that if such spaces 'become too visible, you'd need lots and lots of them', because everybody would want to use them. Hence the system works well 'in this transition phase', but could break down as a result of greater visibility and pressure of demand.

Students and staff clearly value such venues, but ideally would prefer them to be a more normative and easily accessible part of the teaching and learning experience – especially when physical space is perceived to be at such a premium. As one student puts it, ideally there would be a 'Palace of Creativity' to which all students would have the privilege of access to such spaces on an extensive scale.

Figure 6.2. Centre for Excellence in Learning and Teaching through Design (CETLD).
Photograph: Clare Melhuish.

THE FUNCTIONAL ROLE OF SPACE: FLEXIBILITY,
INTERACTIVITY, AND REGULATION

The symbolic value of these new learning spaces is partially represented through
material and organisational features conceived in response to the new pedagogical
paradigms emphasising social and informal learning. These paradigms highlight interactivity, peer-to-peer discussion, 'brainstorming', and team work. In the case of the
Creativity Centre, both staff and student respondents identified the brightly coloured
beanbags as its most distinctive feature, with significant functional implications for
teaching and learning (Figure 6.3). They described 'rolling around on beanbags' as
a positive contributing factor to informal discussions enhanced by physical
interactivity and movement: 'you don't get distracted about being uncomfortable,
which is a benefit'. According to staff, the unconventional seating arrangements
prompt reflectivity and new ideas: 'they sit in the beanbags and they reflect or
come up with new ideas'. In other words, beanbags alter spatial perception and
behaviour patterns in a particular way, loosening people up and providing a medium
for personal engagement with the learning environment. Students spoke of sitting
in the beanbags, as well as *on* them: 'You sit down and make a place and you're
done'. The fact that the beanbags can be moulded into a distinct shape to suit the
individual constitutes a level of 'place-making', or taking possession, at a personal
level within what is ordinarily perceived as an institutional space.

Overall, physical comfort was highly valued as a condition for allowing greater
concentration, despite the occasional risk of falling asleep: 'the only possible
downfall of that room is that sometimes it becomes too relaxing... they're so
comfortable that you don't want to get up again'. Combined with an increased
level of physical mobility and interaction, through lifting and rearranging the
beanbags in the space, and manipulation of the moveable whiteboards, it maintains
student attention levels during teaching sessions: 'beanbags are good, walls that
move around, they're good...That's the sort of interaction that works for us...
lessons in there are far more mobile ... let's move the tables out, and everyone's

Figure 6.3. The Creativity Centre, University of Brighton. Photograph: Clare Melhuish.

sitting on beanbags and stuff, let's go up and write on the whiteboards'. Students also indicated that the beanbags suited their style of working and self-image as design students: 'the beanbags are a definite plus... because of the nature of design, we're a bit more relaxed, and we like to be able to feel relaxed while we're doing our designs'. The beanbags not only fit with their image of what a designer should be and the way a designer should work, but, perhaps, helps them to differentiate themselves from their peer groups in the engineering courses within the same block – students who, according to one tutor, are more accustomed to traditional transmission-based teaching methods: they are 'used to being lectured at'.

The potential for reconfiguration at the Creativity Centre is exploited by some tutors, 'where the theatre bit comes in was the modification and change of scene. You face one way and face the other'. There is an awareness of the room's performative dimension. The teaching process becomes a dynamic performance, actively engaging the students' attention, forcing them to shift and re-focus their attention through physical adjustments to their position. Although the fixed focus of the room is the curved screen in the corner, it is also possible to create a multi-focal environment by manoeuvring the furniture and fittings (including the pot-plants on wheels) into different positions. The students draw a clear contrast between this experience and that of conventional teaching spaces: 'in our first year there were a lot of boring lectures and that space would have made it a lot better... a lot of us sitting in rows like in a classroom'. 'We do a lot of that ... now get into groups and do this, then come back, all join together, so that room's good in that sense, it can cater to that sort of set-up'. As one tutor suggests, it's 'a model which says you're working in groups'. But, for another, that is precisely why it has not been as well-used by design tutors and students as had been hoped, since this model does not fit with coursework and working methods, based on individual project development, that remain more traditional in character.

Beanbags are also a key feature of the InQbate Creativity Zone, but in this study attracted less explicit comment from participants. They seem to prompt more spontaneous and playful behaviour during teaching sessions, perhaps because of the smooth floor surface which makes them good for sliding on, but also highlighting the fact that different groups respond to spatial settings in different ways, depending on their make-up; in other words, spatial factors should not be understood as deterministic, but rather as having varying effects on behaviour patterns. In this case, the student group in question is described by a tutor as having a 'macho dynamic', and 'almost not grown-up enough to use the beanbags'. At InQbate beanbags can be seen to facilitate group working at the whiteboards around the perimeter of the space, and there is comment on the comfort which they offer, although it is somewhat qualified: 'it's nice to sit in beanbags, but... that just induces sleep if it's not interesting... if you're sat on a chair, you're forced to sit up,' says one. This in fact provides the basis for the tutor's request that students do not to bring beanbags into the presentation space, because she finds concentration levels improve if they sit up straight in chairs for lectures.

Within the CETLD space, the layout and furniture are perceived as not only inviting, but also as creating an informal and relaxed atmosphere which is not immediately associated with a teaching venue: 'When I first saw the space my impression was it looked like a café or something because of the tables and the mix and the funny chairs, and I thought, that's a bit strange. But... it does actually encourage you to relax'. Another student describes it 'as a lot less formal'. On the other hand, it is not viewed as especially comfortable. One tutor maintains the chairs are 'quite uncomfortable', though less so than 'those awful chairs [in traditional classrooms] with the little fold-down table, which are really uncomfortable and isolating for students'. She would like to introduce some beanbags, and perhaps a sofa. Another tutor (an architect) maintains it doesn't make a big difference whether you have 'an Eames chair or a standard plastic bucket chair', but on the other hand, distinguishes the furniture here from that of other teaching spaces which have 'not very nice chairs and tables, are not well lit, and have IT equipment that may not work', so that 'you feel like second class citizens'. In other words, functionality and quality combine together to have a perceptible impact not just on the way that teaching and learning is carried out, but also on the way that users feel in a space and – just as importantly – about their own value as users. Yet at the same time, furniture that clearly looks 'designed', and even out of place in this environment, may be experienced as both aspirational and intimidating by users. One student describes it as 'so modern... I want to come up with innovative ideas here', and another concurs, 'it seems more modern here, not just the interior, but also the way of working here seems more millennium-ish'. But another perceives it as daunting: 'because of the design, chairs and the colours and the tables and the fabric on the sofas, it seems very sort of modern and creative and innovative... I sometimes feel slightly pressured into being creative and I'm not really...'. Hence the imagery presented by furniture and fittings may be interpreted in a variety of ways that can impact on feelings about the learning and teaching going on.

However, there is a consensus around the perception that informal furniture arrangements facilitate group interaction and ease with each other. The fact that it is all moveable, and the tables relatively small in size, is valued as allowing easy reconfiguration and grouping, which also promotes discussion and voicing of individual opinions: 'the way we're sat means that if someone says something and has an opinion, you can then make eye contact with them and you have a discussion and other people can join in. It's not one-way'. The students contrast this setting with that of the traditional seminar room, where it is easy to feel trapped around a big table, and incapable of making a worthwhile contribution to a discussion, either because of the feeling of being under a spotlight, with all eyes directed at one point, or because of the difficulty of waiting for a gap in the conversation – 'like crossing a busy street'. In the CETLD room, the fact that 'there's chairs facing away from you and in different directions', means there are multiple focal points which eases the flow of conversation – 'with small tables you're sure to have your opinion heard... everybody does have respect for other people's ideas. It's quite a sort of comfortable feeling'.

All of these participant responses are prompted by the way in which such informal furniture arrangements can promote physical movement and interaction among its users, effectively loosening up the sessions and enhancing participation.

However, an existing level of cohesion within the student group and sub-groups using the space is important to achieving this. A student who attended a special event in the Creativity Centre which required participants to dress up in green and eat green cupcakes, remarked that 'it only worked because it was a small group of people, we already were involved... almost friends and knew each other'. She maintains that, when people don't know each other well (and therefore the group dynamic is weak or non-existent) the experience of using that particular space can be 'really stiff', and not successful. Informal furniture and layout arrangements are not likely, on their own, to be sufficient to sustain interactive learning processes A further point raised by the students – in relation to the Creativity Centre but applicable to all three facilities – is that, although the space might be seen as *liberating* in some ways, it is not necessarily perceived as *empowering*, and that one should not automatically be equated with the other. Although furniture and layout appears informal and to invite rearrangement, it may in reality be closely regulated. Students complain that they rarely have the opportunity to engage with the organisation and set-up of the room themselves, which is effectively constrained by the demands of the technological infrastructure and controlled by teaching staff. There seems to be little sense of ownership of the space, or even of the possibility of taking possession of it, although one student suggests 'maybe you need to be bold, just go, here, I'm going to go in and have a go at this today, use this'. In parallel, one tutor maintains that although his pedagogical practice has 'always empowered students', there is minimal scope for students to enter these new learning spaces and seize control of its spatial and physical properties – because 'it's not open enough and free enough for people just to wander in and do something'.

CONCLUSION

The JELS report[4] highlights the need to find new methods of assessing the impact of innovative, technology-supported learning spaces that go beyond conventional post-occupancy evaluations and surveys (Bligh and Pearshouse, Chapter 1). The aim of this small study was to use the ethnographic methods introduced in Chapter 2 to investigate how the physical environment of innovative types of learning spaces (supported and enhanced by technology, but not exclusively defined by that technology) affects the teaching and learning experience of users.

On the whole, the new spaces explored here may be seen as presenting fragments of innovatory thinking around the physical setting of learning, wrested from a context of recycled, everyday, institutional space. The borders and thresholds between the ordinary and the unusual, the pre-existing and the re-formed, are somewhat ambiguous. This has resulted in a frequently articulated sense of their physical 'invisibility' within the institutional setting which militates against their wider impact, notwithstanding a clear institutional intent to deploy them as advertising resources in the competitive market for higher education. It was striking that all student respondents expressed enthusiasm for opportunities to mix both with other students across courses and year groups, and to meet outside visitors within the university context. Both appear to be facilitated by the three new learning spaces in question which play a significant role in loosening up institutional boundaries in a way which is appreciated by students; however, they are at the same time perceived as being quite tightly bounded by institutional frameworks, and their 'place' within the university system, in a way which effectively limits access to the resource and creates a sense of exclusivity around it.

In design terms, the three facilities reviewed are all fairly neutral, white-painted rectilinear spaces. What makes them stand out is their intended educational function and purpose, the fact that they are sub-dividable and re-configurable, and express a different kind of symbolic identity to 'normal' educational space. As such, they are perceived as venues which offer something 'special'; which acknowledge and accommodate students' right to material and physical comfort; facilitate and enhance their sense of participation and the value of their contribution; and represent, through the medium of material culture and a particular type of student-teacher relationship, an explicit link between the educational process and the professional world of work beyond the university. This perception is generated not simply by the availability of technology (about which, and contrary to expectations, some students express some scepticism) but through the whole configuration, materiality, and image of the rooms as orderly, sophisticated venues in which students feel more like 'adults' and less like 'children', or can have more 'fun', that is, partake in a kind of serious play. The students' comments on the new learning spaces also highlighted the value they placed on the discursive, interactive nature of the teaching conducted in them, described as 'learning' in opposition to 'education' by one focus group. They noted the way in which the sessions encouraged students to feel that their own opinions on the teaching material were of importance and interest, in contrast to standard university teaching procedures which emphasised the acquisition of quantities of knowledge in forms which sometimes seemed indigestible, and did not necessarily invite or facilitate feedback. In this sense, the new spaces have both responded to and provided a resource for the further development of new student-centred paradigms of flexible and responsive teaching which go beyond the deployment of technology, and recognize the need to produce creative, confident, employable students. The key design questions revealed by this case study, then, may perhaps be summarised as: visibility, access to, and ownership of the learning space resources. The data suggests that new learning spaces may be designed with all the appropriate features to meet the criteria specified for effective, technology-supported or enhanced learning, but if they are not visible and accessible to students and staff, due to physical dislocation, lack of public frontage, over-complicated technology, lack of staff time and expertise in using it, or institutional and cost constraints, their use and effectiveness is limited.

Finally, it should be noted that while the findings highlight the significance of spatial factors in student and staff experiences of the learning and teaching process, they also underline the importance of simultaneously considering social factors, showing that spatial and social interactions cannot be artificially separated. What is more, students and staff perceptions of a specific space are continuously and explicitly informed both by wider institutional agendas and through the immediate context of particular learning encounters. This brings to the forefront issues normally invisible in many existing evaluations and student satisfaction assessments, that is the – very sophisticated – perceptions of material space which can be elucidated. By offering more open and engaged frameworks, participants can easily range across symbolic, social, personal and functional concerns, and can interpret spatial experiences at multiple levels, from 'reading' institutional intentions through to personal feelings of comfort or belonging. Only with this kind of rich data, can we begin to really understand how perceptions of material space affect the experiences of learning.

NOTES

[1] The Centres for Excellence in Teaching and Learning were a UK Higher Education initiative, consisting of 74 centres across a variety of educational institutions, which ran from 2005 to 2010. The two CETLS studied here were the Centre for Excellence in Teaching and Learning through Design, known as CETLD (http://arts.brighton.ac.uk/research/cetld) and InQbate, the Centre for Excellence in Teaching and Learing in Creativity (http://www.sussex.ac.uk/cetl/)

[2] Melhuish, C., (2009) Ethnographic case study: perceptions of three new learning spaces and their impact on the learning and teaching process at the Univeristies of Sussex and Brighton: unpublished paper commissioned by InQbate (the Centre for Excellence in Teaching and Learning in Creativity) and the Centre for Excellence in Teaching and Learning in Design (CETLD). Full paper accessible at http://arts.brighton.ac.uk/__data/assets/pdf_file/0011/18488/LS-Case-Study-3.pdf. The study was limited in timescale, sample sizes, and range of respondents, but achieved some valuable qualitative insights. The research was comparative and multi-sited, involving a focus group of students at each site in addition to 1–3 members of staff, and took place in the summer and autumn of 2009.

[3] All quotations in this chapter are from student focus group interviews and interviews with staff carried out during the ethnographic research cited above.

[4] Pearshouse et al (2009). As Bligh and Pearshouse consider in Chapter 1, this study is also aware of the tensions and complexities raised between the kind of situated and detailed analysis undertaken here - its specificity - and the potential for making generalisations about, and enabling transferability to, other situations and contexts.

MAGGI SAVIN-BADEN

7. RESEARCH SPACES

INTRODUCTION

I have been teaching in higher education for over 20 years and during that time I have always undertaken research, to a greater or lesser extent. Like many people I really began with a Masters, then a PhD and progressed to writing a few papers. In all the institutions where I have worked, research was recognised as a component of my activities as an academic, yet there was little if any guidance on how to do it, where to focus it or how to fund it. Most of what I have done over the years has been guided by a few helpful, critical colleagues who have 'paid it forward' in terms of offering help and hints, but much of it has come about through personal discipline and failure. Such research spaces, I believe, are not easy spaces to inhabit, and are often ones which demand spending time wrestling with ourselves as much as with data associated with other peoples' stories. So whilst at one level research spaces might be seen as windows into other(s) worlds, they are as much windows into our own.

Undertaking research in higher education in the current UK context is both personally and academically costly. Small-scale projects with fast outputs seem to satisfy many managers. Complex and in-depth research that requires academics to struggle with data and make space for confronting the often challenging consequences of the findings is invariably seen as more troublesome. As cuts in higher education increase globally, student numbers expand and the pressure to improve research outputs grows, research spaces in higher education seem to be collapsing. Simultaneously there has been an increasing interest in the notion of 'space' in higher education and more recently on physical space. For example, a literature review was undertaken to 'inform the design of learning spaces for the future, to facilitate changing pedagogical practices to support a mass higher education system, and greater student diversity' (Temple 2007, p. 4). This review examined the built environment, the organisational nature of higher education, and how universities are governed and managed, including changing relations with their students and factors influencing the learning process. However, it showed that there has been relatively little consideration of the ways in which space is seen both as a site of learning and as a site of power. For instance, the social architecture of universities tends to represent different ideologies – the lecture theatres of tradition and knowledge, the carpets and beanbags of innovation. Yet the control of space and the way in which it is valued and represented is evident through timetables, meetings, teaching and office spaces and organizational practices. Research spaces,

A. Boddington and J. Boys (eds.), Re-shaping Learning: A Critical Reader: The Future of Learning Spaces in Post-Compulsory Education, 93–103.

like learning spaces, are vital for the development and sustenance of the higher education community. Lefebvre (1991) suggested social space might be seen as comprising a conceptual triad of spatial practice, representations of space and representational spaces; where the term spatial practice indicates the way in which space is produced and reproduced in particular locations and social formations (Boys, Chapter 4). Such spatial practices are largely covert and informal, in which research of different sorts is mediated across and beyond discipline-based pedagogies. Research spaces also tend to be ones that are intense and demanding and thus for many academics they are spaces to be avoided; and the opportunity for using the spaces is often circumvented by filling them with conference hopping or the over-teaching of students. Yet research spaces, like learning spaces, are vital for the development and sustenance of the post-compulsory education community. Research spaces are defined here as transformative spaces and places in which innovative ideas and new investigations are progressed. Such spaces may occur through dialogic learning or writing spaces, but what is important about them is that they currently remain largely unrecognised, despite being where vital transformative ideas originate, are cultivated and flourish. This chapter will present the concept of research spaces, delineate different types of research spaces and suggest ways in which these can be sustained, enhanced and developed in and for post-compulsory education communities.

LOCATING RESEARCH SPACES

It would be tempting at this point to become both utopian and vague about research spaces or alternatively to provide a clearly delineated table of what they might constitute. However, I suggest that although there might be some generalisable ideas or characteristics than can help us understand and locate research spaces, in the main the constitution of a research space relates to individual perspectives and preferences. For example, whilst I might ponder and resolve questions about how to iterate data while running along a tow-path or scribbling in a coffee shop, others might need the silence of a single office or a long discussion with a colleague. Research spaces are thus different for different people and distinct research spaces are used in diverse ways throughout people's career trajectories. Although this perspective might seem somewhat liquid it will be evident from the spaces discussed here that we will not all use these, nor do we use them all of the time. The aim here is to open up to view the kinds of spaces that currently remain invisible. Consider for example, five good researchers at your institution, preferably from diverse disciplines, and reflect on what you know about how they 'do' research:
− Do they have a strong view about whether there is difference between research methods and research methodologies?
− Where do they do their research?
− How do they do it?
− What do they do with their data when they have got it?
− Do they believe there is difference between analysis and interpretation?
− How and where do they write it up?

In undertaking this activity myself I realised that I can answer relatively few of these questions in-depth about people I have known for some years. So by suggesting different understandings and possible 'types' of research spaces we can begin to come to know what counts as research spaces for us. It will also help us to consider what other options might be available that we have perhaps not considered, or considered and rejected in the past. In addition, this activity helps us to realise that myths about research can prevent us from using research spaces as effectively as we might.

TYPES OF RESEARCH SPACES

This section provides an overview of a number of research spaces, suggesting how they tend to be used and arguing that all of these spaces are important in order to progress research.

Interactive Spaces

Interactive spaces are often taken for granted and are invariably not seen as spaces, but as busy meetings. Yet re-interpreting them as 'spaces' can help us to consider them in terms also of time. For example, Castells argued that flows of capital, information, technology, organisational interaction, images, sounds and symbols go from one disjoint position to another and gradually replace a space of locales 'whose form, function and meaning are self-contained within the boundaries of physical contiguity' (Castells, 1996, p. 423). Space is inseparable from time; it is 'crystallized time' (Castells, 1996, p. 411). What I am referring to is not merely about managing time, finding time or rearranging one's day, although these are important factors in working towards what Eriksen refers to as 'slow time' (Eriksen, 2001, p. 50). To see research spaces as slow time renders them more open, dialogic and imaginative, and enables them to be seen less as 'getting through the agenda' and more as creative spaces.

Conferences

Conferences are often too big, busy and full of content, but hopefully include important papers that relate to our current ideas. Ensuring that you meet like-minded and/or challenging colleagues to discuss both conference content and future research proposals and articles can make these spaces more versatile, interactive and productive, rather than just trying to absorb as much knowledge as possible or networking with the 'names'. Too often conferences are packed with papers where the presenters speak for too long and opportunities for discussion are prevented. Those presenting keynote speeches often fail to challenge and provoke debate and instead present a few pleasant thoughts for the day.

Bid, Funding and Grant Meetings

Using these spaces for discussion with colleagues about grant processes and procedures, working across disciplines and arguing about priorities can be hard work.

Yet these research spaces are vital opportunities for learning from researchers with greater experience and from those who have familiarity with a particular funder. Such meetings not only prompt us to focus on refining ideas, but also help us to explain them to other people and consider what would be seen as value for money.

Sandpits

The use of sandpits has grown in use in UK higher education during the early 2000s. They are spaces where groups of (often diverse) people meet to build and create research ideas together. Some of these are funded and facilitated by grant awarding bodies such as the Economic and Social Research Council (ESRC), while others are formed and led by a university research support group in order to promote inter-disciplinary research. Sandpits are generally creative and interesting networking spaces where ideas are developed and new and effective research teams fashioned. Yet they can also be disastrous talking shops full of those who love to affiliate and network, but do not really want the challenge of actually getting the funding and doing the research.

Seminar Series

Whilst seminar series are common across universities they do need a committed core team to sustain them over time. These do seem to be more successful in discrete research-based units who use a range of internal and external speakers, rather than in faculties where there are many and varied research interests. What is important however is that they are highly dialogic rather than experts just talking for an hour at the 'audience', since arenas for discussion can become spaces of interruption and exploration that will be critical to the development of ideas.

Collaborative Spaces

These research spaces are highly collegial in nature and are spaces in which ideas are refined, honed and argued about. However, the notion of collaboration can be problematic in terms of power dynamics. For example, I would argue that it is un-acceptable to talk about collaborative spaces when there is no evidence of collabo-ration; to advocate participant-centred methods (such as cooperative and collaborative inquiry) but leave the research participants voiceless in the discussion of the data and reporting of the study; or to lay claim to an interpretive study but show no evidence of interpretation or, even if it is undertaken, it is not an interpretation shared with other participants as part of that study. The argument here is that in these research spaces learning and criticality are central to the growth and development of all those involved. For example, in a recent supervision meeting with a PhD student we were discussing the difficulty of informed consent from participants with learning disabilities. The discussion centred around whether if participants realised they were disadvantaged in society as a result of questions and queries raised through the research, that this would in fact result in anger and unhappiness with systems and procedures that they would not be able to change. The student argued it was wrong to allow them to know too much information while as supervisors we disagreed. There was a sense that as supervisors we believed in the importance of consciousness raising as Freire (1974) has argued, yet the student suggested that ultimately this may hinder rather than help vulnerable people. Annette, herself, explains:

> There are issues around who holds power and whether power can be given or must be seized. People with learning disabilities have very limited forms of all capital, but in everyday life, difficulties with communication often create significant barriers to social engagement and hence cultural and economic capital. Within health and social care, empowerment policy drivers push for power sharing with service users ... The ways in which power is shared include sharing of knowledge (expert patient schemes), economic capital (personalised budgets) and symbolic capital (partnership boards). Differences in linguistic capital are theoretically acknowledged (different versions of literature), although in practice literature may still prove to be inaccessible. There is an emphasis on user choice in both health and care settings (health and personalised budgets).

> Participants who lack linguistic capital may be marginalised within a research process. Even if alternative forms of research are undertaken (for example, arts-based research), it is usually the researcher who selects a form with which they are comfortable (and which generally will result in enhanced social, cultural and economic capital for the researcher). By borrowing a leaf from health and social care and using choice as a means of empowerment, participants may use their skills to select a method of engagement that reflects their strengths – not that of the researcher. For people with a learning disability, being able to use media that they are comfortable with (for example, art, drama, photography) may enable them to tell their stories in ways that are meaningful to them and this disenfranchised group may have a marginally greater voice within the research process. If it works for this client group, maybe it should be considered as a principle for all research participants where the aim of the research is empowerment. (Annette Roebuck, 2010, personal communication)

Lonely and Alone Spaces

One of the reasons research does not get undertaken or does not get published is because doing it is often challenging, troublesome and lonely. For example, there is only so much help you can get writing a grant application when you are the subject expert, or receive when re-writing a paper that has been accepted but requires a sound response to complex critical questions. Working at research – really working at it – is often lonely and necessitates perseverance. However, undertaking such tasks demands discipline and often requires that we work alone and wrestle with the message we are trying to get across or the arguments for the provision of funding.

Dialogic Spaces

Dialogic spaces are not only those that are created on campus through meetings and research forums, they also need to be recreated at conferences. Dialogic spaces for debate will only begin to re-emerge when the importance of such spaces is realised. However, dialogic spaces are not only those that occur in the cafes and at the end of meetings, rather they are formed and formulated through our positions and identities as academics. Invariably when dialogue or dialogic learning is discussed in academic circles, there is an underlying assumption that dialogue necessarily involves conversation – that the focus is always oral. Yet dialogic spaces also encompass the complex relationship that occurs between oral and written work and the way, in particular, that written communication is understood by the reader. Thus dialogic spaces transcend conceptions of dialogue, which is invariably conceived as the notions of exchange of ideas, and dialectic as the conception of transformation through contestability. This is because dialogic spaces encompass both written and verbal communication with others and one's self, but also dialogic spaces have at their core the sense that through encountering and engaging with such spaces transformation will result. Furthermore, what is often forgotten in dialogic spaces is that language is drawn from contexts and embedded meanings in texts, what Boughey refers to as the 'received tradition'. Drawing on Boughey (2006) in relation to research spaces it is worth considering:

– Producing texts – when writing grant applications assumptions might be made that if the funder guidance is broadly followed it does not matter that there is a typographical error or two. Or alternatively that following the detailed guidance to the letter will mean gaining the grant. However, grant writing is more of an art than a science. It requires creativity and often flair, whilst at the same time understanding the subtext of what the call is really all about. It is not just about producing flat text and ticking the boxes, it means also recognising that those who review it will probably offer conflicting feedback.
– Distinguishing voices – there is often the sense that research reports comprise multiple voices, those voices used by the author to substantiate their position as well as their own solo voice. Whilst academics are able to recognize and locate different voices, those new to research are not always able to distinguish such voices and see articles as flat textual pieces.
– Didactic texts – we tend to assume research-based articles can inform us as to how things *should* be, when in fact they often omit data that did not fit, difficulties that occurred during the study and the challenge of fitting the findings into the publications requirement of a high impact journal.

Writing Spaces

Writing spaces are opportunities not only to write but also to reconsider one's stances and ideas, yet such opportunities tend to be both demanding and challenging. The difficulty with the idea of creating writing spaces and of just writing itself, is that there is often a sense that others know how to use these spaces and write better than we do. Other people are intrigued by the way in which someone else writes, and they want to know their tips, their strategies and their exit routes from being stuck. There seems to be an assumption that there are hints and tips about how to go about creating writing spaces or the task of writing itself; short cuts that help to avoid the struggle and the pain. Yet this is one of the main challenges of being in a writing space, it is a space that no one else can create or inhabit. As writing spaces are our own spaces, they are places where we also have to deal with our own disjunctions, or what Woolf (1931) terms her 'angel'. Disjunction is used here to refer to a sense of fragmentation of part of, or all of the self, characterised by frustration and confusion, and a loss of sense of self. This often results in anger, frustration, and a desire for clear guidance about how to move forward.

For each of us there are issues that prevent us from writing. In a recent study (Wisker & Savin-Baden, 2009), we explored the idea of conceptual threshold crossing in the writing process. The idea of threshold crossings is based on the work by Meyer and Land (2005), who suggest that threshold concepts are discipline related concepts essential for understanding and creating knowledge in a discipline, while conceptual thresholds are moments of enlightenment and learning leaps in the learning journey, often referred to as 'aha!' moments. Building on theories of threshold concepts developed in undergraduate disciplines, notions of conceptual thresholds have been evolved to identify those moments at which postgraduates make 'learning leaps', define their identities as researchers, and start to work at a critical, conceptual and creative level suitable for the achievement of a doctorate (Kiley & Wisker, 2008). Stuck moments, the process of moving on and shifts towards focused, formed writing were examined. We found that diverse levers existed, which enabled writers to breach stuckness. Although we identified places in which some writers become stuck, some of the activities they are involved with can, it seems, be both elements of being stuck and also stages and/or strategies they use to move through that stuck state and get on with the writing. What became apparent was that there were elements of the writing process itself which helped writers to lever their way into or back into writing, over the conceptual thresholds of being stuck, and on into forming the written work. These included the process of moving on, patchwriting (cutting and pasting from existing sources), valuing preliminality (the space occupied before transformation), the vision of a possible movement through a portal and the creative learning leap into focused, formed writing.

The creation of a writing space has to relate to one's own lifestyle and ways of working best. For some people this may mean the use of a writing retreat, a place without telephones and email, in a beautiful setting with someone to help to guide the writing process. For others writing in cafés or noisy rooms is a writing space. The creation of a writing space is neither straightforward nor easily delineated; it is something that relates very much to who we are as individuals. For me a writing space is somewhere quiet, with no music, with opportunities to walk, with beautiful views and as few opportunities as possible to talk to anyone about anything. Yet I have a colleague who positions her desk in the middle of the family living space where she can see the television and where she can write around the chaos of family life. However, it is not just the physical space that is important, the psycho-logical circumstances are also important. For example, some people have a need to clear their mind of clutter whilst tidying a physical space in which to write. Some individuals prefer to trust the unconscious and just write, whilst other people write better in warm climates away from home where they can both physically and psychologically withdraw.

SOME MYTHS ABOUT RESEARCH AND RESEARCH SPACES

For many staff who come into higher education primarily to teach, research is seen as a hurdle and a problem. For those who have done PhDs and taken up research posts the challenge is to carve out their own research spaces whilst working on the principal investigator's research grant. In both these instances it is important to recognise some myths.

You Have to Be Ready

You are never 'ready to do it' and this is probably one of the most mistaken views about research for those relatively new to it post-compulsory education. There is not a particular time when someone will be ready, equipped and prepared. Even those who have been doing research for many years often feel they are struggling and ill equipped. Research, whether applied or fully funded, requires both commitment and perseverance.

It Gets Easier

It doesn't get easier, just different. While in former years I had a research assistant, small chunks of time from colleagues and the odd research grant, gaining a new large grant brought a whole team. The difficulty was that I became a manager rather than a 'blue skies' thinker for a while and this took some adjustment. I also had to learn to delegate effectively. Furthermore, I did not realise how easily upset full-time PhD students could become over issues such as small changes in the university regulations. Attempting to be collegial, encouraging and supportive often seemed at odds with keeping the projects moving and being 'the money' that kept the research unit going. It wasn't any easier just because I had more money and more help, it was just different.

It's a Privilege

Doing research isn't a privilege, it is a discipline and a commitment. The increase in student numbers across the sector in the UK at the same time as financial cuts are occurring is resulting in senior management in many universities seeing research units as privileged places. The perception is that research costs too much with little real return. Yet research is central to teaching and informs the progress of the discipline, something that is often lost sight of. Research should not be about metrics and publishing just in high impact journals. Instead it should be a committed part of all academics lives, whether vice chancellor, dean or new lecturer. It does require discipline and making time, and it is absolutely vital to the health of the academy and what it means to be a university.

DISCUSSION: SUSTAINING AND ENHANCING RESEARCH SPACES

There is currently increasing pressure in UK higher education to improve outputs, publish in high impact journals and mentor staff to improve their research standing. While arguments about ownership and intellectual property flourish, it is difficult to see research spaces as being something that can be creatively reclaimed as central to the university. Yet without research spaces, the shift to high level, well conceptualised research is unlikely to occur. What is needed are support systems which enhance rather than constrict research spaces. These could be encouraged through:

– Collegial research support groups where staff present their recent studies in a critical discussion space;
– University supported writing retreats with clear guidance, support and outputs;
– Writing days;
– Pre publication peer critique;
– One day methodology workshops to share diverse practices from different disciplines;
– Working with peers to use such approaches as qualitative research synthesis over a 2–4 month period in order to develop team research skills and become familiar with this method. Qualitative Research Synthesis is an approach in which findings from existing qualitative studies are integrated using qualitative methods. The purpose is to make sense of concepts, categories or themes that have recurred across a particular data set in order to develop a comprehensive picture of the findings (see for example Major & Savin-Baden, 2010);
– Reading groups that focus on critiquing research text books.

Whilst all these activities might seem as if they require extra and rarely available time for staff, the long-term benefits will be effective research spaces, enabling existing academics to become better researchers and publishers, and giving newly appointed academics a strong research culture with a supportive peer group. The creation and development of such research spaces will enhance all kinds of research whether evaluation, applied research or high cost, high impact studies. All this will hugely benefit both the host university and the wider academy.

However, perhaps what is really needed is to locate and understand space differently, not just in a space–time continuum but as a vector. A trajectory tends to have a sense of linearity and instrumentality about it, of a journey from one place to another. Thus in higher education the direction of travel in research is invariably conceived as a trajectory through fixed points which mark beginnings and endings. To see the direction of travel as a vector, a line of fixed length and direction but not a fixed position, would mean that research and research spaces with a sense of fixed linearity and position would be diminished and dislocated. Rather the act/ motion of travelling is opened up. It could be suggested that there is little difference between a vector and a trajectory but in fact the divergence is one of power. Such research spaces can transcend the existing structures of higher education and start to become a power beyond metaphors of a linear journey, becoming instead more fluid and creative. Such a perspective might also be seen as a sense of living with the oblique, the idea that spaces should be the fusion of movement and dwelling (Virilio, 1997), so that the space is essentially ludic (i.e. playful). Learning, play and research are issues that have always been linked for me, possibly because fun and play brings with it a sense of boundary pushing and pedagogic interruption. For me such change is currently predominantly occurring in spaces which Bruns (2007) calls produsage – characterised he suggests by community-based production, fluid roles, unfinished artefacts and common property, and through emerging technologies which increasingly challenge government and academic imposition of power and control. The consequence is that the influence not only of the internet but different types of spaces merging within it and through it, seem to be shaping and producing ways of thinking and operating, which are always on the move and are therefore constantly unfamiliar. Yet there is also an almost inherent stress that appears to be associated not just with fast time (Eriksen, 2001) but also with 'continuous telepresence'. Such an unrelenting sense of immediacy might at one level be linked to a sense of constant busyness, but also appears to result in reduced time for thinking, a feeling of time being taken away by others, and a means of avoidance of activities that are central to research spaces, such as reflection, reflexivity and critical thought. Indeed Virilio suggests:

> The paradoxes of acceleration are indeed numerous and disconcerting, in particular the foremost among them: getting closer to the 'distant' takes you away proportionally from the 'near' (and dear) (Virilio, 1997, p. 80).

We are in a world in which we are, as Virilio predicted, universally telepresent without moving our physical bodies. Thus there is often a sense that we arrive and depart from spaces and encounters without actually doing so. The question, then, is whether we are victims or beneficiaries of this 'chronic telepresence'.

CONCLUSION

To ignore the importance and essential development of research spaces is perilous and could damage criticality in the academy. Research spaces are often seen as difficult and separate spaces. Yet they are (or should be) part of the life of every academic. They should be seen as 'movement image', where research spaces are not seen as separate sites but as interconnected intersections. As Thrift argues:

> ...every place is regarded as a knot tied from the strands of the movements of its many inhabitants, rather than as a hub in a static network of connectors. Life is a meshwork of successive foldings, not a network, in which the environment cannot be bounded and life is forged in the transformative process of moving around. (Thrift, 2006, p. 143)

Using the metaphor of research spaces as vectors and linking Virilio's notion of the oblique with research spaces can perhaps offer some purchase on the ways in which research in the future might be effective in challenging notions of stability, performativity and equilibrium. Thus, rather than normalising research spaces in post-compulsory education, we can see them as the lost spaces of interruption that should be (re) inhabited.

REFERENCES

Boughey, C. (2006, July). Texts, practices and students learning: A view from the South. *Keynote Speech Higher Education CloseUp, 3,* 24–26. University of Lancaster.

Bruns, A. (2007). *Beyond difference: Reconfiguring education for the user-led age.* Paper presented at Ideas in Cyberspace Education 3, Ross Priory Loch Lomond. Retrieved March 21–23 from http://www.education.ed.ac.uk/ice3/papers/bruns.html

Castells, M. (1996). *The information age: Economy, society and culture* (Vol. 1). Oxford: Blackwell.

Eriksen, T. H. (2001). *Tyranny of the moment. Fast and slow time in the information age.* London: Pluto Press.

Freire, P. (1974). *Education: The practice of freedom.* London: Writers and Readers Co-operative.

Lefebvre, H. (1991). *The production of space* (15th ed.). Oxford: Blackwell.

Kiley, M., & Wisker, G. (2008). *'Now you see it, now you don't': Identifying and supporting the achievement of doctoral work which embraces threshold concepts and crosses conceptual thresholds.* Kingston, ON: Threshold Concepts Conference.

Major, C., & Savin-Baden, M. (2010). *An introduction to qualitative research synthesis: Managing the information explosion in social science research.* London: Routledge.

Meyer, J. H. F., & Land, R. (2005). Threshold concepts and troublesome knowledge (2): Epistemological considerations and a conceptual framework for teaching and learning. *Higher Education, 49*(3), 373–388.

Temple, P. (2007). *Learning spaces for the 21st century – A review of the literature* (pp. 1–84). Retrieved January 25, 2010, from http://www.heacademy.ac.uk/assets/York/documents/ourwork/research/Learning_spaces_v3.pdf

Thrift, N. (2006). Space. In M. Featherstone, & C. Venn (Eds.). Special Issue on Problematizing Global Knowledge. *Theory, Culture and Society, 23,* 139–146.

Virilio, P. (1997). *Open sky.* London: Verso.

Wisker, G., & Savin-Baden, M. (2009). Priceless conceptual thresholds: beyond the 'stuck place' in writing. *London Review of Education, 7*(3), 235–247.

Woolf, V. (Ed.). (1931). *Professions for women. Women and writing.* London: The Women's Press.

SUSAN SHERRINGHAM AND SUSAN STEWART

8. FRAGILE CONSTRUCTIONS

Processes for Reshaping Learning Spaces

INTRODUCTION

From the emergence of modern educational institutions in the wake of the 18th century western Enlightenment, until the early 21st century, the spaces of learning appeared to have attained an ideal type-form. Within this institutional tradition, learning takes place in rooms that provide a stable, neutral environment; free from external distraction. Teacher and class face each other, the teacher backed by a clearly visible surface upon which shifting arrays of information can be temporarily inscribed or projected. The classroom and the lecture theatre reflect this basic configuration. The seminar room and library provide variants catering to group discussion and individual study respectively. For well over a century these arrangements seemed unquestionably to provide the right kind of environment for learning. However there is nothing natural or necessary about such arrangements. They are a construction arising out of a negotiation of cultural assumptions and institutional priorities. The robustness of this construction, its continuing, and virtually unquestioned dominance throughout the radical technological and social changes of the 19th and 20th centuries, seems finally to be about to be unseated.

Learning in higher education is experiencing revolutionary change; some say as dramatic and significant as the scientific and industrial revolutions of the 18th and 19th centuries (Burrowes, 2001). The communications revolution driven by new, digital technologies over the past quarter-century, alongside new conceptions of learning, have posed a decisive challenge to both institutional ideas about the nature of learning, and learners' assumptions about the role and authority of learning institutions. Revolutions de-naturalise previously unquestioned configurations of the world; the interests that have held these configurations in place are unsettled and rendered vulnerable. Apparently robust orderings of the world are newly revealed as fragile constructions, holding sway only provisionally. Equally fragile is the re-negotiation of relationships within a new or emerging order. Stakeholders, though recognising the failure of existing arrangements, struggle to conceive of how things could be done differently.

It is in the character of our times that apparent 'matters of fact' reveal themselves to be 'matters of concern'; solid-seeming artefacts disclose themselves as assemblies of contradictory issues (Latour, 2004; 2008:4). Bruno Latour has argued that design plays a special role in helping us negotiate such matters. He terms design 'a cautious Prometheus' that brings to the task of making and *re*-making, a

A. Boddington and J. Boys (eds.), Re-Shaping Learning: A Critical Reader: The Future of Learning
Spaces in Post-Compulsory Education, 105–118.

radically careful, and carefully radical, sensibility. (2008:3–7). This characterisation of design belongs more to an emergent, 21st century context of collaborative and participatory design than to the legacy of heroic claims and stances associated with design in the 20th century (Loewy, 1950, 2002, 2007; Bel Geddes, 1932 etc[1]; Fry, 2002). Opposed to the culture of designer as celebrity, this more modest (and more crucial) conception positions design at the heart of an ongoing negotiation of "complex and contradictory assemblies of conflicting humans and non-humans [things, ideas, agendas, interests]" (Latour, 2008:6).

The project that this chapter draws upon belongs within this new conception of design. The focus of the project was the brief development process for next generation learning spaces. A design brief is a crucial document, crystalizing and communicating stakeholder desires for the outcome of a building program. The process that leads to the formulation of a design brief is often compromised by the complexity attendant on inclusion of multiple stakeholder voices, and by the constraints presented by limited time, communication difficulties and the inertia that tends to reproduce habitual dispositions within new gestures. The aim of the research project was to design tools, models and other supports for enabling a collaborative and participatory brief development process. It was hoped that the tools and other supports developed, would help to overcome some of the barriers that currently hinder the production of insightful briefs that open up alternate futures and facilitate the design of innovative, next generation learning spaces.

This chapter focuses on two aspects of the research. First, we give an outline of practice theory, which provided researchers with a theoretical starting point for orienting the brief development process to the requirements of 'authentic' learning. Second, we discuss the centrality of participatory processes and playful engagements for fostering inclusive conversations between diverse stakeholders. Within the liminal space that play affords, visual tools are introduced to prompt generative dialogues. The special role of the visual in eliciting understandings that can cross boundaries between different stakeholders, negotiating their often-conflicting values and concerns, is discussed. Together these two approaches - practice theory and the use of participatory processes and playful, visual prompts - may enable the construction of dialogues, and ultimately briefs, that envision new kinds of learning spaces, more appropriate to our new century.

PRACTICE THEORY

Within contemporary, discipline-specific education which aims to prepare, or further qualify, students for participation in particular professions, there has been an emerging emphasis on 'authentic learning'[2]. Authentic learning is understood to take place when the learning scenario experienced by the student reflects contexts for action typical of those for which the student is being prepared. In other words, authentic learning is authentic to the practice context within which the learned skills and understandings will be performed (Herrington & Oliver, 2000).

In many ways the desire to foster authentic learning has arisen from recognition of the centrality of 'practices' to human motivation and striving. In referring to 'practices' we draw upon a body of theory that builds on 20th century pheno-menological, hermeneutic, anthropological and sociological arguments. This emergent theoretical direction, which references influences from (late) Wittgenstein and Heidegger, gained impetus in the wake of Bourdieu's *Outline of a Theory of Practice* (1972), Giddens's *Central Problems in Social Theory* (1979) and MacIntyre's *After Virtue* (1981), and has been further mobilised since the turn of the century in the texts of Theodor Schatzki (2001), and Andreas Reckwitz (2002). Within this theoretical context, and especially in the most recent arguments by Reckwitz, the term 'practice' refers to an identifiable constellation of activities, know-how, orientations, values and striving that is entered into, embodied and performed by those who are engaged in the practice.

Practices range from the everyday, including activities such as cooking or gardening, to complex professional practices, such as medicine and law. Each practice encompasses myriad activities and, conversely, activities can belong to multiple practices. For example the activity of cooking can belong within a parenting practice, a friendship practice and a culinary practice. Not all those who perform an activity are participants in every practice to which that activity can belong. If I cook a family meal, but am more concerned (on such occasions) with nutritional balance and with pleasing the limited palette of my child than with the delicate blending of flavours and aromas that informs the culinary art, then the striving that informs my cooking, my effort to produce something that will be enjoyed, arises from a desire to parent well, rather than a desire to further the culinary arts. It is possible, however, that my participation in the activity of cooking, whether as a part of my parenting practice or in the quite different context of socialising with friends, may open me to an engagement with cooking as a culinary practice. Activities lie in the intersection of multiple practices, and so open participants in one practice to the potential pleasures and disciplines of another.

Practices are not just clusters of related activities and associated know-how, but are rich collections of associations, embodied experiences, and engagements with the world through designed things, environments, and interpretive frameworks (Oosterling, 2009). For example, gardening is a practice characterised by particular activities such as soil preparation, planting, watering, weeding, fertilising, pruning and so on. Expert gardeners share a body of know-how, enabling them to recognise the condition of the soil and the plants; they have an eye for the flourishing of the garden, and for its latent possibilities. They know where to cut, what to remove, how deep to dig. However the true gardener is one who has become disposed, through gardening, to particular pleasures and pains, bodily disciplines and sensitivities. For a gardener, activity in the garden is accompanied by a deep sense of joy in the responsiveness of the garden to their care. The aching of knees and back, the feeling of dirt under the fingernails, calluses on the hands, and sunburn on arms and legs; the registration of labour and exposure upon and within the body; these sensations are shared and understood by those who garden. Similarly the embodied experience of loose-fitting or protective clothing, of broad-brimmed hats and cumbersome gloves, the feel of spade against hand and boot, the slight crunch or scrape of the soil against its blade; these sensuous accompaniments to the activity are cumulatively embedded in the experience and memories of the gardener.

Other practices, such as nursing, law, design or journalism, each share their own particular set of embodied ways of doing, feeling and knowing. In each, the body and the understanding of practitioners are disciplined in different ways; attuned to different subtleties. Further, and importantly, those who share in a practice share particular pleasures and motivations. The rewards for striving within the practice are given through specific joys experienced through exemplary performance within that practice. A gardener feels keen pleasure in the budding of plants; notices this budding in a way quite different from the noticing of such things by those outside the practice. For those who have been inducted into a practice and have become bearers of that practice, pleasure is felt in the accomplishment of goals that are meaningful within the practice itself.

Because practices motivate people, and make their activities meaningful, practices are the site of learning. Although learning can happen outside a practice, the learning is grasped as meaningful only insofar as it relates to a practice in which the learner is a participant. This has consequences for those who seek to induct learners into new practices, especially in formal learning contexts, where entrants to a practice may have no initial desire to learn, or context for making that learning meaningful. Learners are not yet bearers of a practice. They do not automatically embody a disposition for particular kinds of striving; they may not be attuned to the dispositions of the world that are desired within that practice, nor do they yet feel pleasure in the subtleties of expert performance. The transitional process of learning (Boys, Chapter 4; Sagan, Chapter 5) gradually opens them to feeling and performing in these ways. The learning environment can play an important role in supporting this process of attunement, this cultivation of a disposition for what is best within a practice.

PRACTICES AND LEARNING SPACES

Not all practices are the subject of formal education. Those that are have become so because the particular disciplines that educational institutions seek to impart are held to also be necessary to the wellbeing of that practice. Western educational institutions took their modern form during the 19th century as vehicles of the enlightenment project of 'bildung', the development of a "scholarly consciousness ... within which the mind has a special, free mobility" (Gadamer, 1989:15). The cultivation and performance of this scholarly consciousness belongs to a practice of its own, distinct from those other practices, such as medicine, engineering or urban planning, that are now also cultivated in institutions of higher education. The gradual assignment to the university of responsibility for induction into these other practices, which took place from the 19th to the late 20th century, was done out of a desire to endow each of those practices with the same capacity for scholarly and critical self reflection, and the same qualities of free mobility, that were the goals of university education. Contemporary students of higher education are being inducted into a particular practice of their choice, whether it be mathematics or law or music, but they are also being inducted into the enlightenment culture of scholarship, intellectual mobility and critical reason (Boys, Chapter 4). The mix of harmonious or dissonant dispositions created by each particular conjunction of enlightenment agendas and practice-specific orientations, and the weighting of each at different moments within the student's education, colours the student's learning experience.

Recognition that what is learned is made meaningful in the context of the practice in which the learner is engaged has important implications for the design of learning spaces. If learning is a process of induction into a practice or practices, and the purpose of education is to ensure that the next generation of practitioners will be capable of taking their practices in new and promising directions, then spaces catering to authentic learning need to enable and support the informal transmission of attitudes, disciplines and dispositions as well as know-how and more explicit formal understandings relevant to each practice. In other words, the learning environment can play an active role in the acculturation of the student to the practice they are being trained for.

Traditional institutional learning spaces reflect the enlightenment emphasis on the universality and neutrality of a mobile, inquiring, scholarly disposition. The classroom and lecture theatre strive to support a focussed, disembodied attention to the information being imparted by the teacher. Chairs support the body; tables support the activity of note taking; lighting and climate control eliminate inter-ference by weather or temporal cycles. The learner is placed, as far as possible, in a space that allows the mind to be engaged and the body to be neutralised. However the idea that learning should be primarily a cultivation of mind, supported by a disciplined, but passive, body, is not only inadequate to authentic learning, but also to the overarching project of the university, *bildung*; the production of a mobile and critical consciousness. The profound 20th century critique of the enlightenment project overturned the divorce of mind from body. Institutional learning spaces have yet to follow suit.

How, then, can an attention to the specific practices that students are being inducted into inform learning space design? Focus groups with students reveal the ease with which they are able to identify incongruities between their learning spaces and the practices they seek to engage. Students enrolled in *Leisure, Sport and Tourism* at one institution complained of the almost windowless rooms in which they were taught, and the long corridors that separated them from outdoor playing fields. "We are students of *sport*!" they exclaimed. Similarly, students and staff in design schools constantly grumble about the impossibility of fostering a 'design culture' within the over-scheduled spaces of their schools. Design culture requires you to "hang around in the studio together," informally engaging with each other's projects. Evident to both learners and experienced participants within the practice, these mismatches are not readily addressed within the over-stretched efficiencies of contemporary, production-oriented, education provision.

Although incongruities between educational spaces and the practices they cater for can be identified with relative ease by those within a practice, these incongruities tend to be accounted for in terms of function. The rooms in which students of sport are taught ought to open onto outdoor spaces, preferably sporting spaces; the studios in which design is taught ought to be available for students to 'hang around in'. Yet such amendments to the layout and accessibility of these spaces do not address more subtle questions concerning the fitness of institutional spaces for the acculturation of students into particular practices. Those questioned in focus groups about their learning spaces are able to mobilise the language of functionality in their attempt to pinpoint what does not work, but have no means of articulating - no language for - the failure of their learning spaces to evoke the proper 'mood' and disposition for their practice. Practice theory alerts us to the need to attend to the emotional tenor of stakeholder discussions about their learning spaces. Often an exclamation of frustration will signal an absence, a lack, in existing learning experiences; an expression of affection for a particular space may signal its particular fitness to the practice being learned, perhaps in some quite subtle respect. These communications are more likely to be indirect than direct. Practice theory helped us to notice and interpret such moments within stakeholder engagements. Recognition of the importance of such moments has had consequences in our research project for the design of the tools for stakeholder engagement within the participatory design process[3]. It was important to elicit informal and tacit under-standings of both the practice and of what works and what fails in existing learning experiences. The following section outlines the thinking that informed our articulation of a particular participatory design process for the collaborative development of briefs for learning space design.

PARTICIPATORY DESIGN

Higher education is a complex system that involves external drivers, institutional values and directives, funding, preconceptions, curricula, pedagogy, teachers, learners, space, resources, infrastructure and technology, each contributing to the learning experience and the quality of that experience. When new learning spaces are proposed, these various forces, stakeholders and facilities mobilise, or are mobilised, to determine what kind of space is to be provided. The pre-briefing conversations, that set in place the agendas and constraints that will dominate decision-making throughout the design process, have been typically driven by high-level agendas and institutional values. Within such contexts, the particularity of the practices that the new spaces are to house is discounted, because largely unknown to those admitted to these high-level discussions. In recent years, however, there has been an active endeavour to open up this process, to enable more innovative and practice-relevant possibilities to be considered. It was as part of this endeavour that our project for developing protocols to guide processes for generating innovative and appropriate design briefs for new learning spaces, was conceived. The inclusion of our project team leader in working parties for the development of a number of new learning spaces, for 18 months prior to the formulation of the project, provided insight into the challenges presented by established processes. The urgency of developing new processes to better meet the needs of changing learning agendas was evident, and was felt at the highest institutional levels. Thus the project was well supported, and opportunities were readily available for trialling proposed new processes and tools within a number of real building projects.

Observation of the dynamic within typical stakeholder meetings revealed several important obstacles to the generation of innovative and appropriate new learning spaces within these institutional settings. The first, and perhaps most intractable difficulty, lay in the tendency of stakeholders to advocate for, and defend, territory traditionally controlled by their own interests. Stakeholders represent and embody an array of conflicting priorities, values, opinions, and agendas and a range of professional vocabularies. They see their own position as being of the utmost priority and are unwilling or unable to relate to other stakeholders' concerns. Often the conversations between stakeholders in such groups are inflexible, laden with biases, politics and power play. Facilities (estate) managers' concerns about efficiency and value for money, managers' concerns about cost, public profile and student experience, teachers' concerns about 'deep learning', curriculum and engagement, learners' concerns about understanding, achievement and resources; all are legitimate and have their place within the conversation. The adversarial character of many traditional stakeholder meetings works to push less powerful voices aside in order to reduce the complexity of the task. A first concern of the project, then, was to find ways of diffusing power play, to allow decision-making to be informed by a more balanced negotiation of priorities.

A second, and perhaps even more challenging, concern, lies in the difficulty experienced by almost all stakeholders in imagining possibilities other than those they have experienced and are familiar with. Despite the volumes of research showing that students learn little in traditional lecture theatre based, information-delivery oriented, learning scenarios (Bligh, 1998; Gibbs & Jenkins, 1992; Ramsden, 1992), students consulted in focus groups continue to identify lecture theatres as desirable learning spaces. Despite the desire of educators to encourage active learning, many continue to advocate for spaces configured to allow their own voice to dominate. Despite the ongoing maintenance workload for facilities managers, generated by a perceived need to maintain predetermined configurations of room furnishings, the specification of such configurations remains a focus of their concern. Despite the awareness that industry representatives have of rapidly changing practices within their workplaces, both their criticisms and their expectations of learning spaces tend to draw on their own educational experiences, often twenty or thirty years previously. In each case the problems attached to existing ways of doing things, although often acknowledged, remain largely unaddressed in the pre-briefing conversations about new facilities. Assumptions about the nature of learning spaces, informed by habit and a preference for the familiar, are built into the brief, and so fuel the designer's own tendency to reproduce known models (Heimstra, 1991). The power of design to re-configure, rather than simply reproduce, educational practices, is thus elided within these traditional brief-development processes. Participatory design processes, developed and popularised since the 1990s, (Schuler & Namioka, 1993; Muller, 1991, 1993; Blomberg, 1998; Sanders, 1993), offered a way of addressing the above concerns. Interestingly, participatory design has rarely been used in developing spatial design briefs; and where it has been used in developing briefs for educational environments, these have typically been in the context of school-based K-12 learning[4].

The issues identified above as inhibiting the development of innovative and appropriate design briefs within higher education contexts are characteristic not just of learning-space design scenarios, but are typical of complex settings within which change is being collaboratively negotiated. It is to address the needs of such settings that participatory design has been developed as a strategy over the past two decades. The success of participatory design, in meeting this need, stems primarily from its recognition of the enabling power of play (Sagan, Chapter 5). Play is a universal experience. Like learning, play permeates our lives. As humans, we are characterised 'not just by our thinking or achievements, but by our playfulness: our curiosity, our love of diversion, our explorations, inventions and wonder' (Gaver, 2002). The efficacy of play within participatory design arises from three of its enabling capacities; play defuses the power relations that exist between players prior to (and outside of) the game; it opens up a liminal space within which unreflective and tacit understandings can come to view; and it enables players to deal with change and envision alternate and open-ended futures in a risk free space (Gaver, 2002; Kolb 2010). Play within participatory design is initiated and directed through tools, prompts and frameworks devised for the particular design context. These tools can be of various character, however often they emphasise the visual.

The use of visuals or images as triggers or conversation pieces is not new. The introduction of the visual provides a non-linguistic way of developing generative narratives and interpretable artefacts. Anthropologists, social scientists and psychologists have been using images in their practice, through photo elicitation, photo ethnography, photo journals and photo interviews, for their potency to draw forth memories and emotions and their capacity to record events or scenes in their entirety (Banks, 2001; Harper, 2002; Hurworth, 2003; Styhre & Gluch, 2009). Vision, as an embodied intelligence, connects to the multiplicity of human experience without the linear or analytical distraction of language (Styhre & Gluch, 2009) or its socio-political power (Meier, 2007). The visual speaks to tacit understandings of culture, values, and their associated action; they speak to embodied knowing. Images, drawings and photos can be conceived of as socio-cultural probes that elicit feelings, draw forth thoughts and beliefs, and provide triggers for projecting alternate futures through the ascribing of meaning onto the image (Robinson & Parman, 2010). If play is the first strategy of participatory design, then, elicitation of ideas and understandings through engagement with the visual is the second. Of the participatory tools developed in previous projects that we examined, none provided the right focus or level of granularity needed for the development of briefs for next generation learning environments. Here the complex relationships between curriculum, technology, space, the practice(s) and myriad stakeholders needed to be made visible.

One of the primary tasks of our project was therefore the development of playful, visual stimuli, and guiding frameworks for engagement with these stimuli, that would enable communication between stakeholders and encourage them in open-ended exploration of innovative possibilities for future learning spaces in

Figure 8.1. Early development and testing of tools and models - 'Day in the Life' exercise, Scaffold Workshop, Sydney 2009. Photograph: Susan Sherringham.

Figure 8.2. An activity-scape being developed – 'The Parallel University' game, Scaffold Workshop, Interdisciplinary and Social Sciences Conference, Cambridge, 2010. Photograph: Susan Sherringham.

higher education. The tools designed for our project have been specifically conceived of as 'group thinking' and 'epistemic tools' (after Henderson, 1999 & Brecht, 2003) and 'playful triggers' (after Loi & Burrows, 2006) with the capacity to bridge different professional and practice groups (Styhre & Gluch, 2009). They are what Henderson refers to as visual meta-indexicals (Henderson, 1999).

The workshops with stakeholders focus on imaginative development of what we have termed 'activity-scapes'. An 'activity-scape' is the supportive experiential, spatial, equipmental and service environment immediate to the performance of a particular activity. For example the 'activity-scape' relevant to the writing of this paper includes a particular focussed attentiveness to both the unfolding argument and to the voice of the co-author, an equipmental environment of digital software and hardware, lighting, table-top and chairs, coffee-cups, reference texts and so on, and a background supportive environment of services connecting us variously to texts and colleagues, and to sustaining supply lines of food and caffeine. The boundaries to the activity-scape determine how open the activity is to other influences, to the bleeding of sounds, smells and temptations from adjacent environments, or to more distant influences that penetrate the space either virtually or by other means.

From the above account we see that an activity-scape develops from an exploration of five dimensions;
1) what kinds of orientations, embodied experience, communications and interactions need to be supported within the activity;
2) what different aids, inputs and facilities are needed;
3) what tools and technologies will be taken up;
4) what is needed to support those technologies;
5) what the boundary conditions of the activity should be.

These dimensions then need to be considered in terms of practice-oriented preferences for a particular atmosphere or aesthetic that may further support the learning activity. Within our participatory design workshops for a specific group of learning space stakeholders, the starting point for developing an activity-scape is the identification of a practice-relevant disposition or set of dispositions that educators wish to develop within the students. For example, nursing educators may wish to develop a disposition within their graduates, for being observant of the body language of their patients, and a capacity for recognising the relationship between bodily conditions and medical need. In this example, the generators of the activity-scape focus upon the need for students to develop a focussed attentiveness to bodies and then begin to explore the different ways that bodies may be made present to students within the learning space, how those bodies might be experienced, what can be observed and how that observation can be impacted by the immediacy of access to inputs and aids, the environmental conditions and available technologies of the space. Workshop participants are supplied with sets of cards offering multiple options for identifying various needs, supports or conditions for learning from which they can discuss and choose preferences. The cards range from fairly abstract visual prompts to explicit words and cues. Once an array of cards that successfully evokes stakeholder desires for the activity-space has been selected, the second phase of the workshop begins.

If the first phase of the workshop is generative of a desired learning activity-scape, the second critically tests and iteratively develops that conception. Workshop tools enable rapid development of user-personas and learning scenarios. A set of 'what if?' cards introduces possible shifts in the context for learning, including broader changes to the physical, technological, social, political and economic environment of the educational institution. The activity-scape is also tested against both present and future institutional identity and industry expectations. In this way the workshops are modelled to create a form of reciprocal learning, within which

Figure 8.3. Persona Development - Scaffold Workshop, Sydney, 2010.
Photograph: Susan Sherringham.

stakeholders and designers engage in playfully framed exchanges. The interactions with others and the generation of narrative through justifying, resolving, actively listening and achieving consensus, shapes understanding around what is being discussed (Costa in Hyerle, 2009). The process facilitates learning about self, about others and about different futures. Through the social construction of new possibilities, suggestions for change can be generated and owned by the stakeholders (Kolko, 2010). A sense of ownership creates positive engagement with the workshop outcomes, and encourages ongoing commitment to realisation of the vision generated. Such principles are central to participatory and co-design processes and draw on the principles of appreciative enquiry and positive psychology (Whitney & Bloom, 2010; Passmore & Hain, 2005).

CONCLUSION

The relationships between space and learning are not straightforward. Rather they are fragile and constructed, personally, culturally and institutionally. These constructions are subtle, often invisible, and generally unspoken. The traditional processes of brief development often fail to access these webs of significance, or to mobilize stakeholders toward promising change. To enable the envisioning of promising change these processes must be looked at anew.

The social and technological revolutions of our times call for a new consideration of how and where learning takes place. The processes and tools being developed through this project offer a particular way of enabling looking, noticing and 'relooking' at what we want students to learn and the supportive contexts and environments within which learning might take place.

Practice theory brings a new focus to conceptions of learning environments where practices are understood as the site of learning. It acknowledges learning as situated within authentic activity, experience, context and culture. Practice theory provides ways of highlighting the dispositions that are valued and desired within a practice, the learning activities and performances central to the development of these dispositions, and the support and technologies that need to be at hand. Through practice theory we are drawn to those embodied aspects of practice that call for authentic spatial responses.

As an exploratory process the development of activity-scapes enables creative, imaginative and interrogative engagements with new learning scenarios. The participatory design tools developed within the project aim to 'scaffold' stake-holders in their collaborative development of these activity-scapes. Through this participatory process stakeholders are invited to play, to spin webs of meaning, of action, of affectation, and of embodied knowing. Thus a rich tapestry of socially constructed information, a 'thick description', is developed for the designer to interpret and translate. Thus, through the lens of practice theory, the aesthetic and embodied dimensions of what might constitute an authentic learning environment can be articulated. The creative processes of participatory design engage stakeholders in design moves, framing and reframing perspectives and under-standings in their co-generation of a design brief for new learning spaces, relevant to them and to the educational requirements of the contemporary generation.

NOTES

[1] The 20th Century, in the vein of connoisseurship and modernism, continued the tradition of heraldry, that of great men, great objects, great stories within which architects and designers as individuals were held up as heroic figures, and their work as canons.

[2] Authentic learning draws on situated and experiential learning. It aims to provide authentic contexts to support authentic activities that reflect the way information is accessed and shared, the way knowledge is created and used in real life practice. This includes access to and or integration of appropriate tools, equipment, technologies, access to expert performances and modelling of processes providing opportunities for students to engage in multiple roles, to collaborate in the construction of knowledge and to promote reflection to enable abstractions to be formed. Whilst the authors here refer to Herrington and Oliver (2000) and practice theory, see also Boys, Chapter 4, for reference to a related but differently framed idea of practice, the community of practice models of Lave and Wenger (1991).

[3] This chapter outlines research stemming from an Australian Learning and Teaching Council (ALTC) Priority Project Grant "A protocol for developing curriculum-led human-centred next generation learning environments in higher education"; initiated in 2008 and involving a partnership between the University of Technology, Sydney as lead partner with Monash University and the University of Melbourne. The ALTC is an initiative of the Australian Government Department of Education, Employment and Workplace Relations. The views expressed in this paper do not necessarily reflect the views of the ALTC. http://www.altc.edu.au/project-protocol-developing-uts-2008.

[4] There are a few examples of participatory design tools specifically developed for higher education environments; the Learning Landscape project lead by Lincoln University partnering with design consultancy DEGW (http://learninglandscapes.lincoln.ac.uk/) and the Explore It Toolkit: Effective

Spaces for Working in Higher Education (http://exploreacademicworkplace.com/) are exceptions. These projects use evaluation, diagnostic, mapping and charting tools to define shared parameters for expression, efficiencies, and effectiveness within an institution and draw on the institution's own identity, aims and values to build models of learning and work as specific patterns of social and spatial organisation (see also Duggan, Chapter 11).

REFERENCES

Banks, M. (2001). *Visual methods in social research*. Oxford: Oxford University, UK.

Bel Geddes, N. (1932). *Horizons*. New York: Dover Publications.

Bligh, D. A. (1998). *What's the use of lectures?* (5th ed.). Exeter: Intellect.

Blomberg, J., & Kensing, F. (1998). Participatory design: Issues and concerns. *Computer Supported Cooperative Work (CSCW)*, *7*(3–4), 167–185.

Blomberg, J., Giacomi, J., Mosher, A., & Swenton-Wall, P. (1993). Ethnographic field methods and their relation to design. In D. Schuler & A. Namioka (Eds.), *Participatory design: Principles and practices*. Hillsdale, NJ: Lawrence Erlbaum Associates.

Brandt, E., Messeter, J., & Binde, T. (2008). Formatting design dialogues - games and participation. *Co-Design*, *4*(1), 51–64.

Bourdieu, P. (1977). *Outline of a theory of practice*. Cambridge: Cambridge University Press.

Burrowes, G. (2001). *Gender dynamics in an engineering classroom: Engineering students' perspectives*. Australian Digital Thesis Program, University of Newcastle.

Fry, T. (2002). Approaches to historical study of design in Australia. In M. Bogle (Ed.), *Designing Australia: Readings in the history of design* (chap. 2, pp. 7–13). Annandale, Sydney: Pluto Press.

Gadamer, H. G. (1989). *Truth and method* (2nd rev. ed., J. Weinsheimer & D. G. Marshall, Trans.). London: Sheed & Ward.

Geertz, C. (1973). *The interpretation of cultures*. New York: Basic Books.

Gibbs, G., & Jenkins, A. (1992). *Teaching large classes in Higher Education: How to maintain quality with reduced resources*. London: Kogan Page.

Giddens, A. (1979). *Central problems in social theory. Action, Structure and Contradiction in social analysis*. London: Macmillan.

Harper, D. (2002). Talking about pictures: A case for photo elicitation. *Visual Studies*, *17*(1), 13–26. Routledge.

Heimstra, R. (1991). Aspects of effective learning environments. In R. Hiemstra (Ed.), *Creating environments for effective adult learning*. San Francisco: Jossey-Bass.

Henderson, K. (1999). On line and on paper: Visual representations. In *Visual culture, and computer graphics in design engineering*. Cambridge, MA: The MIT Press.

Herrington, J., & Oliver, R. (2000). An instructional design framework for authentic learning environments. *Educational Technology Research and Development*, *48*(3), 23–48.

Hurworth, R. (2003). Photo-Interviewing for research. *Social Issues Update*, Issue 40, Spring, Department of Sociology, University of Surrey, Guildford.

Hyerle, D. (2009). *Visual tools for transforming information into knowledge* (2nd ed.). California: Sage Publications.

Kolb, Y., & Kolb, D. (2010). Learning to play, playing to learn: A case study of a ludic learning space. *Journal of Organizational Change Management*, *23*(1), 26–50.

Kolko, J. (2010). Sensemaking and framing: A theoretical reflection on perspective in design synthesis. *Design Research Society*, conference proceedings.

Latour, B. (2004). Why has critique run out of steam? From matters of fact to matters of concern. *Critical Inquiry*, *30*(2).

Latour, B. (2008, September 3). A cautious Prometheus? A few steps towards a philosophy of design (with special attention to Peter Sloterdijk). Keynote lecture for *Networks of Design*, meeting of the Design History Society, Falmouth, Cornwall.

Loewy, R. (2007). *Industrial design*. London: Duckworth.

Loewy, R. (1950, 2002). *Never leave well enough alone*. Baltimore: Johns Hopkins University Press.

MacIntyre, A. (1981). *After virtue. A study in moral theory*. Notre Dame, IN: University of Notre Dame Press.

Meier, P. S. (2007). Mind-mapping a tool for eliciting and representing knowledge held by diverse informants. *Social Research Update*, 52, Autumn. Department of Sociology, University of Surrey, Guildford.

Muller, M. J. (1991). *PICTIVE – an exploration in participatory design*. CHI Proceedings of the SIGCHI conference on Human factors computing systems: Research through technology.

Muller, M. (1993). Participatory Design. *Communications of the ACM, 36*(6), 24–28.

Passmore, J., & Hain, D. (2005). Appreciative inquiry: Positive psychology for organisational change. *Selection & Development Review, 21*(5).

Oosterling, H. (2009). Dasein as design or: Must design save the world? In *Premselalecture 2009* (L. Martz, Trans.).

Ramsden, P. (1992). *Learning to teach in higher education*. Routledge.

Robinson, L. B., & Parman, A. T. (2009). *Research-inspired design: A step-by-step guide for interior designers*. Fairchild Books.

Reckwitz, A. (2002). Towards a theory of social practices: A development in culturalist theorising. *European Journal of Social Theory, 5*(2), 243–263.

Sanders, E. B. N. (1992). Converging perspectives: Product research development for the 1990's. *Design Management Journal, 3*(4), 49–54.

Sanders, E. B. N. (2000). Generative tools for co-designing. In Scrivener, Ball, & Woodcock (Eds.), *Collaborative design: Proceeding of co-designing 2000*. London: Springer-Verlag London Limited.

Schatzki, T. (2001). *The practice turn in contemporary theory*. New York: Routledge.

Schuler, D., & Namioka, A. (Eds.). (1993). *Participatory design: Principles and practices*. Hillsdale, NJ: Lawrence Erlbaum Associates.

Styhre, A., & Gluch, P. (2009). Visual representations and knowledge-intensive work: The case of architect work. *VINE, 39*(2), 108–124.

Whitney, D. A., & Trosten-Bloom, A. (2010). *The power of appreciative inquiry*. San Francisco: Berrett-Koehler (first published 2003).

PART 3: LEARNING SPACES AND INSTITUTIONAL IDENTITIES

ANGELA THODY

9. 'LEARNING LANDSCAPES' AS A SHARED VOCABULARY FOR LEARNING SPACES

INTRODUCTION

Is it a café? Is it lawn with lake? Is it lecture room, professor's office, virtual architecture of computer phone and web cam, corridor ...? No – they're all spaces on, or connected with, university lands. These lands, as empty spaces, exist irrespective of users. Once the spaces are used, they become 'landscape', 'the projection of human consciousness, the way the land is perceived and responded to' (Becher & Trowler, 2001, p. 16). As landscape, university students and teachers, researchers, caterers, estates managers, governors and administrators create learning opportunities by interacting in the multiple dimensions of all these different spaces. Thus a university campus offers possibilities for holistic and ubiquitous education with its design as a physical signal of this; every element of a campus can offer a learning opportunity. Collectively, this is its learning landscape.

This chapter investigates 'learning landscapes' as shared vocabulary for universities' collectives of on- and off-campus learning spaces; with the aim of enabling architects, designers and educators to consciously develop a university campus that can offer the most learning opportunities. Firstly reviewed is how the terminology of learning landscapes has been employed outside universities and its gradual absorption into university planning during the early 2000s. Discussed secondly are the forces that have been the impetus to develop the concept of learning landscapes: university conceptualisations, sociological and political imperatives, learning theories and practices, technology-based learning and last, our need for belonging. Finally demonstrated are some proposed techniques used for the initial design of learning landscapes – mapping and user consultation.

LEARNING LANDSCAPES: EARLY 2000S' TERMINOLOGY

The very limited literature overtly using learning landscape terminology launched the concept metaphorically as geography (Noyes, 2004; Quinn, 2004). This emphasised concepts of space and place so much neglected in education (Hutchinson, 2004) but within boundaries too limited for the scope of whole university space (school maths, undergraduate geography). Outside of its geographical metaphor, the learning landscapes concept was adopted by project-based companies. These 'discontinuous... complex interdependencies...[with] uncertainties...variations in knowledge activities, levels of formality, technologies, social relations and communicative

A. Boddington and J. Boys (eds.), Re-Shaping Learning: A Critical Reader: The Future of Learning Spaces in Post-Compulsory Education, 121–135.
© 2011 Sense Publishers. All rights reserved.

interactions' (Brady, Marchall, Prencipe & Tell, 2002, p. 1–2) understand learning landscapes as mechanisms that enable project-to-project learning to take place (ibid., p. 11–12), in a way very akin to how universities operate. Such interconnectedness is also central to post-compulsory learning landscapes since these too are trying to link all campus provision into seamless learning opportunities.

Colonisations of the words 'learning landscapes' in spheres other than post-compulsory education confuse definitions. Norfolk Children's Services (UK) New Landscapes for Learning (2006) seems little more than a way to link training workshops, discussion seminars and conferences about personalised learning; the 'Learning LANDSCAPE for Schools' (sic) (LL4 n.d.) is about safe blogging for schools. However, these usages do pick up emergent themes for universities' learning landscapes: student-centred learning and e-structures. Learning landscapes are used to sell ideas or products: the US's Bureau of Land Management has Learning Landscapes as 'America's big backyard', promoted to provide enrichment opportunities from the environment (BLM n.d.); management training games are sold as learning landscapes (Bonner Networks n.d.); *webanywhere* (n.d.) titles its catalogue 'Learning Landscapes' selling personalised e-learning; Natural Learning Landscapes for Schools (n.d.) advertises outdoor learning purchases. While disconnected from universities, all point to the significance in learning landscapes of not only e-learning architectures but also of eco-interpretations related to the actual physical landscapes of campus grounds.

Physical landscapes are central to green schemes for university grounds in the USA (Starik, Schaeffer, Berman & Hazelwood, 2002). Denver public schools' and the University of Colorado's Landscapes for Learning (US) (Denver, n.d.), aimed to improve school grounds but it is noteworthy that its processes involve much of what is now becoming central to our understanding of learning landscapes anywhere – community involvement, collaboration on designs and participatory learning (Brink & Yost, 2004). 'Northumberland Learning Landscapes' (n.d.) (UK) is themed on the landscape as teacher. The same idea, nationally promoted, was behind the part-UK government sponsored charity, Learning through LANDSCAPES (2010), championing school grounds as out-door classrooms.

Before learning landscapes, as a term indicating complete entities, entered the lexicon for universities, the words sometimes surfaced for libraries - as information landscapes (Russell, Criddle & Ormes, 1998) using construction analogies of e-architectures and building systems for knowledge management (Quinn, 1992). To this technological area, have been added the terminologies of personal learning landscapes created from a variety of open source tools including e-portfolios (Kalz, 2005; Tosh, Werdmuller and Haywood, 2005) and through discussion of the impact of technology on the design of learning environments (Francis & Raftery, 2005). These ideas have affected, for example, the views of one of the originators of the learning landscapes concept for universities – DEGW – an architectural practice. Their learning landscapes concept is of increasingly flexible work spaces, innovatively used to encompass physical and virtual learning space, delineated as central hubs, learning spaces, lifestyle facilities, informal physical environments whether as new build or redesign, based on co-operative planning between architects, designers and educators (Harrison, 2006b, pp. 3–4). Such a conceptualisation has been realised in projects at Newcastle, Warwick, Lincoln, Reading, Loughborough and York *inter alia* (CERD, 2010, pp. 20–25)[1].

LEARNING LANDSCAPES: FORCES FOR FORMULATION

What, then, have been the forces behind the development of the concept of learning landscapes as a means to describe educational institutions as holistic entities? I will outline some of these next (see also Barnett on ecologies, Chapter 13).

University Conceptualisations

Using historical referencing in university architecture, design and education matters has an important symbolical power since universities are seen to be societal conservators and have a work force often perceived as conservative (SPOT+ 2001-4, p. 97) or slow to be re-educated (Gore & Gore, 1999). Universities' learning landscapes must also be places tax-payers, fee-payers or donors as external stakeholders, can *recognise* as universities. Concurrently, an understanding of history must combine with universities' missions to lead new thinking, preparing 'students for the future in an increasingly complex society' (Starik et al., 2002, p. 339). This tension has been constant whether we return to the thirteenth century when universities began, or later; there were always empires in confrontation, new weaponry, inventions and social changes. Then it was the Holy Roman Empire, long bows and feudalism; now it is democracy, satellite attacks and student diversity. Twenty-first century universities' learning landscapes are akin to a new town, established to house increasingly diverse, mass student populations in central hubs. These hubs are also electronically linked for any-time learning to even more suburban/rural/isolated crowds of students. For some philosophers and practitioners, these changes are cause for rejoicing and offer new conceptualisations (Kelly, 2002, p. 106; Barnett, 2005; CERD, 2010, pp. 20–25). Others report reasons for mourning (Gilbert, 2000; Cutright, 2001; Maskell & Robinson, 2001; Scruton, 2001). For both, the learning landscape concept provides an opportunity to reflect on the value and objectives we want for university education (Sarles, 2001).

With universities conserving tradition and simultaneously confronting the future, one borrows from the ideas of nineteenth century Cardinal John Henry Newman. He aimed to reconcile the competing landscapes of old collegial and new professorial systems in his establishment of a Catholic University of Ireland in the mid-1850s, from whence came his influential writings on what universities should be (Newman, 1852/1858, collected in Newman, 1907). He envisaged learning as holistic and therefore led by disciplines united in the university, not divided into colleges (Cameron, 1956). Learning would be led by university professors teaching existing knowledge to educate whole minds, to help men learn how to think and value knowledge for its own sake (Kerr, 1999, pp. 20, 22, 24, 27). His contemporary, Benjamin Jowett, stalwart of the Oxford college tradition (Balliol tutor, 1842–1893, Professor, 1855, Master of Balliol from 1870) with his own acclaimed personal tutorial style, bequeathed the centrality of the staff-student tutorial to university education (Abbott & Chambers, 1897/2010; Ashley, 1897/1966) and therefore the need for learning landscapes to accommodate such individualised learning. Personal academic offices sufficed in the 1800s. While these survive in 21st century universities, experimentation with alternative workspace for tutors has begun. Wolverhampton University's New Technology Centre, for example, gives staff and students equal access to computer stations on an open floor space, each bookable on line. Some smaller rooms survive for staff working collaboratively or with students (www.learninglandscapes.lincoln.ac.uk/case-studies/university-of-wolverhampton-new-technology-centre, accessed 23/11/10). In common with other learning landscapes configurations, the aim is to facilitate informal staff-student tutorial experiences in as many locations as possible such as seating nooks in corridors or quiet areas in cafés. E-architecture, with its web links, skype telephoning and web cams, also aims to ensure that individualised guidance for students can continue – this despite the distance-learning diaspora that has developed since Jowett expounded the virtues of face-to-face tutorials with students. Leap forward to an apparently anti-Newmanesque period of corporate Macdonald's, Disney's or L-Oreal's universities and discover even these aiming to 'stimulate co-creative thinking and develop instruments of integrative transition…[to] innovate…break out of traditional mind-sets…of knowledge transfer…into more proactive and broader learning landscapes' (Dealty, 2002, pp. 340–341). Contrasting romantic interpretations of universities (1770–1850) advocated cultivating 'in the young a heightened sense of aesthetic and cultural appreciation' (Henley, 2002, p. 418). This latter resonates with that part of learning landscapes that is about the style of the architecture, preserving historical buildings, the joy of interior design and the provision of gardens that delight the senses.

Sociological and Political Imperatives

Universities have always both reproduced and created elites. The balance between these two for the 21st century is towards creating an ever more elite 'elite', or the removal of the 'idea' of there even being an elite. As the 19th century comic librettist W. S. Gilbert noted, when everyone is somebody then nobody is anybody (Iolanthe), which Scruton might see as a suitable requiem for our mass intake universities (Scruton, 2001). This mass enlargement is mandated by pressures from an ever-more educated and certificated school and parent population, economic needs for highly trained workers, society's needs to extend childhood (if only to justify its own existence as carers and to delay unemployment) and governments' needs for efficient resource management. The latter has brought together massification with an intention of improving space usage across the university estate; such as Shirley Williams, 1969 UK Secretary of State for Education and Science, proposal to make universities more efficient through more intensive use of buildings and equipment. By 2009, there was still only 15–20% occupancy of university buildings during core working hours (CERD, 2010, p. 8) contributing to the more recent coalition UK government's 2010 call for 2-year degrees.

But whatever the sources or rationales for this mass student influx, it has to be accommodated, physically and virtually in landscapes that must appear both 'special' and as encouraging all to enter this 'special' world. Reconceptualising universities as learning landscapes thus becomes a way of coping with the size, complexity and objectives of their socio-politics. Re-conceptualisation must result in effective social reproduction, but from a much wider base of entrants, so that elites are extended. University landscapes must therefore both create awe in their users and on-lookers while also symbolising universal accessibility.

Students' identities and cultures in part arise from students' accessibility to staff and peers outside of formal educational settings (Brennan & Jary, 2005). From this comes the significance of bringing the entire learning landscape within formal purview; all learning opportunities are given equal status thus either enabling more elites or no elites depending on your personal perspectives. Sociological topography recognises place as 'partisan and ideologically charged' (Hutchinson, 2004, p. 14). As such, learning landscapes can cause total alienation (Illich, 1973) but they also have responsibility to renew (or perhaps transform); 'the social fabric of society… [schools] are the institutional bridge that ensures our cultural continuance, that connects one adult generation to the next' (Hutchinson, 2004, p. 9). Staff, in these sociological reproduction scenarios, are usually assumed to be academic staff and the significance of administrators and service staff tends to have been overlooked. However, the latter do appear in university organisational models arising from power constructs such as professional bureaucratic, collegial, political and anarchic (Baldridge, 1983; Bourgeios & Frenay, 2003). In the greater holism of learning landscapes, administrators and other non-academic staff, gain status, a change already noted in school learning (O'Sullivan, Thody & Wood, 2000). Thus academic staff elites must open to admit other staff as well as students; learning landscapes must facilitate this, recognising all participants as sources of learning – often overlooked in the informal elements of university architecture and design.

Learning Theories and Practices

Amongst the many debates about the desirability of these social and political developments (Smith, 1999, pp. 163–166), there seems general agreement that learning is most effective when at least part self-initiated, holistic, requiring action-learning, recognising everyone's involvement to create total learning and culminating in the student as producer as well as recipient (Neary & Winn, 2008). Find too, ideas in university learning of early-years educators (Froebel and Montessori for example) who created 'a Landscape for Learning…from self-directed play', stimulating all the senses (Torelli & Durrett, 2006, p. 2). This reminds us again of interconnectedness, integral to twenty-first century learning landscapes. This arises from twentieth century learning theorists such as Kolb (1984), with his circle of learning for adults, Greene (1978), with her merging of students' interior worlds with the landscapes of their exterior worlds, and nineteenth century Newman who wanted students to have a 'connected view and grasp of things' (Kerr, 1999, p. 17). This connectivity is mediated around naturally occurring or formally encouraged collaboration with learners, as in the UK's Oxford Brookes University's thinking about a new learning landscape (Francis & Raftery, 2005). All this social learner collaboration does not preclude equal emphasis on solo learning (cf Lincoln University's Great Central Warehouse Library, CERD, 2010, p. 21). Collaboration is, however, accorded prime place because shared learning is deemed so significant in advancing learning (Arthur & Lindsay, 2006).

From these ideas emerge practices to be facilitated by architects, designers and educators in universities' learning landscapes. These include students' active engagement in real world issues in a supportive, relational social environments (Pascarella & Terenzini, 2005), 'flexible, distributed learning' (Francis & Raftery, 2005, p. 1), 'constructive alignment' between course aims and their environments to enable student active learning on 'authentic real tasks' (ETL project proposal, 2000/2001) and learning from a green environment (Starik et al., 2002). All this is to foster creativity and experiment. So, for example, the InQbate project, at Brighton and Sussex Universities (http://www.inqbate.co.uk) is not so far away from Newman's desire to cultivate energetic mental action around new ideas (Kerr, 1999, pp. 20, 22). This mental action must today, however, ideally be in-the-world (Barnett, 2005, p. 795) though this can be through virtual or physical means. Traditional formal lecturing, whether in person or on internet screens, is still integral to post-compulsory education, but here designers need to create, for example, wired lecture theatres that enable students to have concurrent access to sources other than the lecturer and seating that twirls to facilitate group work, sleep or attention to a podium-based lecturer – the type of innovations that reconsideration of learning landscapes' designs might bring.

This reconsideration recognises connections between university learning landscapes, student behaviour and achievements (ETL university learning landscapes project) which was a major rationale for the UK's Labour Government's Building Schools of the Future (BSF) policy for the pre-18s (Harrison, 2006b, pp. 8–12). BSF aimed to change the appearance of secondary school buildings and their settings to be innovative, collaborative and diverse, all concepts that appear in various university learning landscapes projects where similar connections are made with student learning outcomes (ETL, 2001, p. 2). These outcomes are extended as students add informally to a university's structured learning spaces, for example colonising corridors and cafes (Brennan & Osbourne, 2005), which have been neatly categorised as 'the bits in-between (Harrison, 2006b, p. 16). Such informal learning can be aided by conscious design promoting learning interactions but good architecture in itself should also become a learning tool. It should 'teach people to analyse and be sceptical' (Sussex, 2002).

E-Technology

The learning theories and practices discussed above can fortunately be provided for massified 21st century universities using e-technological tools, now regarded as integral in creating learning landscapes' interconnectedness and individualised learning. This was tested in the Cambridge University learning landscapes project by removing technology tools for a week from volunteer students and staff to find out where, and if, they were really vital (Riddle & Arnold, 2008). The general consensus was that current learning theories can be implemented without e-technology but with much greater difficulty than with it.

Major exemplars have been the UK Joint Information Systems Committee (JISC), advising universities on ways in which e-learning tools can support teaching, learning and research, and the SPOT+ study (2001–4), investigating ICT use for teaching and learning in twelve European universities. This extended university opportunities through facilitating outreach to outlying geographical areas and social classes, linked to the socio-political changes referred to above. Parallel developments are seen in businesses where virtual classrooms were introduced in corporate universities for economic reasons and thereby re-engineered their learning landscapes (Aldrich, 2006). An example from school children's learning is the University of Illinois at Chicago which produced an 'immersive learning environment [a whole room virtual reality experience]...where children build virtual ecosystems', enjoying a multi-user experience (Roussos, et al., 1997, p. 917).

Some sound caveats about this virtual world of detached experiences for educational environments; many findings suggest that technology alone does not change learning (Bain, 1996; McWilliam & Taylor, 1998; OECD, 2001; Serafin, 2006). E-tooling, however, permits ubiquitous, immersive learning around the whole university learning landscape and connects it to its outside world of, for example, commerce. The London School of Economics BOX project is a learning space with whiteboard walls, plasma screen and PC and with a substantial area for moving around the seating to facilitate various learning modes. To stimulate learning, the room has books, boxes of artefacts more usually viewed in museums, and unusual furnishings (Harrison, 2006a). This illustrates the integration into a common immersive landscape, of e-tools, knowledge architectures, virtual learning, traditional facilities, space and stimuli to, as one might say, 'think outside the box'. However, expectations that e-technology will replace human teachers may be 'naïve' (Smith, 1999, p. 164). But there is no longer 'an unquestioning belief in the efficacy of classroom delivery...[Everything is moving to learners controlling] their own learning programme in terms of time and space' (Harrison, 2006b, pp. 5, 14). E-tools facilitate student control but design must facilitate academic staff having the same rights of control too.

Need for Belonging

All the preceding topics require recognition of the centrality to effective teaching and learning of space and place (Edwards & Usher, 2003; Hutchinson, 2004) and from that to the significance of interconnected *placings in spacings* (see also Temple, Chapter 10). These give human beings the necessary feeling of belonging to an intellectual home, summed up in the phrase alma mater. For an excellent example of a campus demonstrating physically an intellectual home, view the inter-connectedness, speciality, difference and combination of tradition and innovation, at the University of Texas at El Paso where all its learning landscapes have echoed Bhutanese architecture ever since its inception in 1914. Visit my own University of Lincoln, UK; locate yourself amidst its award-winning post-modernist campus and see how its design frames the view above of the mediaeval Cathedral, how its new buildings convert older structures such as railway warehouses whilst – when straggling up the hill to that Cathedral – find other university colonies dotted in various historic locations.

A lack of this place recognition/space bounding for the learning landscape may have contributed to the short life of the UK's unsuccessful e-university project, which I would describe as a de-schooling experiment in the post-compulsory sector, and which was wound up in 2004 (House of Commons Education and Skills Committee, 2005). We were ready for an extension to the traditional idea of a university (as the success of the UK's Open University has shown) but perhaps not to its obliteration as a bounded space with a physical HQ and Regional Centres to which we can mentally relate even if we never go there. This may arise from the human need to be able to relate to what we see (Hutchinson, 2004, p. 13). In planning their learning landscapes, architects, designers and educators therefore need to enable that relationship by reducing the strangeness of teaching and learning opportunities while preserving expectations that a university is traditionally something special and different. Into that special and different space, students enter as transients; administrators and academics are more rooted with permanent offices and designated teaching areas; estates, and other service, staff tend to come some-where between these two extremes with work bases and meeting places from which they emerge into their fairly mobile lives. Combining these communities in the learning landscape and admitting academic staff and students to decisions about that landscape, means changing their 'places' to some extent. This alters existing views of power as the socio-political perspectives and learning theories discussed above indicate. To facilitate this, students and staff have been promoted to design partners in some of the learning landscapes projects, albeit not without some caveats being expressed as to the respective roles of each group (Lincoln Learning Landscapes, n.d.). For example, those reporting on the leadership and governance of the project to create the Reinvention Centre at Oxford Brookes University, a centre to encourage student independent and autonomous research, state:

> academics should provide leadership in terms of the development of the estate…students are only here for a short time so their views are very much the current view. I think we have to be brave enough to say that we have a vision, we have the experience and the evidence to back it up. (Oxford Brookes, n.d.)

BEGINNING DESIGNS FOR LEARNING LANDSCAPES

Finally in this paper I will briefly look at issues around participatory design, and then at how mapping techniques can support user consultation in the initial design of learning landscapes.

Student/Staff Consultations

Including students and staff in decisions previously reserved to architects, engineers, designers and senior education managers has so far been little researched in university projects but it has in school design projects. UK, US and Australian findings point somewhat cautiously to stakeholder input in planning school buildings creating 'a healthier, more inclusive and fairer society' (DfES, 2006, p. 4). The resultant buildings can reduce inequities of gender, ethnicity, socio-economic status and differential abilities while enhancing student achievements, physiological wellbeing and improving behaviour (Pearson, 1972: Beck, 1980; Allen 1988, p. 10; Lucas & Thomas, 1990; Gordon & Lahelma, 1996; Nelson, 1996; Lyons 2001, p. 6; Featherstone, 2002; Martin, 2006, pp. 91, 102; DCSF, 2007, p. 13; Mason, 2008; NCSL, 2008). Creativity also ranks highly as a reason to extend client influence on design plans (Castaldi, 1969, pp. 15, 97, 101; Dudek, 2000, p. 125; CABE, 2004, p. 4) as does client advice on how buildings can best satisfy social and psychological needs as well as the merely technical (Davis, 1982, pp. 261–262). The influence of client groups joining the decision-making is deemed central to major social and economic changes according to an 'enormous international literature' (Black, 2003, p. 4). For this to happen, architects and designers must be committed to 'colla-boration and accepting that…insiders who use the building may see it differently from outside observers' (Elliott-Burns, 2005, p. 8).

Of the insider groups, pupils' opinions are rated as the most important of all client perspectives (Leeds, 1995, p. 15). They have been particularly studied in UK school design projects (Flutter, 2004) as part of involving student voice in all matters educational (Flutter & Rudduck, 2004; Rudduck & Flutter, 2003). Student voice and school design is noted in US organisations such as DesignShare (Designing for the Future of Learning) and the NCEF (National Clearing House for Educational Facilities) both of whose web sites report collaborative projects involving student input and how this has been organised in countries around the world. Generally the tone of the literature glowingly supports involvement. There are examples of children's great ideas (Building4Education, Nov 2006, p. 7) and lack of vandalism and graffiti in school premises is attributed to ownership engendered by pupil participation in design (DfES, 2006, p. 29). One caveat is sounded: children's ideas are not necessarily as original and useful as they might be (Mason, 2008).

While students are welcomed, teachers as consultants appear to attract only muted support, and are insufficiently involved (DCSF, 2007) or sidelined to minor furniture choices (DfEE, 2000, pp. 86–88). Inclusion of teacher committees in the planning processes in US school building 'met with varying degrees of success' (Castaldi, 1969, pp. 15, 27). Architects 'expressed their disillusionment with teachers whose experience has extended little beyond the conventional methods still so widely practised' (OECD, 1975, p. 10). These same attitudes to teachers have been reported from Australia where 'the process of designing or refurbishing an existing facility is not certain to include systematic consultation with resident educators' who are hindered because the language of architecture and design is unfamiliar

(Elliott-Burns, 2005, p. 5). Architects and designers have tried imaginative ways to involve students and staff in school design (Thody, 2008, p. 25) but getting such clients to participate is expensive, increases designers' workload by up to 40% (Clark, 2002, p. 15) and overburdens school participants with meetings (CABE, 2004, p. 22). These may be the reasons why staff are not mentioned as consultative university design partners in a 2010 definition of learning landscapes principles (CERD, 2010, pp. 46–47).

In creating post-compulsory learning landscapes some university projects, like schools, have focussed almost exclusively on collaboration with students as 'recognised stakeholders…essential components to the implementation of effective and practical systems' (SpotPLUS, 2001–4, n.d., p. 1). Cambridge University's Learning Landscapes project developed tools to let students map their own learning experiences as a central focus of this research (Riddle & Arnold, 2007). Involving students in their own learning and ownership of places within which it occurs, in settings that encourage collaborative learning, underlie the aims of most innovative university learning centres (CERD, 2010, pp. 20–25). The ETL project (2001–5) included staff as well, organising evaluation and dissemination through collaborative workshops.

Mapping Techniques

Mapping can be both a precursor, and post-implementation evaluator for maximising learning connectivities in university landscapes. Mapping reveals how 'people navigate and make their way through a place. Individuals build their own cognitive maps through a campus, linking boundaries, paths, embedded spaces, activity nodes and reference points through which they recognise where they are' (Hutchinson 2004, p. 14). Once staff and student usage is mapped, campus adjustments can be designed and buildings created or altered to fit formal and informal learning. Do corridors need wired alcoves with window seats for semi-private tutorials and peer-chats? Would the café be used more outside refreshment times if higher backed seating or booths were provided? Should the Vice-Chancellor's office (President, Rector) be at the end of a wing if the leading administrator's open-door policy is to work successfully? Are staff offices large enough to facilitate the seminars often crammed into them?

Mapping evidence has emerged from, inter alia, the Open University's project, Social and Organisational Mediation of University Learning (SOMUL) which developed maps from interview data (Richardson & Edmunds, 2007). Cambridge University's Learning Landscapes Project developed The Day Experience Method for recording staff and student teaching and learning experiences (Riddle & Arnold, 2007). Scotland's Local Lifelong Learning Landscapes tracked provision and linkages of adult learning opportunities (2006/2007). Oxford Brookes University's E-Learning Modes of Engagement cartographers followed basic course adminis-tration, blended learning arrangements and on-line architectures (Francis & Raftery, 2005). Knowledge systems apparently need road-maps too (Lytras, Naeve & Pouloudi, 2005) not surprising if one takes the University of Edinburgh's

Enhancing Teaching and Learning (ETL) project's definition of a teaching-learning environment as 'the whole set of teaching, learning support, assessment and administrative arrangements, as well as the facilities and resources' (project website p. 1; University of Edinburgh, 2000/2001). In the UK's mapping attempts, insights can be gained from the US's 'college experience' literature about the significance of student residence patterns (Pascarella & Terenzini, 2005) although there are doubts about its transferability (Houston & Lebeau, 2006).

Transferability is, however, perhaps best offered by a mapping example from the project teams within a commercial company. They found mapping learning landscapes a valuable reference frame for reflection on varieties of learning modes in their company (Brady et al., 2002). Their map showed where individual, group and community learning happened and where it could be exchanged. They sub-divided the learning into experience accumulation, knowledge articulation and codification - categories also suitable for university analyses (see also Boys, Chapter 4). Within these, learning mechanisms mapped ranged from the very informal 'scribbling notes' to the most formal of meeting minutes. From this emerged a useful typology for learning landscapes: socio-technical, advanced ICT development and socially driven (Brady et al., 2002, pp. 13–14).

CONCLUSION

University learning landscapes are conceptually holistic, loosely coupled inter-connections of all formal and informal, on- and off-campus, virtual and physical facilities, sites and services - crucially framed by how stakeholders use them. A learning landscapes approach is distinguished from mere site management by academics', administrators' and governors' conscious decisions to manipulate all these traditional and innovative facilities so they offer continually and ubiquitously available, collaborative opportunities to enhance learning. Preparations for this approach require understandings of why universities are still wanted, based on an examination of their socio-political needs and contexts, on developments in learning and teaching theories and practice including e-technology and on concerns with both belonging/sense of place and innovative risk taking. To facilitate learning landscapes as collaborative entities includes usage mapping and student/staff involvement in design and architecture choices.

NOTES

[1] Illustrations of, and detail about, each of the projects listed here can be found at www.learning landscapes.lincoln.ac.uk/case-studies.

REFERENCES

Abbott, E., & Campbell, L. (1897/2010). *Life and letters of Benjamin Jowett, master of Balliol College, Oxford*. Memphis, TE: General Books.
Aldrich, C. T. (2006). E-Learning in the workplace. *Training and Development, 60*(9), 54–56.

Allen, P. (1988). *Playstructures participation and design by children.* London: Community service volunteers.

Arthur, M., & Lindsay, V. J. (2006). *Knowledge at work: Creative collaboration in the global economy.* London: Blackwell.

Ashley, W. J. (1897/1966). Jowett and the university ideal. In *Surveys historic and economic* (pp. 445–463). New York: Augustus M. Kelly.

BLM (Bureau of Land Management). (undated). *Learning landscapes.* Retrieved July 1, 2010, from www.blm.gov/wo/st/en/res/Education_in_BLM/Learning_Landscapes.htmlp

Bain, A. (1996). The school design model at Brewster Academy: Technology serving teaching and learning. *T H E Journal (Technological Horizons in Education), 23*(10), 72–79.

Baldridge, J. V. (1983). Organisational characteristics of colleges and universities. In J. V. Baldridge & T. Deal (Eds.), *The dynamics of organisational change in education.* Berkeley, CA: McCutcheon Publishing Corporation.

Barnett, R. (2005). Recapturing the universal in the university. *Educational Philosophy and Theory, 37*(6), 785–797.

Becher, T., & Trowler, P. R. (2001). *Academic tribes and territories* (2nd ed.). Buckingham: Society for Research into Higher Education & Open University Press.

Beck, T. (1980). An Australian study of school environments. *Australian Journal of Education, 24*(1), 1–12.

Black, R. (2003). *Thinking community: New Australian partnerships for public education.* Australia: The Education Foundation.

Bonner Networks. (n.d.). *Simulation sightings.* Retrieved July 1, 2010, from www.learninglandscapes.com

Bourgeois, E., & Frenay, M. (2003). Widening participation and the European Union: Direct action – indirect policy. *European Journal of Education, 38*(1), 99–116.

Brady, T., Marchall, N., Prencipe, A., & Tell, F. (2002). *Making sense of learning landscapes in project-based organisations.* Paper presented at the Third European Conference on Organizational Knowledge, Learning and Capabilities, Athens, Greece.

Brennan, J., & Jary, D. (2005). *What is learned at university?* SOMUL Working Paper 1, York: Higher Education Academy.

Brink, L., & Yost, B. (2004). Transforming inner-city school grounds: Lessons from learning landscapes. *Children, Youth and Environments, 14*(1), 208–232.

Building for Education (B4E). (2006, November). *Students help design new academy.* Reading: B4E.

CERD (Centre for Educational Research and Development). (2010). *Learning landscapes in higher education.* Lincoln: CERD, University of Lincoln. Retrieved August 11, 2010, from http://learninglandscapes.blogs.lincoln.ac.uk/files/2010/04/FinalReport.pdf

CABE (Commission for Architecture and the Built Environment). (2004). *Being involved in school design.* London: CABE.

Cameron, J. M. (1956). *John Henry Newman.* London: Longmans, Greene and Co.

Castaldi, B. (1969). *Creative planning of educational facilities.* Chicago: Rand McNally.

Clark, H. (2002). *Building education: The role of the physical environment in enhancing teaching and research.* London: Institute of Education.

Cutright, M. (Ed.). (2001). *Chaos theory and higher education: Leadership, planning and policy.* New York: Peter Lang.

DCSF (Department for Children, Schools and Families). (2007). *Evaluation of building schools of the future – 1st annual report (final version).* Report prepared by PricewaterhouseCoopers for the DCSF. Retrieved January, 26 2010, from http://www.teachernet.gov.uk/_doc/12318/BSF%20Final%20 Report%20December.pdf

DfEE (Department for Education and Employment). (2000). *Furniture and equipment in schools: A purchasing guide.* London: The Stationery Office.

DfES (Department for Education and Skills). (2006). *Sustainable schools for pupils, communities and the environment.* Nottingham: DfES Publications: London: Her Majesty's Stationery Office.

Dealty, R. (2002). The real-time corporate university becomes a reality. *Journal of Workplace Learning, 14*(8), 340–348.

Davis, R. H. (1982). Sociotechnical theory – managing boundaries to enhance student learning. *Human Relations, 35*(4), 261–181.

Denver Public Schools. (n.d.) (2001-ongoing). *Landscapes for learning.* Retrieved July 1, 2010, from http://bond.dpsk12/org/learning_landscapes

Dudek, M. (2000). *Architecture of schools. The new learning environments.* Oxford: The Architectural Press.

ETL (Enhancing Teaching-Learning Environments in Undergraduate Courses). (2001–2005). *Project proposal; project annual progress reports.* Retrieved August 10, 2010, from www.tla.ed.ac.uk/publications.html

Edwards & Usher. (2003). *Space, curriculum and learning.* Charlotte, NC: Information Age Publishing.

Elliott-Burns, R. (2005). Designing spaces for learning and living in schools: Perspectives of a 'flaneuse'. In *Proceedings 2005 Australian curriculum studies association biennial conference.* Queensland, Australia: University of the Sunshine Coast. Retrieved June 12, 2008, from http://eprints.qut.edu.au/archive/00004345

Featherstone, M. (2002). The physical environment: Some thoughts about design and design processes. *Journal of the Reggio Emilia Information Exchange Australia, 6*(2), 12–19.

Flutter, J. (2004). *Student participation and the architecture of change.* Connect Journal (published by the Youth Research Centre of the University of Melbourne, Australia). Winter Issue.

Flutter, J., & Rudduck, J. (2004). *Consulting pupils: What's in it for schools?* London: RoutledgeFalmer.

Francis, R., & Raftery, J. (2005). Blended learning landscapes. *Brookes eJournal of Learning and Teaching, 1*(3), 1–5.

Gilbert, A. D. (2000). The idea of a university beyond 2000. *Policy, 16*(1), 31–36. St Leonard's Centre for Independent Policy Studies in Australia and New Zealand.

Gordon, T., & Lahelma, E. (1996). School is like an ants' nest: Spatiality and embodiment in schools. *Gender and Education, 8*(3), 301–310.

Gore, C., & Gore, E. (1999). Knowledge management: The way forward. *Total Quality Management, 10*(4 & 5), 554–560.

Greene, M. (1978). *Landscapes of learning.* New York: Teachers College Press.

Harrison, A. (2006a). London school of economics: BOX. In D. G. Oblinger (Ed.), *Learning spaces.* E-Book. Retrieved from http://www.educause.edu/learningspacesch23

Harrison, A. (2006b). Working to learn, learning to work: Design in educational transformation. In *DEGW 4th annual founders lecture.* Retrieved August 11, 2010, from www.degw.com./founderslectures/Founders%20Lecture%20Booklet%2006_A%20Harrison%20Final.pdf

Henley, B. (2002). Hofstetter, the romantic idea of a university. *History of Education Quarterly, 42*(3), 418–420.

Houston, M., & Lebeau, Y. (2006). *The social mediation of university learning.* SOMUL Working Paper 3. York: Higher Education Academy.

Hutchinson, D. (2004). *A natural history of place in education.* New York: Teachers' College Press.

Illich, I. D. (1973). *Deschooling society.* London: Penguin.

JISC (Joint Information System Committee). (2001 ongoing). *Innovation in the use of ICT for education and research.* Retrieved July 5, 2010, from http://www.jisc.ac.uk

Kalz, M. (2005). Building eclectic personal learning landscapes with open source tools. In F. de Vries, G, Attwell, R. Elferink, & A. Todt (Eds.), *Open source for education in Europe – research and practice.* Proceedings, Conference on Open Sources for Education in Europe, Heerlen.

Kelly, A. V. (2002). The idea of a university revisited. *Irish Education Studies, 22*(2), 101–116.

Kerr, I. (1999). Newman's idea of a university. *Higher Education Policy Series, 51*, 11–29.

Kolb, D. A. (1984). *Experiential learning.* Englewood Cliffs, NJ: Prentice-Hall.

LL4. (n.d.). *LL4 schools: e-Safe social networking.* Retrieved July 1, 2010, from www.ll4schools.co.uk/

LSE (London School of Economics). (n.d.). Retrieved November 23, 2010, from http://www.degw. com/project.aspx?id=38&p=BOX%2C+London+School+Economic and http://www2.lse.ac.uk/business AndConsultancy/LSSEEnterprise/Facilities/box.aspx

Learning through LANDSCAPES. (2010). *Inspiring outdoor learning and play*. Retrieved August 10, 2010, from http://www.ltl.org.uk

Leeds, J. (1995). A seven-step method for building effective learning environments. In D. M. Gayeski (Ed.), *Designing communication and learning environments*. Englewood Cliffs, NJ: Educational Technology Publications.

Lincoln Learning Landscapes. (n.d.). Retrieved November 23, 2010, from www.learninglandscapes. lincoln.ac.uk

Lucas, D., & Thomas, G. (1990). The 'geography' of classroom learning. *British Journal of Special Education, 17*(1), 31–34.

Lyons, J. B. (2001). *Do school facilities really impact a child's education?* Council for Educational Facilities Planners International (CEFPI); brief on education facilities for the School Building Association. Retrieved June 15, 2008, from http://schoolfacilities.com/pdf/School% Facilities%20 Impact%2012–27–01.pdf

Lytras, M. D., Naeve, A., & Pouloudi, A. (2005). A knowledge management roadmap for e-learning: The way ahead. *International Journal of Distance Education Technologies, 3*(2), 68–76.

Mcwilliam, E., & Taylor, P. (1998). Teacher im/material: Challenging the new pedagogies of instructional practice. *Educational Researcher, 27*(8), 29–35.

Martin, S. H. (2006). The classroom environment and children's performance – is there a relationship? In C. Spencer & M. Blades (Eds.), *Children and their environments* (pp. 91–107). Cambridge: Cambridge University Press.

Maskell, D., & Robinson, I. (2002). *The new idea of a university*. London: Haven Books.

Natural Learning Landscapes for Schools. (n.d.). Retrieved July 1, 2010, from www.naturallearning.co.uk

Mason, W. (2008). *Student voice in building schools of the future*. Unpublished EdD thesis, University of Lincoln, UK. Retrieved from http://eprints.lincoln.ac.uk/1631/

Neary, M., & Winn, J. (2008). The student as producer: Reinventing the student experience in higher education. In L. Bell, H. Stevenson, & M. Neary (Eds.), *The future of higher education* (pp. 126–138). London: Continuum.

NCSL (National College for School Leadership). (2008). Research Intelligence Service. Issue 41, High quality school buildings are central to BSF's success; Vandalism and bullying decrease in 'inspirational' BSF school. Retrieved January 26, 2010, from www.partnershipsforschools.org.uk/ search.jsp?q=research+intelligence+41

Nelson, J. R. (1996). Designing schools to meet the needs of students who exhibit disruptive behavior. *Journal of Emotional and Behavioural Disorders, 4*(3), 147–161.

Newman, J. H. (1852/1858/1907). *The idea of a university defined and illustrated*. London: Longmans Greene and Co.

Norfolk Children's Services. (2006). *New landscapes for learning*. Retrieved July 1, 2010, from http://schools.norfolk.gov.uk/index.cfm?s=1&m=1364&p=942,index

Northumberland Learning Landscapes. (n.d.). *Northumberland local authority*. Retrieved August 10, 2010, from http://ngfl.northumberland.gov.uk/nll/index.htm

Noyes, A. (2002). Learning landscapes. *British Educational Research Journal, 30*(1), 27–41.

OECD (Organisation for Economic Co-operation and Development). (1975). *School building and educational change*. Paris: Author.

OECD. (2001). *Designs for learning: 55 exemplary education facilities*. Paris: Author.

O'Sullivan, F., Thody, A. M., & Wood, E. (2000). *From bursar to school business manager*. London: Financial Times, Prentice Hall.

Oxford Brookes. (n.d.). *The reinvention centre*. Retrieved November 23, 2010, from www.learningland scapes.lincoln.ac.uk/oxford-brookes-university-the-reinvention-centre

Pascarella, E. T., & Terenzini, P. T. (2005). *How college affects students (vol. 2): A third decade of research*. San Francisco: Jossey-Bass.

Pearson, E. (1972). *Trends in school design*. London: Macmillan.

Quinn, J. B. (1992). *Intelligent enterprise: A knowledge and service based paradigm for industry*. New York: The Free Press.

Quinn, J. (2004). *Mapping 'geographies of the possible' for contemporary academics*. Unpublished conference paper, British Educational Research Association Conference, UMIST.

Richardson, J. T. E., & Edmunds, R. (2007). *A cognitive-developmental model of university learning*. SOMUL Working Paper 4, York: Higher Education Academy.

Riddle, M., & Arnold, T. (2007). *The day experience method: A resource kit*. Cambridge: Cambridge Learning Landscapes Project.

Riddle, M., & Arnold, T. (2008). *The shutdown method: A resource kit*. Cambridge: Cambridge Learning Landscapes Project.

Roussos, M., Johnson, A. F., Leigh, J., Barnes, C. R., Vasilakis, C. A., & Moher, T. G. (1997). The NICE project: Narrative, immersive, constructionist/collaborative environments for learning in virtual reality. In *Proceedings of Ed-Media/Ed-Telecom* (pp. 917–922).

Rudduck, J., & Flutter, J. (2003). *How to improve your school giving pupils a voice*. London and New York: Continuum.

Russell, R., Criddle, S., & Ormes, S. (1998). *Information landscapes for a learning society*. Unpublished conference report. UKOLN, Bath University. Retrieved August 9, 2010, from http://www.aridane.ac.uk/issue16/landscapes/intro.html

SPOT+ (2001–4). Students' perspectives on technology in teaching and learning in European Universities – participation and learning of university students. Case Studies Report for Socrates/Minerva n.90310-CP-1-2001–1-MINERVA-M. Retrieved August 11, 2010, from http://www.spot.plus.odl.org/

Sarles, H. (2001). A vision: The idea of a university in the present age. *Organization, 8*(2), 403–415.

Scotland. (2006/7). *Local lifelong learning landscapes*. Retrieved April 10, 2008, from www.lds4centres.com/News/Local+Lifelong+Learning+Landscapes.htm

Scruton, R. (2001). The idea of a university. *Salisbury Review, 20*(1), 4–8.

Serafin, E. (2006, September). *Learning landscapes: The use of landscape as a metaphor for the design and implementation of learning systems*. Unpublished conference paper. Association of Learning Technology conference. Retrieved March 10, 2008, from http://www.alt.ac.uk/alc2006

Smith, D. (1999). The changing idea of a university. *Higher Education Policy Series, 51*, 148–174.

Starik, M., Schaeffer, T. N., Berman, P., & Hazelwood, A. (2002). Initial environmental project characterisations of four US universities. *International Journal of Sustainability in Higher Education, 3*(4), 335–346.

Sussex. (2002). *Why learning landscapes need to change*. Announcement of conference on 'Building Universities: The 1960s and Beyond'. Retrieved March 18, 2008, from http://www.sussex.ac.uk/press_office/media/media207.shtml

Thody, A. (2008). *What lessons can be transferred to higher education learning landscapes from the leadership, governance and management processes of school design projects?* Working Paper II, Learning Landscapes Research Project, Centre for Educational Research and Development (CERD) University of Lincoln.

Torelli, L., & Durrett, C. (2006). *Spaces for children's resources. Landscape for learning: The impact of classroom design on infants and toddlers*. ALT conference paper. Retrieved March 8, 2008, from www.alt.ac.uk/altc2006/

Tosh, D., Werdmuller, B., Helen, C., & Haywood, J. (2005). *The learning landscape – a conceptual frame for e-portfolios*. Retrieved August 11, 2010, from http://homepages.ed.ac.uk/jhaywood/papers/The%20Learning%20Landscape%20preprint.pdf

Webanywhere. (n.d.). *Learning landscapes*. Retrieved July 1, 2010, from www.learninglandscapes.co.uk

PAUL TEMPLE

10. LEARNING SPACES AS SOCIAL CAPITAL

THE UNIVERSITY SPACE AND PLACE

The premise of this chapter is that space (and place: which I define here as what people make of the space they inhabit) is an under-acknowledged independent variable in understanding how higher education institutions work. Space in the university takes the form it does as a result of the decisions and actions of its designers, its users, those who manage it in various ways, and those who look after it. But may there also be a sense in which space and place help to determine what the university *is*? As Hillier and Hanson (1984, p. 2) argue, 'the ordering of space in buildings is really about the ordering of relations between people'. Considering this complex set of space/life relationships, Lefebvre (1991, p. 26) suggests that space 'serves as a tool of thought and of action...it is also a means of control...of power; yet...it escapes in part from those who would make use of it.' Or as a writer on the theory of place has put it, 'the relations of architecture to social behaviour are complex and culturally embedded' (Dovey, 2008, p. 2). Following these ideas, it seems necessary to ask if, once space is created, or re-created, for the university, then is an institution with particular characteristics likely to emerge? And if so, which elements of the built environment bring about these characteristics?

In the education literature, the term 'space' is typically used metaphorically, although, increasingly, its physical sense is now being taken into account. Edwards and Usher (2003) make a case for its physical significance to be properly examined, and Savin-Baden (2008) suggests links between metaphorical or conceptual senses of space and its physical reality. These writers, though, are the exceptions: although built environment-driven costs are the second-largest item in nearly every UK higher education institution's budget – after staff costs – space remains an almost invisible topic in the higher education literature, taken for granted (though much complained-about), and left as a matter for technical discussion between architects, designers, space planners and estates managers.

Discussions about the relationship between spaces and the activities that go on within them are often fascinating, but for me, frequently unsatisfactory. Hayden (1995), for example, has tried to pursue thinking about the connections between social and economic activities and the built environment in her historical study of working-class and ethnic minority neighbourhoods in Los Angeles. She argues that 'social history is embedded in urban landscapes' (p. 43): but the difficulty here is that this must either be a truism (if Chinese workers once lived in an area, then an accurate history of that area must indeed indicate this) or a kind of pathetic fallacy,

A. Boddington and J. Boys (eds.), Re-Shaping Learning: A Critical Reader: The Future of Learning Spaces in Post-Compulsory Education, 137–146.

which claims to see a continuing presence of long-departed social groups in the ordinary buildings they once inhabited but which have now quite different uses. One critique of this line of thought notes that 'it is not obvious…[how the] values that are related to the non-physical qualities of the institution are exchanged into the building' (Gabrielsen & Saugstad, 2007 p. 532). Nevertheless, the wish to project onto bricks and mortar, or steel and glass, an ideological conception is widespread in writing about university space: Edwards's *University Architecture* (2000) provides some good examples.

Chapman (2006: xxiii), though, reminds us that some designers of university buildings did, and do, want their creations to 'say' something about what the university is, or does; which is not the same as claiming that buildings must necessarily tell a historical story. The difficulty here is that while the built form of an institution can certainly tell *a* story, it is easy to see (without necessarily buying the whole post-modernist ticket) that alternative readings of the 'text' must be possible. The imposing neo-gothic Victorian buildings of the University of Manchester (UK), for example, might be thought to speak of the city's civic pride and wealth at the height of its 19th century commercial power; another reading might reflect that, perhaps in contrast to today, it was once seen as natural that learning and scholarship should be generously supported by private wealth; and yet another observer might detect in Waterhouse's elaborate designs capitalism's exploitation of factory workers, producing the surplus wealth to spend freely on prestige projects. As Dober (1992) suggests, iconic university buildings 'are cultural currency…charged with allegorical significance and perceptual connotations and meaning' (p. 5) – though this currency will be valued differently between individuals and over time.

THE PHYSICAL CONTEXT OF UNIVERSITY WORK

The culturally significant aspects of the university built environment have now often been incorporated into thinking about the university 'brand' (Temple & Shattock, 2007). Some universities are almost defined, or branded, at least in the public mind, by their physical presence – Cambridge, Heidelberg, or Cornell, for example. However, student satisfaction surveys, internationally, tend to attach relatively low importance to physical issues as contributors to the overall student experience (Temple, 2007, p. 64): possibly a counter-intuitive finding, but one supported by a good deal of empirical evidence. A recent study on student recruitment adds weight to this finding, reporting that buildings-related issues appear to have minimal impact on the choices of potential students (Belanger, Syed and Mount, 2007). This must be a disappointment to universities that have invested in expensive iconic buildings for this precise purpose. There may be a threshold effect operating here: providing universities offer physical facilities that are perceived as broadly acceptable as a whole, then features more directly associated with the value of the degree and the organisation of academic work may assume greater importance in students' minds. When asked directly about how *particular* sorts of space could support their learning, a recent US study did find students expressing clear preferences (Bennett, 2007).

These somewhat contradictory (superficially, at least) conclusions seem to point to the central yet variable and hard-to-define role of space in the educational process. A deeper level of theoretical understanding seems to be needed. I want to suggest an understanding of space and place in the university that goes beyond suggestions that certain ideas are embodied in buildings, or that buildings help to create the brand, and instead to propose how space becomes place, and how it may affect the academic work of the institution. And space and place have almost always been central features in thinking about the university. The universities of medieval Europe quickly acquired a physical identity and, arguably, a sense of place. By the late 12th century, the University of Paris was located on the left bank of the Seine near the Ile de la Cité (Cobban, 1975, p. 77), where much of it yet remains. Once they acquire a physical home, universities are hard to shift. The University of London would almost certainly be organisationally different today if its central administration and most of its colleges had relocated to what was then an industrial area on the south bank of the Thames (where the Festival Hall and National Theatre now stand), as was proposed in the debates about the University's future in the years immediately before the First World War (Harte, 1986, p. 191). The creation of a new campus would probably have resulted in a unitary institution, on the lines of the other British urban universities of the day, and this physical form would then have probably continued to condition future organisational developments.

How, then, might the university's physical form be linked with academic effectiveness? One way may be through the contribution of space to the creation of a sense of community, and thus of *place* – in the sense of space which (in academic settings) is bound up with the ways in which we live and understand ourselves, what we value, as well as what we do. Other writers have suggested, somewhat speculatively, that a sense of place arises when 'spatial stories' can 'inhabit our dreams, and produce a kind of spatial unconsciousness, and…a continuing sense of social critique' (Amin & Thrift, 2002, p. 48). Sennett writes of 'narrative space', space designed in ways which permit people to develop their own uses for it, so becoming 'personified places' (Sennett, 1990, pp. 190, 192). A role has been claimed for public places in helping social integration within a community, bringing together people who might not otherwise come across one another (Williams, 2007, p. 191). Savin-Baden (2008, p. 115) discusses one aspect of space/place – the notion of 'boundary spaces' in terms of learning/cultural boundaries, disciplinary boundaries, boundaries between student and staff expectations, as well as boundaries relating to physical interactions. I will suggest that such physical boundaries are particularly important in analysing university spaces: that designing permeable boundaries, inviting interactions, even intimacy, can be used to create a distinctive university experience. In addition, Massey (2007, p. 15) observes that places, once created, can assume particular powers, which may be projected to affect the wider world: and there are certainly examples of how some university places have been able to set intellectual agendas. One thinks perhaps of economics at the University of Chicago (the names of Friedman and Becker might come to mind), or applied mathematics at the University of Cambridge (Dirac and Hawking, say) where influence, perhaps power too, has certainly been projected onto a global stage. But, to return to an earlier observation, it is surely the people inhabiting the place – who have been able to attract other gifted people to join them – which is the significant factor in these cases, rather than the place as such.

PLACE AND INSTITUTIONAL EFFECTIVNESS

Here, I want to make a connection between these different ideas of place, and wider understandings of institutional life and effectiveness, by bringing in the concept of social capital. There is theoretical and empirical work suggesting that high levels of social capital are associated with strong institutional communities, and that this may lead to the improved effectiveness of that institution (Lesser, 2000; Preston, 2004). 'Effectiveness' is itself, though, a rather elastic concept. While the engineering-based idea of efficiency, involving the measurement of outputs as a proportion of inputs, is in principle at least relatively unproblematic – just such an input-process-output relationship is the assumption behind most university internal resource allocation models – effectiveness carries with it the wider sense that processes are being directed in ways which achieve valued goals. Measures of relative effectiveness may then be the extent to which the goal was achieved; how quickly it was achieved; or the quantity of resources used to achieve it – the latter point showing why discussions of efficiency often become about effectiveness, and vice-versa.

In this case, the physical form of the university, considered at the levels of both the whole campus and of individual buildings, may be linked to institutional effectiveness (and indeed efficiency) indirectly, through its role in assisting in community formation. This physical support for community formation, and hence (I suggest) social capital creation, might be done in various ways. Designing a campus on a human scale is one approach, with attention to design details such as pleasant places to sit and talk, which encourage social interactions and connectivity (Chapman, 2006, p. 180). An account of the design of Miami University, for example, tells us that, seeking this human scale, 'it was designed to feel small' (Kuh, Kinzie, Schuh & Whitt, 2005, p. 106); and student learning, it is argued, may be improved through the informal interactions which result.

In a broadly similar way, it has been proposed that the original layouts of human settlements around the world can be interpreted as various attempts to manage encounters between locals and strangers safely and efficiently, and to provide appropriate amounts of public and private space (Hillier & Hanson, 1984, p. 20). The form of many towns in medieval Europe was determined by the need to provide a workable marketplace – where townspeople and outsiders could come together – usually in the very centre of the town, with security apparently in mind (Schofield & Vince, 1994, p. 33). Designs of modern shopping malls seek, similarly, to manage commercial encounters in a secure environment – one planned, obviously, with a view to parting visitors from as much of their money as possible (Gladwell, 2004). University design poses some similar questions: how to manage insider/outsider interactions (between the 'resident' staff members and 'visiting' students) effectively and safely; how to maximise the possibility of beneficial encounters; how to locate facilities to make them easily accessible; and, perhaps, how to use design to convey particular messages about the kind of place that one is in – how to manage 'the semantic field' (Dovey, 2008, p. 143). The challenge for architects working on university projects, particularly those undertaking campus master-planning, is to achieve these results within the constraints imposed by budgets, site availability and so on.

We might think of this task as being about 'encounter management': using design features to bring people together in settings where mutually beneficial inter-actions may occur. Knowledge-intensive companies seem to have reached similar conclusions: 'Visit Google, and you'll see a lot of public spaces that seem to serve multiple purposes. On one visit, I noticed a grand piano, a billiards table, several large whiteboards, and a sandwich station all within a few meters of one another...the eclecticism of the furnishings suggested a conscious attempt to create opportunities for unscripted interaction' (Hamel, 2007, p. 176).

Modern cities have rather similarly been theorised as places that support encounters between different social networks, providing complexity and the un-expected, and so enabling the city to become 'a potent generator of novelty' (Amin & Thrift, 2002, p. 41): the medieval marketplace, updated - and some may even find novelty in shopping malls. City-regions, similarly, are major centres of creativity, as measured in the US by Florida's 'creativity index' (Florida, 2004, p. 245), because they 'can offer abundant options.' As Florida argues, 'places with diverse mixes of creative people are more likely to generate new combinations [of ideas]' (p. 249). In the UK, local government is increasingly seeing its role as one of 'place-shaping', focusing on local identity and community cohesiveness, and how these relate to economic activity, rather than simply managing a collection of separate local services (Lyons, 2007). The comparisons with the university space and place – interlinked networks of creative people, with a shared sense of community – are surely suggestive. But it would be a mistake to think of these effects as happening necessarily in a benign, supportive type of setting: it is necessary to remember that countervailing forces will be at work, ones perhaps causing the 'diminishment of informal trust among workers, and weakening of institutional knowledge' (Sennett, 2006, p. 63), among other organisational dysfunctions. Certain features of place might affect some people positively (say, a researcher who wants to relax by strolling around a landscaped campus) and others negatively (an administrator who is irritated by the need constantly to move around the same campus). Dealing with such conflicting requirements constitutes part of the university management challenge.

CREATING PLACE

In the University of York's (UK) campus, we see an encounter management approach apparent in its early 1960s design. York is one the campuses that Muthesius (2000, p. 6) describes as 'utopianist', in that its design had particular educational aims in view, which involved directing its inhabitants' behaviours. One of these aims was specifically the encouragement of informal interactions. An important way of achieving this was through a collegiate organisation, bringing together living, working and leisure activities for manageable numbers of people, and which mixed staff and students from different disciplines. But, as the original University development plan made clear, the campus design was intended to do more than simply provide organisational units small enough for people to relate to:

> Meeting, both accidental and deliberate, must be provided for by the greatest possible number of intersections en route (without producing congestion) and it should ideally be impossible to go from one unit of accommodation to a similar one without coming into contact with at least one of completely different academic or social character on the way (University of York, 1962, p. 13).

This is surely a remarkable statement: that a key design principle was to create complexity, to mix people up, regardless of what their own wishes might be. This was one step on the way to changing space into a particular kind of place. There is a striking contrast between York's planning and that of recent buildings of the University of Copenhagen, where a design aim was to ensure 'that students and visitors should be served without disturbing...the scientific personnel' (Gabrielsen & Saugstad, 2007). No accidental meetings here. Inasmuch, then, 'that the spatial structure of each building embodies knowledge of social relations' (Hillier & Hanson, 1984, p. 184), we may see in York's designed dislocation, in its complexity, a way of trying to erase the 'embodied' knowledge of separate subject specialisms and to allow those living there to create their individual, original, sets of social relations: their own place. Nor was the branding issue (as it would now be described) overlooked: as the project architect responsible for York's original design has said, the aim was to provide a 'quality of remarkability...to express the particular identity of place and experience' (Derbyshire, 2005). But these senses of 'remarkability' and identity seem to go beyond mere branding: they surely contribute to community-building by providing a memorable setting in which new social relations can develop.

While design features of the kind noted here may relate positively to learning and research outcomes, it is extremely difficult to find convincing evidence of this linkage. Most of the work in this field comes from the schools sector: here, despite many attempts to show a link between building design or quality and learning, the evidence is at best inconclusive – and much of the empirical work is flawed (Temple, 2007, p. 57). One of the methodologically strongest studies of the contributors to secondary school effectiveness is known as the 'fifteen thousand hours' study: it is unusual in seeking correlations with achievements in external examinations, rather than simply reporting on changed student perceptions. It concluded that while the physical environment generally (school size, and age of the buildings) had negligible effects on learning, a good standard of cleaning and day-to-day maintenance did appear to lead to improved results. This was almost certainly because of the standard-setting effects of being in cared-for premises, leading to more harmonious social relations, more cohesive social groupings, and so to better learning (Rutter, Maughan, Mortimore & Ouston, 1979, p. 195). Again, we see the suggestion that the link to better educational outcomes comes through complex interactions between space and people, rather than simply by providing people with a particular working or social environment.

SPACE AND PLACE, AND WHAT THEY DO

In higher education, it has been noted that the relationship between campus design and the quality of the student experience has not been adequately defined (Jamieson, 2003). Ronald Barnett and I, in agreeing with this, noted that 'few conceptual frameworks exist for understanding the connections between the physical form of the institutions and their academic effectiveness – and perhaps their sense of place' (Temple & Barnett, 2007). How, then, might we relate ideas of space and place, and link them to ideas of social capital, and other forms of 'capital'?

The quality of university space may be considered in various possible dimensions: its setting, its unique design and historical features, its scale, internal spatial relationships, and how well it is maintained. These are all features that we may straightforwardly categorise as *physical capital* issues. Once the users of these spaces are brought into the picture, some different considerations arise. I have suggested that the idea of encounter management sums up the process of managing the ways in which people come into informal contact: one study suggests that for university students such encounters can be 'socially catalytic' in developing relationships and supporting learning (Strange & Banning, 2001, p. 146). The idea of *locational capital*, which comes mainly from economic studies of firms' and workers' locations, is useful here: that certain activities have added value when they occur in particular locations. The perhaps self-evident sense that many activities take place where they do because there are special economic benefits arising (IT development in California's Silicon Valley is a well-studied example) – or conversely, that incomes are depressed when activities take place in sub-optimal locations – is well-attested empirically (Cohen & Fields, 2000; Jones, Williams, Lee, Coats & Cowling, 2006; Yamamura, 2009). The creation of a particular university physical setting, which stimulates increased, perhaps higher-quality, interactions among teachers and students, can similarly be thought of as creating locational capital.

These interactions, conditioned by the physical environment, give rise to the community that exists within the institution, and help to form its culture. The notion of a university culture is a contested one (Silver, 2003), but for the present let us say that within organisations people tend to have certain shared, tacit under-standings about the way the organisation does, and should, work that condition their behaviour; and which are often considered to amount to an organisational culture. The creation of a community and its culture turns, I suggest, the university space into a *place*. As a result, locational capital may be thought of as being transformed, through the mediation of an institutional culture, into *social capital*. The debate about the scope and value of the concept of social capital is an extensive one, which I will not attempt to rehearse here (Temple, 2009). I am using the concept in the sense of social networks, the norms of reciprocity and trust that arise from them, and the application of these assets in achieving mutual objectives (Field, Schuller & Baron, 2000; Putnam, 2000, p. 19). These are the assets which probably underlie all effective organisations, especially knowledge-based ones which depend on the effective transfer of information. Information becomes more generally available, and so more valuable, through the networks that are implied by social capital, as it then becomes available to the community at large. (A distinctive characteristic of social capital, in the sense that I am using it, is that it is available for use by those who have not necessarily contributed to the organisation's store of it.) Social capital adds value to the intellectual resources of the university by encouraging sharing and trust. Learning and research outcomes thus emerge from the university as a *place*.

CONCLUSION

Space and place together have a complex effect on the academic life of university institutions and their performance. It is a more nuanced picture than simply one of the university campus, or individual buildings, sending messages or telling a story. The connection between space and place, which I have suggested involves the creation of social capital, is consistent with the ideas of commitment, authenticity, and reciprocity that Barnett (2007) suggests support student learning. But however it happens, there is an interaction between space and the university community, during which both are changed. Physical design features, large and small, seem to be important in ensuring that this interaction is educationally positive, although I do not suggest that these features are on their own transformative. I have argued that considering the ways in which space becomes place, through the transformation of physical capital into locational capital, and the subsequent creation of social capital, is a potentially useful way of studying this relationship. It is time, I suggest, to study these interconnections more thoroughly.

REFERENCES

Amin, A., & Thrift, N. (2002). *Cities: Reimagining the urban*. Cambridge: Polity Press.

Barnett, R. (2007). *A will to learn: Being a student in an age of uncertainty*. Maidenhead: Open University Press/McGraw Hill.

Belanger, C., Syed, S., & Mount, J. (2007). The make up of institutional branding: Who, what, how? *Tertiary Education and Management, 13*(3), 169–185.

Bennett, S. (2007). Designing for uncertainty: Three approaches. *The Journal of Academic Librarianship, 13*(2), 165–179.

Chapman, M. (2006). *American places: In search of the twenty-first century campus*. Westport, CT: American Council on Education/Praeger.

Cobban, A. (1975). *The medieval universities: Their development and organisation*. London: Methuen & Co.

Cohen, S., & Fields, G. (2000). Social capital and capital gains in Silicon Valley (reprinted from California Management Review, 41, 1999). In E. Lesser (Ed.), *Knowledge and social capital: Foundations and applications*. Boston: Butterworth-Heinemann.

Derbyshire, A. (2005, November 24). *The University of York campus: 40 years of growth and change: What next?* Text of lecture given at the University of York.

Dober, R. (1992). *Campus design*. New York: John Wiley.

Dovey, K. (2008). *Framing places: Mediating power in built form*. Abingdon: Routledge.

Edwards, B. (2000). *University architecture*. London: Spon Press.

Edwards, R., & Usher, R. (2003). Putting space back on the map of learning. In R. Edwards & R. Usher (Eds.), *Space, curriculum and learning*. Greenwich, CT: Information Age Publishing.

Field, J., Schuller, T., & Baron, S. (2000). Social capital and human capital revisited. In S. Baron, J. Field, & T. Schuller (Eds.), *Social capital: Critical perspectives*. Oxford: Oxford University Press.

Florida, R. (2004). *The rise of the creative class: And how it's transforming work, leisure, community and everyday life*. New York: Basic Books.

Gabrielsen, M., & Saugstad, T. (2007). From identity to facility – the new buildings for the Faculty of Humanities at the University of Copenhagen. *Scandinavian Journal of Educational Research, 51*(5), 531–546.

Gladwell, M. (2004, March 15). The terrazzo jungle. *The New Yorker*.

Hamel, G. (2007). *The future of management*. Boston: Harvard Business School Press.

Harte, N. (1986). *The University of London 1836–1986*. London: The Athlone Press.

Hayden, D. (1995). *The power of place: Urban landscapes as public history*. Cambridge, MA: MIT Press.

Hillier, B., & Hanson, J. (1984). *The social logic of space*. Cambridge: Cambridge University Press.

Jamieson, P. (2003). Designing more effective on-campus teaching and learning spaces: A role for academic developers. *International Journal for Academic Development, 8*(1/2), 119–133.

Jones, A., Williams, L., Lee, N., Coats, D., & Cowling, M. (2006). *Ideopolis: Knowledge city-regions*. London: The Work Foundation.

Kuh, G., Kinzie, J., Schuh, J., & Whitt, E. (2005). *Student success in college: Creating conditions that matter*. San Francisco: Jossey-Bass.

Lefebvre, H. (1991). *The production of space*. Oxford: Blackwell.

Lesser, E. L. (2000). Leveraging social capital in organisations. In E. L. Lesser (Ed.), *Knowledge and social capital: foundations and applications*. Boston: Butterworth-Heinemann.

Lyons, M. (2007). *Place-shaping: A shared ambition for the future of local government*. Norwich: The Stationery Office.

Massey, D. (2007). *World city*. Cambridge: Polity Press.

Muthesius, S. (2000). *The postwar university: Utopianist campus and college*. New Haven, CT: Yale University Press.

Preston, J. (2004). 'A continuous effort of sociability': Learning and social capital in adult life. In T. Schuller, J. Preston, C. Hammond, A. Brassett-Grundy, & J. Bynner (Eds.), *The benefits of learning: The impact of education on health, family life and social capital*. London: RoutledgeFalmer.

Putnam, R. D. (2000). *Bowling alone: The collapse and revival of American community*. New York: Simon and Schuster.

Rutter, M., Maughan, B., Mortimore, P., & Ouston, J. (1979). *Fifteen thousand hours: Secondary schools and their effects on children*. London: Open Books.

Savin-Baden, M. (2008). *Learning spaces: Creating opportunities for knowledge creation in academic life*. Maidenhead: Open University Press/McGraw-Hill.

Schofield, J., & Vince, A. (1994). *Medieval towns*. London: Leicester University Press.

Sennett, R. (1990). *The conscience of the eye: The design and social life of cities*. New York: Norton.

Sennett, R. (2006). *The culture of the new capitalism*. New Haven, CT: Yale University Press.

Silver, H. (2003). Does a university have a culture? *Studies in Higher Education, 28*(2), 157–169.

Strange, C., & Banning, J. (2001). *Educating by design: Creating campus learning environments that work*. San Francisco: Jossey-Bass.

Temple, P. (2007). *Learning spaces for the 21st century: A review of the literature*. York: Higher Education Academy. Retrieved from http://www.heacademy.ac.uk/ourwork/research/litreviews

Temple, P. (2009). Social capital and university effectiveness. In G. Tripp, M. Payne, & D. Diodorus (Eds.), *Social capital*. New York: Nova Science Publishers.

Temple, P., & Barnett, R. (2007). Higher education space: Future directions. *Planning for Higher Education, 36*(1), 5–15.

Temple, P., & Shattock, M. (2007). What does 'branding' mean in higher education? In B. Stensaker & V. D'Andrea (Eds.), *Branding in higher education: Exploring an emerging phenomenon*. Amsterdam: EAIR.

University of York. (1962). *University of York: Development plan 1962–72*. York: York University Promotion Committee.

Williams, T. (2007). Rationalising public place commodification and the ramifications of this choice in Alberta, Canada. In M. Osborne, K. Sankey, & B. Wilson (Eds.), *Social capital, lifelong learning and the management of place*. Abingdon: Routledge.

Yamamura, E. (2009). The role of social capital in homogenous societies. In G. Tripp, M. Payne, & D. Diodorus (Eds.), *Social capital*. New York: Nova Science Publishers.

FIONA DUGGAN

11. SOME MODELS FOR RE-SHAPING
LEARNING SPACES

When learning space is a scarce resource, there can be a temptation for conversations about space to become increasingly dominated by spreadsheet generated data – sqm/student, sqm/staff, sqm/income, cost/sqm, % utilisation, and so on. It sometimes seems that the more we focus on this kind of data, the more insurmountable the problem of 'not enough space' becomes. But, how much space is 'enough space'? This paper suggests the answer lies with key stakeholder groups who are empowered to collectively explore how the space of their university, college or other educational provision is described, designed, allocated, managed and evaluated. By identifying the primary focus of three key stakeholder groups this paper explores different types of value and how each might be measured. It looks at case studies where educational institutions have sought to identify their space requirements, by drawing upon different types of knowledge and data. It will show how, through an ongoing process of sharing perspectives, agreeing values and moving towards collective *sense-making*, conversations about physical space can become increasingly open and hopeful, no longer so focused on the limitations of scarce space, but rather on ways in which its full potential can be realised. Most crucially, this involves building models of learning as specific patterns of social and spatial organisation and activities, 'grown out of' the identity, aims and values of a particular educational institution.

BALANCING DIFFERENT PERSPECTIVES

Discussions around learning space tend to involve three key stakeholder groups – users, estates and institution. Each group is likely to have different views on the amount, type and quality of space an institution requires to carry out its activities. Dialogues around space needs can be greatly enhanced when participants are clear about their own focus, while also understanding, and respecting, the focus of others. Users (the students, staff and visitors who occupy space) need to feel confident that space can support the learning, working and social experiences they want to provide and receive. Estates (the staff who manage space) need to focus on how space can support user requirements in an affordable way, both in the present and stretching into the future. The institution (represented by senior management staff responsible for allocating space) needs to decide how best to allocate space resources in line with the institution's strategic objectives and the parameters set

A. Boddington and J. Boys (eds.), Re-Shaping Learning: A Critical Reader: The Future of Learning Spaces in Post-Compulsory Education, 147–154.

by outside influences (e.g. government policies and market trends). In assessing their space resources, institutions have a considerable amount of expertise to draw upon, including organisational, pedagogical and spatial knowledge. They also have a considerable amount of data at hand, including academic plan, corporate plan, financial plan, student satisfaction survey, retention figures, vision documents, information and communication technologies (ICT) usage, timetabling information, space utilisation surveys, estate strategy, condition survey, masterplan and so on. These different datasets are rarely reviewed together, yet when they are, the gaps or overlaps between them often reveal new and compelling ways forward.

When learning space is scarce, there can be a tendency for these different perspectives to become more starkly articulated. Users are likely to want access to as much space as possible. Estates will want to keep space costs as low as possible. The institution may want to exercise greater control over space, so that it can quickly respond to shifting priorities. If not sensitively handled, dialogue between these three stakeholder groups can become one of rather defensive position-taking, especially when anxiety levels are running high. For effective dialogue, the focus of all three groups needs to be integrated in a holistic way. This requires an explicit development process where debate about amounts, types and quality of space can enable the best-fit solution between diverse priorities, in the particular situation under review. This, I suggest, requires a shift from conflicts over needs and requirements, to engagement with ideas of *value*. Several institutions have already put in place, or are in the process of doing so, management structures that can ensure space needs are more holistically considered. These range from working groups for teaching and learning spaces dealing with day-to-day management to learning enhancement networks focusing on policy and strategic direction. Both groups tend to be made up of students, teachers, timetablers, ICT support, facilities managers and development staff. Activities include regular meetings, production of materials, assessing space requirements, reviews of upcoming projects and evaluations of spaces in action. One institution has set up a learning enhancement programme which includes regular events with in-house/guest speakers addressing particular aspects of learning spaces, and site visits to places of interest.

In my own experience as a consultant, multi-disciplinary discourse seems to be the most effective means of achieving results that can both surprise and delight, yet up until recently, there has been little guidance on the difficulties and complexities that such a multi-faceted approach can encounter. In the UK, research projects such as the University of Strathclyde's Explore It project (www.explore academicworkplace.com), Loughborough University's Innovative, Effective, Enjoyable project (www.academicworkspace.com) and the University of Lincoln's Learning Landscape project (www.learninglandscapes.blogs.lincoln.ac.uk) go a long way towards improving this, while the work of HEFCE's Space Management Group (www. smg.ac.uk) and HEFCE's Estate Management Statistics annual reports (www. hefce.ac.uk) have provided much needed space data to inform discussion.

UNDERSTANDING VALUE

In addition, there has been some work on value in design. For space to reach its full potential, institutions need to become better at reflecting the priorities and values of all stakeholder groups. Values describe the beliefs, attitudes and principles that drive actions. Values are subjective and each of the three key stakeholder groups identified here will have their own view on the value of space. These groups need to be able to first understand and express value in their own terms, then share and align their expectations for value delivery. When stakeholders recognise space values consistent with their own, they identify with the space, feel a sense of belonging to it and acquire a stake in achieving its objectives (see also Temple, Chapter 10).

The Value in Design model (VALiD, www.valueindesign.com) offers guidance for developing shared values around space. The model is the result of a 3-year (2003–2005) joint industry and academic research study called 'Managing Value Delivery in Design.' Led by Loughborough University, the research team represented a broad spectrum of views and sought to increase customer satisfaction for construction projects in terms of process, product and performance. The study's objective was to develop a common value culture and language for clients, users and designers, by providing shared tools for monitoring overall project effectiveness in delivering value. VALiD advocates a transparent approach that builds confidence and trust in the views of stakeholders, thereby enabling a common purpose to be established. Attention is focused on shared priorities, while solutions are guided by shared values. Benefits include clear and agreed definitions of value to each stakeholder group and a decision-making process that reflects stakeholders' values. The first step is to understand the values of the different stakeholders. The second step is for each stakeholder group to define what value means to them. For example, estates managers may be interested in life-cycle costs whilst academics may be more focused on the student experience. Within the VALiD framework, value is defined as the trade-off between what each stakeholder gets and what they give up. This view of value helps stakeholders appreciate that, while the bottom line (resources) is about improving efficiency, the top line is concerned with effectiveness (user benefits). The third step is for each stakeholder group to assess the value proposition against their own criteria for benefits, sacrifices and resources. This raises the question of what to measure or, as Bligh and Pearshouse ask in this book (Chapter 1) what kind of evaluations can be plausibly undertaken. Their conclusion is that the quality of evaluation is ultimately judged by the insights shared within a community of interested practitioners.

In seeking to understand the value users, estates and institutions put on space, we have found it useful to structure stakeholder discussion around four key elements, what we might call the E4V model – efficient, effective, expressive, enduring. During discussion, each group is encouraged to articulate what value they put on space for each of these four elements. For example, users might describe the value of efficient space as sufficient to deliver programmes, effective space as supporting collaboration and experimentation, expressive as providing a sense of belonging and enduring as contributing to collective memory. Estates are more likely to describe efficient in terms of sqm/user, effective as cost/sqm (i.e. build and operational costs), expressive by the standard of build quality achieved and enduring in terms of the estate's ability to adapt to change. Institutions tend to describe efficient as balancing the books, effective as the ability to respond quickly in an increasingly competitive market, expressive as showcasing the institution and enduring as protecting heritage while ensuring future viability. As the priorities of each stakeholder group become clearer, a collective set of priorities starts to emerge. This not only helps to build consensus, but also enriches the range of issues included when discussing space needs.

LEARNING AS A SOCIAL ACTIVITY

Users, estates and institution tend to agree that the real value of education is the discourse generated by face-to-face interaction, increasingly supported and enabled by technology. Learning is a social activity. In a world where access to information is increasingly available anytime and anywhere, institutions continue to build upon the enduring importance of people and place, their aspiration being to provide high-quality learning experiences that are situated, embodied and social. Institutions connect with their local communities through their events programmes and/or other projects, build learning groups through their academic programmes and create communities of practice through their research and enterprise initiatives.

When considering learning as primarily a social experience, some institutions have found it useful to link space to different levels of staff support. At a basic level of engagement, learners benefit from the co-presence of other learners in open-access settings, such as external grounds, places to relax, social learning settings, ICT zones, libraries and so on. Staff support, when available, tends to focus on general assistance. As the focus on independent and peer-based learning increases, open-access settings become increasingly important. Social learning space, in particular, is gaining in popularity. Staff support for this type of space is rare, although some institutions are beginning to see the value such support could bring in enhancing the overall quality of learning experience offered. At a more enhanced level of engagement, learners become part of learning groups formed by the various programmes on offer. Staff support is more specific and generally timetabled. At an advanced level of engagement, learners create their own communities of practice, becoming co-creators of knowledge. Staff support is tailored to specific interests. Indeed, many of the learners at this level of engagement with an institution are already members of staff. In this way, the ease and generosity with which space (both physical and virtual) can support learning at different levels of engagement may become an increasingly important issue for institutions, as they continue to aim to offer a comprehensive range of life-long learning opportunities to past, current and potential learners, in times of increasing financial constraint (Boddinton, Chapter 14).

Across these different levels of staff–student relationships the desire for flexibility is a common theme voiced by users, estates and institution. Yet when each stakeholder group is asked what they mean by flexibility, the answers are rarely straightforward. 'We want flexibility' can sometimes mean 'we don't know what we want yet', or 'we need to keep all our options open', or 'we're afraid to make a decision'. Further clarification can be gained through questions such as, 'what aspects in particular need to be flexible?', or 'what kinds of learning experiences should flexibility enable?', or 'where might we find good examples of flexibility in action?'. In the discussions generated by such questions, it becomes clear that space is not flexible until its users are enabled to enact that flexibility. Space is one of many inter-related factors, including curriculum, learners, teachers, technology and more. It thus becomes useful to have more sophisticated models for understanding what flexibility means in different contexts.

The following case studies look at three different institutions undergoing major building projects. Common to all is a discourse-based, collaborative approach to identifying space requirements that incorporate enhanced flexibility. The first space model, which we have called Learning by Working, explores how space might be better deployed to reflect students' view that learning is about working for real. The second model, Negotiated Boundaries, overcomes the limits of traditional space boundaries to meet the needs of changing practices in art and design disciplines. The third model, Bonding and Bridging, uses space to support the needs of learners at each stage of academic progression.

Case Study 1: Learning by Working

The starting point for the Learning by Working model is a student quote – 'when we wear our uniform, we feel more professional and people take us more seriously'. For these students, at a further education college, learning is about being surrounded by role models, working for real, having pride in their profession. It is not about learning for learning's sake or hanging out on campus. These students want their college to provide them with the skills and confidence to become competent professionals in the workplace. The college has responded by seeking more employer and sector skills council involvement in its curriculum advisory groups and placing more emphasis on spaces that provide industry standard facilities. It is promoting greater community use of college services provided by students and locating business activities on campus where students can work alongside professional colleagues or as a fully integrated member of the team. A key component of this new space model is to create two distinct realms of learning – one private, the other public. The latter features a number of learning platforms where students can progressively showcase their learning achievements as they advance through their programmes of study. The 'prepare and make' platform will include cooking demonstrations, everyday dining, events catering, online bookings and recipes. The 'create and exhibit' platform will include gallery management, exhibitions and sales, community projects. The 'rehearse and perform' platform will include an improvisation club, partnership performances, events marketing, online booking and music blog. And so on. The LSC space guidelines (Learning Skills Council, www.lsc.gov.uk) recommend the following breakdown of gross space: 50% teaching and learning, 10% amenities, 10% administration and 30% balance (circulation and core). An optional +10% is suggested for atrium space. Using these guidelines as a starting-point, the Learning by Working model brings together almost half of the total proposed teaching and learning space (20%), all amenities (10%) and atrium (+10%) to create a market-place of learning platforms. In this way, greater opportunities are provided for students to work in order to learn, as well as learning in order to work.

Case Study 2: Negotiated Boundaries

The Negotiated Boundaries model is a response to the ongoing blurring of boundaries in many subject areas, in this case art and design, where some discipline-specific departments are finding it increasingly difficult to meet the multi-disciplinary preferences of many learners, such as graphic designers who want to write in stone (literally) and painters who want to work with film. This space model explores the idea of boundaries defined by activities rather than departments, where thinking, reflecting, sharing, making, presenting, performing, exhibiting, storing, etc., might happen in any one of several settings along the full spectrum offered. The starting point is a series of studios based on material types, which are then supported by a range of generic and specialist spaces. Two types of staff support (on-hand and timetabled) are offered with each space type. Studios come with studio assistants and tutors, libraries with librarians, computer rooms with information technologists, workshops with materials specialists, laboratories with lab specialists and so on. The amount and level of staff support available is clearly visible to learners and the staff costs associated with each space type can be considered from the outset. In this model, space ownership criteria for each space type are redefined as shared (freely available), borrowed (bookable and/or open-access) and allocated (annual rent required). Flexibility characteristics are mapped in terms of agile, adjustable and adaptable. Agile focuses on furniture flexibility, adjustable focuses on fit-out flexibility (e.g. movable screens, bleacher seating), while adaptable focuses on a building's ability to support major fit-out change over time. Thus, users are enabled to exercise change and to shape their environment at different levels of control.

Case Study 3: Bonding and Bridging

The Bonding and Bridging model sees learning as a process of increasing levels of participation in the learning communities and networks of the learner's chosen profession. Broadly speaking, the stages involved might be described as finding our way' (undergraduate), 'going deeper' (postgraduate), 'leading the way' (research and enterprise) and 'sharing widely' (public engagement). In this model, the institution looks at how the social skills required for participation in both communities and networks might be enhanced at each stage of academic progression. Bonding skills focus on defining 'who we are' by making connections with our immediate community through everyday activities. Bonding-type relationships are developed via face-to-face communication within space that is preferably owned and has strong boundaries. Bridging skills focus on extending 'who we are' by building an expanded community through participation in activities beyond the subject grouping. Bridging-type relationships are developed and maintained largely through virtual communication, supported by occasional face-to-face gatherings in space, which tends to be borrowed and has permeable boundaries.

In this model, bonding places are provided by homelands – spaces with strong boundaries that allow communities of practice to form and develop distinct identities. Each homeland supports a particular art or design practice via a range of settings including studio (live-in and drop-in), workshop/lab (open-access and bookable), research base and staff base. Bridging places are provided by commons – places with permeable boundaries that allow different communities of practice to interact and overlap. Settings include welcome (meet + greet, deli-counter, gallery, shop, support staff), learning (library, open-access project space, seminar rooms, repro centre, support staff), practice (project space, loans depot, workshops, media-labs, support staff) and research (meet + display, coffee bar, project space, workspace, support staff). The relationship learners have with these two types of space will vary as they progress through their programmes of study. An interesting aspect of this third model is the conversations it generates around where best to locate academic heads. Situating each head in his/her practice homelands provides opportunities to focus on specific practice issues. Situating heads together in a commons location provides opportunities to strengthen relationships between practice areas. The option chosen depends on an institution's current strategic priorities, and needs to be supported by good use of email, phone and timetabled meetings to ensure effective maintenance of both bonding and bridging relationships.

IMPLEMENTING NEW SPACE MODELS

All three models outlined (Learning by Working, Negotiated Boundaries, Bonding and Bridging) accept that an institution's efforts to make more effective use of space are likely to generate new costs. Additional job roles may be required, such as increased staff presence in non-timetabled learning spaces and more complex management of booking systems. Enhanced technology continues to be high on the list of resource requirements – infrastructure to support users own technology, equipment which is increasingly focused on high-end use and technical support that is both general and specialised. Using space more intensively over longer opening hours may also lead to higher operating costs and increased wear and tear.

And there are other factors to consider, such as the likely impact on users and providers. New space models are best learnt through hands-on experience, where participants are given opportunities to engage both actively and reflectively with the stages involved in development, implementation and evaluation. Finding out how participants already perceive space, and asking them to make connections with different types and ways of using it, takes time and can be a traumatic experience for some. Prior knowledge is often hard-earned, embedded over time and highly resistant to change. We therefore shouldn't be surprised when projects involving new ideas about space are not immediately met with widespread enthusiasm. Because learning is seen as a social activity, one of the most effective ways for opening up the possibility for change is to encourage users, estates and institution representatives to spend time together walking around and observing their institution in action, as well as other institutions, such as organisations in commercial or other sectors that have interesting social and spatial arrangements. This process not only deepens individual understanding of space-in-use, but also develops collective understanding by highlighting similarities and differences in priorities, values, hopes and concerns.

Increased understanding is one thing, enhanced dialogue another, while decision-making processes takes institutions into another realm of complexity altogether. Space, we quickly learn, goes right to the heart of what individuals and institutions believe in. It can sometimes seem as though the tools applied to this heart-felt issue are ill-chosen or poorly maintained, with the result that potentially excellent space initiatives can sometimes end up in the 'too difficult to achieve' category. The institutions that appear to understand their learning spaces best tend to be skilled at recognising patterns in their own learning activities and the ways they occupy space. They can help generate and visualise the kinds of social and spatial organisational models outlined above. They also need a willingness to apply a range of evaluation tools to deepen their understanding (Bligh and Pearshouse, Chapter 1). This ability for self-reflection in action enables these institutions to develop space models that are both customised and general, planned for and incremental. By continually drawing individuals' attention back to their role as stakeholder, reminding them of the role of other stakeholders and allowing dialogue to incorporate the values, hopes and concerns of all, the processes outlined here enable the institution's development of learning spaces to focus on opening up new possibilities. The quality and effectiveness of such learning spaces reflect the insights gained by a wide community of practice who are engaged in an ongoing process of sense-making around what makes *their* learning spaces work. The general informs the specific, while the specific informs the general. Having set up the conditions whereby key stake-holders are encouraged to experiment together, change is allowed to happen in a nurturing way, where the best of the new is continually integrated into the most useful of the old.

DAVID ANDERSON

12. LEARNING BEYOND THE UNIVERSITY

The Utopian Tradition

INTRODUCTION

Societies – and this applies as much to societies in our own time as in the past – need public spaces for learning and many other purposes. Such spaces are, of course, a cultural construct, reflecting the characteristics and preoccupations of the communities of which they are part. Public spaces play three key roles: first, they are spaces of opportunity, for provision of public good; second, they are a defence – sometimes a vital defence – against the threats any democratic society can face; and third, they are places for debate and negotiation of the future. Museums at their best play at least one, if not more of these three roles. They do so by being welcoming and accessible to people from all backgrounds; by encouraging participation; inspiring creativity; encouraging intercultural exchange; fostering engagement with uncomfortable issues from the past, and understanding of their significance for the present. This can be summed up as treating all visitors and potential users with equal respect. Of course, no museum achieves all this in practice.

Neil Postman, then Professor of Communication Studies at New York University, set an aspirational agenda in a keynote speech at an ICOM Triennial conference at the Hague in 1989. 'My pet project', he said, 'would be a Museum of Lost Virtues, which would have four sections: one devoted to honour, another to the meaning of civility, a third to the meaning of magnanimity, a fourth to the meaning of loyalty. Well, that's enough of my fantasies...' (Postman, 1991). The losses Postman laments are not small ones. Not lost property, lost visitors, lost cities or even (in keeping with his devotion to fantasies) Peter Pan and the Lost Boys, but lost virtues. We may imagine that Postman's Museum of Lost Virtues would be a rather dull affair – unless, that is, he chooses to indulge our base desire to know exactly how these virtues were lost, by whom and when. Even so, who can doubt that the faithless multitude will abandon Postman's worthy efforts to promote virtue, and instead will flock to a rival attraction, the Museum of the Seven Deadly Sins. Museums can be dystopias as well as utopias.

MUSEUMS AND UTOPIA

It is easy to mock (as I just have) Postman's nostalgia for public spaces to endorse public virtues that in reality may always have been in short supply. But I had better

A. Boddington and J. Boys (eds.), Re-Shaping Learning: A Critical Reader: The Future of Learning Spaces in Post-Compulsory Education, 155–164.
© 2011 Sense Publishers. All rights reserved.

be careful. My own institution, the Victoria and Albert Museum in London (V&A), is itself the product of the grand utopian tradition. The founders of the South Kensington Museum aimed to spread art among all classes of society, to improve the quality of industrial design, and to raise standards of art and design education – a utopian vision of museums as places for universal public education. The Museum aspired, then, to educate designers and manufacturers; to educate consumers; and to educate the young – the designers, manufacturers and consumers of the future. This was a great educational experiment, a project of breathtaking ambition, and before many decades had passed it was comprehensively abandoned. With it died a vision of museums as instruments of public education concerned with the world beyond the walls of the institution. Until the directorship of Elizabeth Esteve-Coll (and with limited exceptions around World War II and Roy Strong's exhibitions programme in the 1970s and 1980s) the Museum's staff were primarily concerned with their collections. The institution slept for 100 years, still devoted to a utopia of a kind – but one that was very different from that of its foundation. William Morris, the 19th century designer, author and inveterate utopian, was a seminal influence on the Museum in its early years and is now well represented in its collections. What had Morris to say about museums and museum education in his writings? It must be admitted that, especially in his later years, Morris was not an unqualified enthusiast for the museums or the education of his day. He had no illusions about the effectiveness of the museum experience which, if we are honest, has not changed in its essentials over the last 100 years in some of our more traditional national institutions. Rip van Winkle could awake tonight in one of several major museums in London and believe, at least for a few hours until the visitors arrive, that he has only had the briefest of naps. As Morris noted,

> I am in the habit when I go to an exhibition or a picture gallery of noticing their [people's] behaviour there; and as a rule I note that they seem very much bored, and their eyes wander vacantly over the various objects exhibited to them, and odd to say, a strange or unusual thing never attracts them, no doubt because it appeals to their minds chiefly through their eyes; whereas if they come across something familiar which a printed label informs them is something, they become interested and nudge each other (1973, pp. 198–199).

In fact, Morris was convinced towards the end of his life that museums as he knew them were of little use to most people. In a lecture, 'The Prospects of Architecture in Civilisation,' he wrote:

> Until our streets are decent and orderly, and our town gardens break the bricks and mortar every here and there, and are open to all people; until our meadows even near our towns become fair and sweet, and are unspoiled by patches of hideousness: until we have clear sky above our heads and green grass beneath our feet; until the great drama of the seasons can touch our workmen with feelings other than the misery of winter and the weariness of summer; till all this happens our museums and art schools will be but

amusements of the rich; and they will soon cease to be of any use to them also, unless they make up their minds that they will do their best to give us back the fairness of the earth (1929, pp. 196–197).

Given Morris' scepticism about museums, it is scarcely surprising to find that they play little part in his utopian visions. For Morris, the past – historic buildings, museums, even works of art and literature – were of use merely as a catalyst for the achievement of an ideal society. Once they had succeeded in their task, as in the future society of his *News from Nowhere*, there were virtually redundant.

Books, books, books, grandfather!' exclaims the young woman Clara, 'when will you understand that after all it is the world we live in that interests us; the world of which we are part, and which we can never love too much! (1993, p. 175).

In view of Morris' distaste for museums in the latter years of his life, it is no surprise to discover that in *News from Nowhere* the South Kensington Museum seems to have disappeared entirely, to be replaced by woods (p. 64). It is not the only historic building to have suffered. The Houses of Parliament have become 'a sort of market and a storage place for manure' (p. 69). The British Museum has somehow survived but in reduced circumstances, as has the National Gallery. 'A place where pictures are kept as curiosities is called a National Gallery', explains one of the characters, 'Of course, there are a lot of them up and down the country' (p. 80). But these surviving buildings need not get ideas above their station. The time traveller is told that 'these silly old buildings serve as a kind of foil for the beautiful ones we build now' (p. 69). Why was the South Kensington Museum made to disappear altogether? Perhaps its failures as a museum of design were particularly offensive to Morris. It is something of a shock to realise that Morris, earlier so closely and personally involved in the development of the Museum, was, by 1890, so determined to humble this same institution and all other national museums. Formal education, in *News from Nowhere*, is jettisoned even more abruptly. Schools are unknown, and children live and sleep out in the open in summer, camping in these same Kensington woods, riding ponies and swimming. They learn to read from the age of 4 years simply by picking up books (p. 66).

Morris was not the only museum utopian of his age. In August 2003, Andrew Carnegie presented the ancient city of Dunfermline, his birthplace, with the then enormous sum of £500,000 to be used as an experiment 'to bring into the monotonous lives of the toiling masses of Dunfermline ... some charm, some happiness, some elevating conditions of life, which residence elsewhere would have denied'. He urged the citizens of Dunfermline selected as trustees to remember that,

you are pioneers, and do not be afraid of making mistakes. Not what other cities have is your standard ... Do not put before their first steps that which they [the public] cannot easily take, but always that which leads upwards as their tastes improve (Anderson, 1993 pp. 9–12).

The first step of the Trustees was to commission a report from Professor Patrick Geddes of Glasgow University, one of the founding fathers of urban planning. This report is a truly remarkable document, inspired by a determination to infuse the whole city with the museum spirit, and museums with an awareness of the needs and interests of the ordinary inhabitants of the city (Geddes 1904). Professor Geddes' proposals – which included a Japanese tea house to be made in Japan and imported into Dunfermline; a rock garden as an open-air geological museum; a zoological garden preserving the natural habitat of the local fauna; and an open air museum to be constructed by the boys of the neighbourhood, complete with workshops for manufacture of furniture and other crafts – might not seem now to be particularly innovative; if so this is only because so many of his concepts have been implemented in one place or another. Geddes' ideas have an additional and deeper significance. They reflect his strong desire to develop an alternative to museums. 'I have no faith in the educational value of the commonplace art museum with its metal masterpieces in a glass case and the smithy nowhere', he wrote. 'Wherever real technical education is beginning, it centres on seeing and sharing the real work, and then applies the paper drawings and the collections of the old system to their right uses' (1904, p. 131).

So Neil Postman is in a long tradition of museum utopians – a tradition that was particularly vigorous in an age when museums themselves were young, and alternatives still seemed possible. What has utopianism to do with the realities of museum work today? More, perhaps, than we might think. In the first place, it is in the nature of utopias that they are concerned with the concept of perfection and the definition of the characteristics of a perfect society (at least, perfect in the eyes of their creators, for we must remember that one person's utopia is another's dystopia). Second, utopias are usually removed either in time or in space (but not necessarily both) from ourselves – that is, they are a version of 'the other'. Third, they are defined by principles, or rules, or characteristics, or articles of faith which, at least in the minds of their creators, explain their perfections. Fourth, they are often a deliberate critique of contemporary conditions (and as such are less removed from the here and now than appearances might suggest). Finally, they are places where (time as) change has ceased. Many of these processes are applied by museums to the objects in their care.

THE USES OF UTOPIAN THINKING

Many twentieth century thinkers were sceptical of the influence of utopian thinking. Karl Popper, for one, was a critic of the corrosive effects of its historicism (Kumar, 1993). Yet it would be wrong to identify utopianism as a vice of the modern age. For the reality is that we have always been surrounded by, or have surrounded ourselves with, utopias. Of course, the classical utopias are removed from us both in place and time, and so by definition we cannot experience them. But we can experience quasi-utopias – hybrid societies that have some utopian features only. The Shakers, New Lanark and other communities have sought to create perfection in miniature. Disney World – the Magic Kingdom – is another example, a dystopia created for commercial purpose. Then there is perhaps the most corrosive micro-utopia of all – McDonalds, the 'McTopia' so elegantly dissected by John

O'Neill in his brief but luminously brilliant article 'McTopia: Eating Time' – the source of words such as McJob that have already entered the language (1993). For O'Neill, McDonalds is 'nowhere because it is everywhere. It is everywhere, because, wherever it is, the "taste" is always the same'. In McDonalds, the ubiquitous 'McArch is both an opening, and not an opening. It is a place where happiness is blocked by the removal of change, variety and imperfection through endless repetition ... [whereas] Outside utopia everything is eaten by time'. Unlike children in the world of Morris' *News from Nowhere*, 'kids work in McTopia ... They do not play there ... The counterpart of McTopia's sweated labour is the hurried McTopia consumer ... In no case does the customer choose or reject the items picked out of the assembly line'.

So much for McTopia. It is only one of the legion of micro-utopias. Everywhere, in everything we experience, in almost everything we think, are micro-utopias – statements and actions that reveal our concepts of the ideal society, or our conscious or unconscious submission to the utopian concepts of others, and our attempts to enact them. When we support the War in Iraq, or eat at McDonalds, or send our children to a state school or a private one, we perform utopian/dystopian acts; they are most successful when we carry these templates unquestioned in our heads. Museums – utopias of the Muses – cannot be exempted from this analysis. Why should O'Neill's critique of McDonalds not be applied to museums? We might care to remember that museums, like McDonalds, consist of a public space (eating space/gallery space) and private space (where the reality of the processing of food/objects is done out of sight). Museums have all of the characteristics of utopias that I listed earlier: objects that reflect a concept of perfection; immortalisation of objects through their removal from the risks to which their continual use in the world of real time and space would expose them; framed by characteristic principles or rules – in this case, a belief in the transforming power of objects; embodying a critique – albeit implicit not explicit – of real life (museums are usually places of ostensible absences of conflict, and behaviour is tightly controlled); and finally, the slowing of change to the point where, in some galleries, it has become almost imperceptible.

If we doubt that museums are as capable of being dystopias as well as utopias, we only need to look for evidence to Yuri Dombrovsky's novel, *The Keeper of Antiquities*, first published in the Soviet Union during the brief spring of the early 1960s (1988). As Nadezhda Mandelstam, wife of the poet Osip Mandelstam, wrote in her extraordinary autobiography *Hope Against Hope*,

> Dombrovsky is the author of a book about our life which was written as they used to say in the old days 'with his heart's blood...' It is also a book which gets to the very core of our wretched existence. Anybody who reads it cannot fail to understand why the camps were bound to become the instrument by which 'stability' was maintained in our society (1971, p. 387).

Dombrovsky's book is a thinly fictionalised account of his experiences as a young man, exiled from 1930s Moscow to Alma Ata in Khazakstan. There he became a junior curator in the National Museum, just as Stalinism was tightening its grip on every aspect of life in this remote region of the Soviet Union. The book had a certain black humour, but the reality of the impact of Stalinism on the Museum and its staff was clearly anything but amusing.

TOWARDS NEW KINDS OF PUBLIC CULTURAL SPACE

If utopianism in an integral part of thought, we must embrace it (with critical awareness). What kind of public spaces do we need today, in our society, and what role should culture play within them? Since at least the 19th century, we have had at least three (and, more recently, four) kinds of public spaces, each with a distinctive cultural role. First, cultural institutions such as museums, libraries, performing arts venues and community arts centres, where specific cultural and educational activities are the primary purpose. Second, there are cultural spaces such as urban parks and protected landscapes, where culture and education are an explicit element of these spaces, but not their only activity. Third, open spaces such as streets, rivers, wildernesses and the air around us, to which the public has access as of right, but are rarely if ever designed for explicit cultural purposes. Finally, in the 20th century, media (now digital) space has emerged as a fourth creative and dynamic area for cultural activities that has both enriched and challenged the primacy of physical space.

Over the last 200 years, in much of the developed world, the first of these categories, cultural institutions, has been the primary focus for public policy and the priority for such limited public funding as has been available, followed some way behind by cultural spaces. The full potential of open spaces has largely been disregarded. A (possibly radical) proposal is that the successful achievement of public policy goals will depend on the systematic and integrated development of all four kinds of public space. This does not diminish the importance of existing cultural and educational institutions – the expertise of their staff will be essential to the success of a project of cultural education in public spaces, but only if curators and educators accept that they cannot and should not control public cultural spaces in the way they do their own institutional spaces. A new model of accountability and governance is needed, that provides a voice for all the key stakeholders and users of these spaces. The formation of the Exhibition Road Cultural Group in an area of West London (see below) is one example of an attempt to provide such accountability. This is becoming an urgent issue. In Britain, public spaces are under pressure from many directions. Commercial pressures can threaten the integrity of cultural institutions as well as other kinds of public spaces, and allow them to become playgrounds of the wealthy. Technology such as CCTV cameras can be used by governments to monitor their populations. Faith groups can demand the right to control the debate on issues they care about (as evangelical Christians have done in protesting at displays on natural selection in US museums). Museum staff themselves can use their control of collections and displays to serve their own professional interests rather than those of the public.

THE SACKLER CENTRE FOR ARTS EDUCATION AT THE V&A

The V&A's Sackler Centre for arts education, which opened in 2008, could be regarded a return by the V&A to its utopian roots. The 1,800m^2 Centre, in the Museum's Henry Cole Wing, was conceived as a state of mind, a way of thinking, as well as a building. It consciously attempted to bring together the expertise, not just of the Museum and its staff, but creative professionals and audiences. The vision of the Centre is that it should be the V&A's centre for learning through creative design, and the brief for the architects specified that visitors should know good design by experiencing it, as well as participating in the Centre's programmes. Through its three studios, the Centre embraces as wide a definition of design as possible; with one studio dedicated to digital learning, another to traditional craft and design practice, and a third to a combination of the two (Figure 12.1). This diversity of design practice, embracing the contemporary as well as the historical, can be seen as a continuity rather than a fracture in the development of the Museum's educational role. Underpinning the architecture of the Centre is a belief that design can (at its best) change the world, and is central to the quality of our lives. Everyone, we believe, has talent and it is our job to help them to develop it through the medium of the Museum's collections. In addition, difference, debate and exchange – between cultures and across disciplines – is, potentially, a source of cultural dynamism. The Centre, with its seminar rooms, auditorium and artists studios, thus aims to embrace different ways of learning. Thinking, making and participating are all essential life skills that the programme attempts to foster. It is, in many ways, an avowedly utopian project, as well as an implicit intellectual and cultural critique of the rest of the V&A, where objects remain in display cases.

Figure 12.1. A studio workspace, with associated computer facilities at the Sackler Centre, V&A Museum, London. Photograph: Hilary Smith.

THE EXHIBITION ROAD CULTURAL GROUP

Over recent years, the V&A has also played a leading role in another ambitious project, the Exhibition Road Cultural Group (ERCG). Formed in 2004, the ERCG is a consortium of 16 national and international cultural and educational institutions and two local authorities. It has two aims: to work together to release the cultural, environmental, creative and intellectual potential of the area through joint cultural and educational programmes; and to work with the two local authorities who manage the streetscape to enhance the physical environment as a public cultural space. Since 2004, the ERCG has run more than 20 major public events, each involving a wide range of its members. These have included the International Music Day celebrations on 21 June each year, an event that has attracted up to 70,000 people to the area. The institutions have also taken a collaborative approach to diversity programmes such as Black History Month and the Notting Hill Carnival. These programmes have a strong international as well as community dimensions, which reflect the extensive international links of many of the member organisations.

In many respects, the Exhibition Road Cultural Group is itself also a utopian project because this area of London was deliberately created as a defined network of institutions, with the same aspirations at its heart to create a better society, and the same faith in the power of education and culture to achieve this, as inspired the foundation of many of its member institutions from the mid-19th century onwards. But it is not just institutions that enact utopian or dystopian aspirations. On the contrary, it is often individuals, without official approval, who articulate most effectively through their actions the utopian spirit in public spaces. In 2007, the *Guardian* reported that, for 1 year from 2005, an underground 'cultural guerrilla' movement known as Untergunther (Untergunther.blogspot.com), whose purpose is to restore France's cultural heritage, had set up a secret workshop and lounge in a cavity under the dome of the Panthéon in Paris. Under the supervision of a group member and a professional clockmaker, Jean-Baptiste Viot, they had pieced apart and repaired the Panthéon's antique clock that had been left to rust since the 1960s. Only when their work was completed did they reveal their audacious act, which included connecting their hideaway to the grid and installing a computer connected to the net. This is not the group's only such intervention. Since the 1990s they have restored crypts, and staged readings and plays in monuments at night. Untergunther was only discovered by the authorities in 2004, when police found an underground cinema, complete with bar and restaurant, under the Seine. Many of its members were students in the Latin Quarter in the 1980s and 1990s, and now work by day in professions such as nursing and the law. 'We would like to replace the state in the areas it is incompetent,' said their spokesperson Lazar Klausmann. 'But our means are limited and we can only do a fraction of what needs to be done. There's so much to do in Paris that we won't manage in our lifetime'. He added that 'The Latin Quarter is where the concept of human rights came from. It's the centre of everything. The Pantheon clock is in the middle of it. So it's a bit like the clock at the centre of the world' (The *Guardian*, London, 26 November 2007). What could be more utopian than that?

CONCLUSION

The foundation of public space is social relationships. Public space both reflects and helps to shape the society of which it is part. Who uses it, and for what? Who controls it, and who should control it? These questions raise fundamental issues of cultural rights and cultural democracy. Three factors in particular seem to be animating culture at the moment: the relationship of geography and cultures in an era of globalisation; the relationship of consumers and producers in an era when the gap between them may be reducing and the question of what disciplines and practices count as culture, in an era when science and technology are now demanding to be taken seriously as part of culture, and Western definitions of culture don't always travel well[1].

A focus on culture in public space would have the advantage of once again drawing into the museum project many of the longstanding critics of our institutions. Untergunther is only one of numerous, thoughtful examples. The anti-museum movement has a thin literature but a long and significant history. It deserves to be taken more seriously. Opponents of the museum solution have included many artists who have resisted the display of their works in galleries, educators who regard museums as irrelevant and reactionary in both their content and their learning strategies, and social reformers who have perceived these institutions as expressions of the ideologies of dominant elites. Finally, one must not neglect to mention the silent majority – that section of society that is often poorer and less well-educated – who rarely if ever visit museums, for a diversity of reasons they may not care to articulate but which remain substantial. It may be that engagement with public space can change museums, as much as museums may change public space.

Should utopian dreams be discarded? Perhaps not. As Milan Simeka, (described by Krishnan Kumar as 'one of the most passionate critics of utopians') has said, 'A world without utopias would be a world without social hope' (Kumar and Bann, 1993). We may believe we should avoid visions – we fear that they will distract us from reality and dim our critical faculties. Of course, utopias are not 'real', any more than dreams are 'real', yet they are a manifestation of our cultural unconscious. They are as necessary and important to the health of our public spaces as dreams are to the health of our minds and bodies.

NOTES

[1] I am grateful to Ken Arnold of the Wellcome Collection: this paragraph is based on written communication between us in the preparation of a Manifesto on Public Space for an event organised by the London Cultural Quarter Group (LCQG) in 2007.

REFERENCES

Anderson, D. (1993). Beyond museums, objects and cultures. *Journal of Education in Museums, 13*, 9–12.
Dombrovsky, Y. (1988). *The keeper of antiquities*. Manchester: Carcanet Press.
Kumar, K. (1993). The end of socialism? The end of utopia? The end of history? In K. Kumar & S. Bann (Eds.), *Utopias and the millennium* (pp. 66–67). London: Reaktion.
Kumar, K., & Bann, S. (Eds.). (1993). *Utopias and the millennium* (p. 75). London: Reaktion.

Mandelstam, N. (1971). *Hope against hope* (p. 387). London: Collins and Harvill Press.

McNeill, J. (1993). McTopia: Eating time. In K. Kumar & S. Bann (Eds.), *Utopias and the millennium* (pp. 129–137). London: Reaktion.

Morris, W. (1887/1973). The society of the future (text of lecture delivered to the Hammersmith branch of the Socialist League on 13 November 1887). *The political writings of William Morris* (pp. 198–199). London: Lawrence and Wishart.

Morris, W. (1929). The prospects of architecture in civilisation. In *Hopes and fears for art: Five lectures by William Morris* (pp. 196–197). London: Longman, Green and Co.

Morris, W. (1993). *News from nowhere* (p. 175). London: Penguin Books.

Postman, N. (1991). 'Extension of the museum concept'. In *Museums: Generators of culture* (pp. 40–48). The Hague, Netherlands: ICOM '89 Foundation.

PART 4: RESHAPING THE FUTURE
OF LEARNING SPACES

RONALD BARNETT

13. CONFIGURING LEARNING SPACES

Noticing the Invisible

INTRODUCTION

The idea of learning space has many attractions, but it holds traps for the unwary. The idea is at once educationally expansive, potentially emancipatory and even subversive. It opens up the hope of students becoming authors of their own learning in spaces that they claim as their own. But the idea of learning space, as it is being taken up, deserves to carry warning signs. There are invisibilities associated with it, invisibilities connected with a potential psychological overload on learners and with a possible down-valuing of knowledge as the student's own learning journey is given prominence. This, at least, is the argument I shall try to make in this chapter. To do that, we shall need, en route, to essay a brief exploration of the conceptual landscape of learning spaces and to attempt a preliminary taxonomy. Finally, having developed a somewhat cautionary account of learning spaces, I shall turn – via the idea of an ecology of learning spaces – to intimate a positive way forward that addresses the challenges sketched out.

VALUING LEARNING SPACES

The idea of learning spaces is – on the surface, at least – emancipatory. It conjures themes of freedom, openness, personal realisation and creativity on the part of the learner. It also conjures a dissolution of the boundaries that have hitherto characterised formal learning – between different forms of knowledge, between forms of knowledge and forms of practice and between the teacher and the taught. Now the learner is free to roam by herself where so ever she wishes, in whichever direction she prefers and in whichever mode of learning she enjoys. In its intimations of the breaking of boundaries of higher education, the idea of learning spaces is subversive as, in its wake, the fixities and barriers that are characteristically so much part of the academy are set aside. This is a pedagogy that offers a new conception of education, in which the learner is much more the designer of her learning experiences.

The idea of learning spaces, then, flies in with large and even universal themes attaching to its wings. It is not shy of its ethical pretensions but proclaims them boldly and loudly. In associating itself with such tropes as freedom, openness, personal realisation and creativity, it stakes large claims for itself, claims that are

A. Boddington and J. Boys (eds.), Re-Shaping Learning: A Critical Reader: The Future of Learning Spaces in Post-Compulsory Education, 167–178.

not only pedagogical and educational but also ethical. The idea of learning spaces is a kind of educational radicalism, an outrider in its energies, its claims and its hopes. It attempts to storm the ethical high ground, to secure a vantage point from which other educational doctrines and dogmas may easily be vanquished.

It has considerable right on its side. Only so long as students have some degree of space to themselves can they flourish. Only insofar as they have space to themselves can they acquire and be authentically themselves in their learning and their own development. The idea of learning space is a radical concept that seeks to grant the individual student – and students collectively – space in which to become truly themselves, free from constraint. There is both negative and positive freedom here (Berlin, 1969/1979): on the one hand, the limitations – of discipline, of bounded curricula and of tight pedagogical frames – are reduced as the student is freed from constraints; on the other hand, the student is thereby empowered and indeed encouraged to take their courage in their hands and to venture forth by and for themselves. There is an existential calling lurking in the idea of learning space.

We should note too that the terms 'learning space' and 'learning spaces' are often here treated as if they were synonymous. This is a telling insight into the way in which language has ideological force. The learning space opens into learning spaces (plural). The one leads naturally to the other; and various *forms of learning space* may be identified. It is not merely that students can have access to different rooms, as it were, of the educational mansion through which they may roam, in and through its different spaces. Rather, the students may now have access to quite different kinds of mansion, configured quite differently and affording quite different kinds of experience.

The idea of learning space, thereby, offers an unending opening up of pedagogical space. Its spaces are presumably – at least in theory – infinite in their scope. The idea heralds, as we may term it, a pedagogy of air (Barnett, 2007). It is a space in which students take off and fly and breathe for and by themselves. They fly with courage and with confidence, and direct their own flight. They become themselves in this space. It is a space not just for greater understanding but a space in which students' own re-becoming as persons becomes possible. It is a space that offers to change students' lives.

TOWARDS A TAXONOMY OF LEARNING SPACES

It is surely already evident that learning spaces are of multiple kinds. Let us, then, hazard an attempt at forming a preliminary taxonomy of learning spaces (cf. Savin-Baden, 2008). I would want to classify learning spaces as forming three broad domains:

- a. *Material space and physical space*: These two – material space and physical space – are intimately related but are crucially different. Or to put it another way, the terms point us to different aspects of the geography of learning space. In relation to the student's material space, we can inquire into the materiality of the student's learning experience, its technologies, and its material structures (are there lecture halls?) and the spaces that they open (or close off). In relation to the student's physical space, we can inquire into the location of the student's learning (to what extent is it on campus or off it? To what degree are the tutors and other students visibly present?). Design can enter both forms of space here but it is the client and architect who come into play in the design of material space whereas it the educationalist as designer who acts in relation to physical space.

– b. *Educational space*: This is a set of intentional spaces that are revealed in the playing out of the curriculum and pedagogy. Curriculum spaces and pedagogical spaces are intertwined but again should be distinguished. *Curriculum spaces* are the spaces intentionally opened to the student, in the ordering of specific knowledge and its practice elements. *Pedagogical spaces* are the spaces of the relationship – the pedagogical relationship – between the tutor and student, and among the students. Curricula and pedagogical spaces are *both* structured and unstructured; but curricula spaces tend more by structure and pedagogical spaces more by improvisation. This is because, in higher education, curricula are formed crucially by assemblies from disciplinary fields that are, to some extent, given, whereas pedagogies are more open to experiment and innovation. Within both curricula and pedagogical spaces are to be found other spatial zones, in particular those of knowledge and of practices; so we can talk of *epistemological spaces* and of *practical spaces*. Issues arise as to the kinds of journey a student is being invited to make and as to the freedom extended to explore forms of knowledge. To what extent are the boundaries between forms of knowledge kept tight and even policed? Are there no-go areas? Issues also arise as to the kinds of actions that a student is enabled to conduct: with what freedom and in which direction might a student go? In some disciplines, related to life-threatening situations, there may be good reason for quite tight boundaries containing practical ventures.

– c. *The student's interior space*: This is a psychic space, but it is more than that. This is a kind of ontological space: it is the space of the student's being. It has a liquid character: her educational being flows in and out of her wider being as a person. It is a zone in which is to be found much of the meaning of that complex concept of *Bildung* (Lovlie, Mortenson & Nordenbo, 2003). Here, the student's own self-formation is implicated. To what extent does the student have a will to venture forth? How secure does she feel in doing so? Does she really wish to explore the spaces that are opened to her? What forms of explorations does she prefer? Concrete and practical or ideational and cognitive? Is she a nomadic learner or a stay-at-home learner? Is her world local or global – or both? How spacious is her interior space?

These three sets of spaces could be depicted as intersecting circles but that would be misleading. There is a dynamic between all three: each interacts with and influences the other two. But they are more like clouds, flowing into each other and setting up turbulences. The unbrokenness and the fixity of Venn diagram circles is far from this situation. The zones of the spaces outlined above are much more fuzzy, inchoate and fluid.

There is another difference between Venn diagrams and clouds. Characteristically, the circles of Venn diagrams are fairly empty; clouds on the other hand are more or less opaque; they are cloudy! Correspondingly, learning spaces may be populated; they may even be congested. There is perhaps too readily an assumption that learning spaces are open, uncluttered and readily available to the student's freely chosen explorations. But the opposite may be the case. Not infrequently, especially in the hard sciences and in the newer institutions of higher education, the learning spaces of the curriculum have been and are unduly full. Students have been sometimes been left with little room to reflect and hardly even to breathe, educationally speaking. So the arrival of the idea of 'learning spaces' is a call to the academic world to remove unnecessary clutter. The new dispensation is an implicit plea for more openness in the students' learning spaces.

LANGUAGES OF LEARNING SPACES

Trailing in the wake of the idea of learning spaces are the different languages through which it is articulated. There is a language that speaks to the pedagogical experience of students as they make their way amongst the learning spaces afforded to them and which they are increasingly invited to design and construct for themselves. There is a language, for example, of 'liminality', of the 'fluid' and 'liquid', of the 'transitional' and 'provisional', of the 'transgressing of borders' and of 'fragility'. There is 'risk' here, risk that learning may not advance effectively or even efficiently; risk that the student's will to learn may falter, as the personal load becomes unbearable. There is also a language of the student as 'traveller', as a 'voyager', as a 'nomad', a 'sojourner', hardly able to put down roots, as the student glides from one learning space (with its experiences) to another (with *its* experiences).

These two languages (of the absence of borders on the one hand and of the student's crossing of borders on the other hand) point to the ephemeralism of the student and her experiences as an ever-continuing traveller. The metaphors – at once of fragility and of personal travel – are metaphors of the contemporary age; or at least, of perceptions of it. For the current age, of 'post-modernity', of 'hyper-modernity', is seen precisely as a fluid age, somewhat rudderless, and lacking in the anchors of sure and uncontestable values and principles. As such, the individual is seen as bearing responsibility for making his or her way in the world, not just materially but also conceptually. A curriculum of learning spaces, accordingly, is a response to the challenges of a liquid world.

The educational philosophy – as we might term it – behind informal learning spaces is one that diminishes the place of knowledge and instead throws its weight behind *being* and *becoming*. Here, it is less important that the student knows or even that she is able to do particular things; what counts is that she is a certain kind of human being, able to take on unexpected challenges and move ahead even in murky waters. This is a philosophy not of filling up (with knowledge) nor even of filling out (with skills) but of opening out; opening out of the person, ready to take on the world; willing to go on a voyage of exploration by and for oneself.

Accordingly, the curriculum is to be characterised much more by relative open spaces, spaces both on and off campus, spaces of the mind and of body. There is a freedom here; it had better be termed not so much 'academic freedom' but a 'learning and personal freedom'. It is a space in which the student's voice can be developed and will be developed; it will be valued and will be heard and even heeded. (Witness the continuing and expanding efforts to monitor and evaluate students' 'satisfaction' with their courses and their entire university experience.)

There are ideological currents at work here. The idea of learning space implies an in-between space. It is a space that is not fully accounted for. Unforeseen experiences may arise in such spaces. There is a tension, therefore, between the idea of learning space and that of learning outcomes. The one speaks of spaciousness, of air, of freedom, of self-authorship; the other speaks of predictability, of control, of lack of freedom. So the idea of learning space is a subversive concept, containing the prospect of challenging the hegemony of contemporary dominant curricular thinking (which in the UK, for example, is predicated on a rigid structure of specific learning outcomes, explicitly linked to defined evaluation criteria which are then used to formally assess each teaching unit).

There are also other strains embedded in the idea of learning space. A key question is this: To what extent are learning spaces designed and who designs them? In other words, the idea of learning spaces could also herald a new kind of pedagogic control. It could presage a kind of Foucaultesque experiment, in which curricula and pedagogies are designed precisely to bring about the kinds of 'subjectivities' felt to be required by a globalised learning economy (Foucault, 1991). For such spaces might be designed and even engineered so as to elicit specifically desired qualities and dispositions – of venturousness, resilience, fortitude, self-endeavour and so forth. Far from heralding a critique of contemporary curricula, learning spaces may just be a device for bringing about a new order of student domestication.

The idea of learning spaces, then, is a discursive space in which different and perhaps somewhat antipathetic agendas come together. It is emancipatory, at least in its self-presentation; and it yet may serve as a pedagogic vehicle for the needs of the market and the global learning economy, and thereby serve the dominant interests in society. Its inner perception of the student as a free spirit, fearlessly exploring the learning spaces being opened may also here be coexisting with an educational response to calls for greater efficiency. And yet the idea of learning spaces, properly pursued, may lead to 'inefficient' learning as students are granted pedagogical space in which to make and to learn from their own mistakes. There is, therefore, in the idea of learning spaces an ideological complex, as competing educational philosophies jostle together.

THE POTENCY OF LEARNING SPACES

Higher education has long been associated with learning through subject disciplines. 'Disciplines' are aptly named: they require discipline for their study. They impose limits (of reasoning, argumentation, truth claims and ways of proceeding) and require understandings, whether of a horizontal character (across a broad range of concepts and schemas, as in the humanities) or of a vertical character (going into a limited range of concepts in an ordered way and to ever greater depth, as in the natural sciences) (Bernstein, 1999; Wheelahan, 2010). Disciplines require that the learner yield to their demands, if learning is to take place. The learner has to displace him or herself, to some extent. Learning spaces, to the contrary, encourage the learner forward. Disciplines provide a kind of learning *super-ego*: they call the learner to account, inviting an internalisation of the standards and forms of life particular of each discipline. Learning spaces, on the other hand, sponsor a learning *ego*: they invite the learner to become more fully him or herself, independently of external expectations.

Within the idea of learning spaces, therefore, lurks a psycho-dynamic dimension in which the individual appears to be freed from the perceived impositional tyranny of disciplines and is instead encouraged to become their own person. But learning spaces are inert in themselves. Under certain conditions, however, they can take on an educational power: they can become potent. Learning spaces can provide – as we may term it – *educational energy*. They can elicit and encourage a self-realisation among students; a new *becoming*. It is through the provision of learning spaces that a student can testify to the fact that her experience at university has changed her life. Nor is this potency a *fixed* quality of learning spaces, even where it is present: learning spaces can be assessed as to their degree of potency. The following theorem therefore presents itself:

availability (of learning spaces) + a will to explore + pedagogical encouragement = potency (1)

Potency here, therefore, is a function of real openness for the student to make their own explorations, combined with a will on the part of the student to take advantage of that openness. This also requires an encouragement to do so from the pedagogical environment. Under such a set of circumstances, the idea of learning spaces can be realized.

But what is this potency? Potency of what? It is, as implied, a potency for student *becoming*. In the centre is the flowering of the student's learning ego. She comes to have confidence in herself and her own understandings. However, as implied too, there are epistemological implications. For, insofar as the student's becoming becomes the pedagogical fulcrum here, there is – or is liable to be – a consequent diminution in the extent to which the student yields to and is initiated into *the discipline of the discipline*. This may be an empty triumph for the onto-logical quest of the student's being and becoming. For, if it is at the cost of the student's effective appropriation of a discipline, the resulting ego may be educationally empty at best and downright dangerous – being full of assertive dogma and personal opinion – at worst.

Another way of expressing these reflections is to observe that the disciplines themselves help to form perspectives on the world. In that way, they illuminate the world: they reveal it in ways not ordinarily perceived. They are themselves vistas of strangeness. They offer, in the words of Deleuze and Guattari, a set of 'striated' spaces as against the 'smooth' spaces of 'learning spaces' (Deleuze & Guattari, 2007). Disciplines are slices into the world; learning spaces are educational vehicles for traversing the world. A course of study, in and by the disciplines, is a programme that runs its course; it is channelled. Perspectives may be limited, therefore, but may run true and steady. Learning spaces offer excitement, a rare freedom and personal exploration; but the very open ended nature of the learning experience may be problematic. Not merely the learning spaces may be empty as the student is encouraged to make her own pedagogical journey; but the resulting experience may be largely empty as well. Without the insights of disciplinary perspectives, little understanding of any rigour may be gained. This is not so much a liquid learning as a glassy learning, in which the student skims across the learning surfaces and, in the process, accumulates very little.

NOTICING THE INVISIBLE

I have been hinting that there are hidden aspects in the idea of learning spaces. That thesis can now be brought more fully into the open. The idea of learning spaces is of its time. It offers – or seems to offer – the sponsoring of a learning 'subjectivity' in which the student embarks on a never-ending journey of self-learning. The learning, too, is a free-floating enterprise, that skates confidently over the existing representations of the world. Both these aspects of learning spaces have a pedagogical appropriateness in and for the 21st century; or so it may seem. The never-ending journey of self-learning that the idea of learning spaces seems to sponsor is a learning style fitting for a liquid world (Bauman, 2000), a world that seems to call forth a nomadism, a learning without roots, a learning that evinces disdain for disciplinary-bound learning. The world presents, so we are continually told, with changing, interdisciplinary and hybrid problems. It is, too, a world of fluid institutions, employment patterns, geographic movements and learning media. No one set of representations can sustain the kind of educational self-help that such a world requires; or so the argument seems to run.

There are a number of exclusions and hidden preferences in this ideology. Firstly, there is the exclusion of attachment. The contemporary world appears to call for a kind of learning promiscuousness in which the individual moves effortlessly from one topic to another, from one concept to another, and from one set of data to another. 'Multimodality' perhaps captures the hallmark of the discourse here and its appropriate learning processes (Kress & Van Leeuwen, 2001). Secondly, there is a preference for learning in the world and a down valuing of learning apart from the world. The reasoning runs this way. Effortless movement across situations – from which individuals learn – calls for a readiness to adopt different schemas. An education in a single discipline is thereby no longer useful. Such an education not merely restricts vision and access to learning tools; it severs the individual from the world, when what is desired is the capability and confidence of negotiating the world in all its messiness. Thirdly, the learning spaces that are encouraged are spaces in which the student is active and preferably literally so; active in visible performances. Spaces for mere contemplation are largely off-limits here. Finally, there is an embedded set of assumptions to the effect that all 'employability' requires this framing of knowledge and skills and that students en masse are in turn open to such malleability.

So, within the working out of the rhetoric of learning spaces, issues arise as to the rules of inclusion and exclusion. Not all learning spaces are equal; some are more equal than others. Some planes of learning – the disciplinary, the visionary, the theoretical, the contemplative – may be largely hidden or occluded; or banished completely. In the curricula construction of these learning spaces, students are carefully enjoined to go on certain kinds of learning journey rather than others. There is thus a major dimension of invisibility attaching to the educational project of learning spaces.

We may distinguish two kinds of the invisible. Firstly, there is the kind of learning spaces that is excluded by reason of educational intention. Opening up learning spaces of action, of 'training', of 'professional education' or even of 'service', whether on or off campus, whether in formal or structured settings or in informal and unstructured settings, can diminish spaces which enable a deep engagement within disciplines. It is not merely disciplines which fade from sight; so too do their perspectives and their power to transform perceptions. Such spaces are closed off *intentionally*. This is a form of *ideological invisibility*: the liberal idea of higher education is implicitly repudiated and banished. Secondly, learning spaces of former kinds may remain but become unnoticed. In an age of increasing e-learning, and group-based projects, books may remain on the shelves of the library but become invisible – less a learning resource and more a symbolic emblem of a former idea of the academy. Students are oriented to the task, the collective and the here-and-now. Private, in-depth and reflective study – of which dedicated reading is an obvious example – is not outlawed as such but instead passes out of sight. We may term this a 'myopic invisibility'.

For Heidegger, 'being' strives for to become transparent to itself. It becomes 'cleared in itself' in such a way 'that it is itself the clearing' (Heidegger, 1962/ 1998, p. 171). A key question for learning spaces, therefore, is the extent to which they allow students a *clearing* to come into themselves, to be disclosed to themselves. Far from encouraging such 'disclosedness' (ibid.), learning spaces may shut off – intentionally or unintentionally – such clearings as would allow a student genuinely to come into themselves, to develop authentic understandings of the world for and by themselves. Far from opening up real and challenging vistas, learning spaces may consign students to the immediate, the familiar and the safe as they move rapidly from one learning space to yet another. The idea of learning spaces loses its meaning if it means yielding one set of closures for another. The very breadth of view, the interconnectedness and largeness of outlook, the vision and even the wisdom (Maxwell, 2009) that the idea of learning spaces holds out may be vitiated if it is implemented as an ideological vehicle for external interests.

AN ECOLOGY OF LEARNING SPACES

We can, therefore, speak of *an ecology of learning spaces*. An ecology of learning spaces points to interconnectedness between learning spaces and thence to modalities of that interconnectedness. Learning spaces primarily of knowing, learning spaces primarily of doing and learning spaces primarily of sheer being: what are their relationships? To what degree and in what ways does the student have freedom to roam across those spaces? What are the values informing the shaping of these various learning spaces? To speak of an ecology of learning spaces, therefore, is not only to advert to patterns and shapes in and between learning spaces, but also it is to underscore their ethical dimensions. What ends are these learning spaces intended to sustain? Which sustainabilities are favoured here? Do these learning spaces look outwards or at least open windows outwards, towards the learning economy perhaps, or to ideas of civic society? Or do they look inwards, to the student's own sustainability and development across her lifespan?

There is literally incredible complexity here. A student's programme of under-graduate studies typically runs its course over three or four years. Each is a set of learning spaces, with their own ecologies. There is a dynamic here, the modules and units in tension with each other, firing off each other, drawing from each other. They open spaces for the students, who take differential advantage of their opportunities. Some venture forward excitedly; others hold back. After all, students need courage to move into learning spaces of their own volition. This courage is a kind of gift on the part of the student to him or herself. But, because of the risks, it is a gift he or she can often barely come to bestow. It is an expression of goodwill, to make good of the open spaces, but the outcome is unclear.

This ecology is a complex of ecologies. It is a knowledge ecology, a learning ecology (itself a complex of learning modalities), an ecology of being and becoming and an ecology of praxis all at once, and all working in an extraordinary dynamic with each other. There is, too, as there has to be, all manner of inter-connectednesses across these domains. These inter-connectednesses are themselves constantly shifting, as curricula, pedagogies, students, learning opportunities on and off campus, changing members of course teams, disciplinary developments and alterations in resources all play their part in helping to shape the ecological landscape. The student makes her way in and across these learning spaces, perhaps hesitantly, perhaps with some confidence; but there is unpredictability here; there has to be. No matter how far some of the spaces are rule-bound – are 'striated' – still there is some glassiness here. The student slides across the 'smooth spaces', just hoping that the ice will not crack.

These are serious learning ventures. They are adventures, ventures of discovery. The potential discoveries are as much discoveries of self – of being in the world – as they are about knowledge and of practice. In these learning processes, there is room inevitably for misadventure, not only for wrong turnings but for learning encounters where the discoveries of self are even, at first, injurious (Meyer & Land, 2006). There has to be always a possibility of genuine learning spaces, but ecologies may founder; may not be sustained.

The idea of ecology, to use a term of Bernard Williams (2008), is a 'thick concept'. It is fact and value at once. So, too, are learning spaces considered as learning ecologies: we can inquire into them as sets of actual curricula and pedagogical spaces and we can inquire into the hopes and commitments circling in them and around them. Learning spaces are always pools of *learning–possible*. They are potentials for learning in all manner of directions, learning that has ultimately to be at least partly under the control of the student. They constitute a retort to the dominant ideologies encircling these learning spaces.

As ecologies, learning spaces are full of hopes for improvement, for the student's own personal improvement, for her being in the world, and for her knowing and for her practices in the world. They hold out the wish for some kind of existential liberation from the pulls and pushes that attend those spaces, even from the existing educational communities of knowers and would-be knowers (the other students) participating in those spaces. Learning spaces, even in their ecological moments, are sites of some anarchy (Barnett, 2010) as students take their chances and realise their own possibilities, amid the inter-connectivities that characterise the many ecologies at work.

To couple the ideas of learning spaces and learning ecologies is to inject both an intention and a value-component into what otherwise might be – *a priori* – a neutral concept, open to any manner of curricula aims. Now, seen as the formation and sustaining of learning ecologies, learning spaces are imbued with high and virtuous hopes and ideals. The idea of learning spaces, which (as noted) is itself inert, is now given a forward and progressive momentum. As the formation of a learning ecology, it is no longer blind to ideological presences (of the kind observed earlier). On the contrary, this ecology now keeps open a watchful eye for ideological presences and directly engages them in combat. This is not fanciful. Students these days are often very aware of ideological presences, of the state or corporations, of discourse and of power structures that affect their learning and their student experience (see Melhuish Chapter 6). As inhabitants of learning spaces, afforded their own autonomy to take some charge of their own learning, they become active and may even adopt a critical and radical stance as they forge their own learning situation, reflective of their own – doubtless developing – values. An ecology of learning spaces is dynamically in favour of improvement of and for a better world, even if just what is to count as a better world is kept under critical review.

CONCLUSION

The idea of learning spaces holds traps for the unwary. It comes full of promises and hopes, of liberation, emancipation and authenticity for the learner, now freed to take charge of her learning experiences and to win through to new stages of her own self-becoming. But its contemporary and forceful arrival as an idea isn't happenstance. It has taken off as an idea because multiple and indeed even antagonistic groupings find it a useful vehicle for furthering their various interests. As well as it being a vehicle for emancipatory hopes, it is also a vehicle for technical and instrumental interests, in a context of mass post-compulsory education, rising student:staff ratios and an attunement to a global learning economy that calls for individuals to have powers of self-renewal throughout their lifespan. The single term 'learning spaces', therefore, denotes a contested ideological terrain.

There are also education pitfalls arising from learning spaces considered as an emancipatory project. If the student's learning spaces are initially empty, to be filled only by the student's creative endeavours, what becomes of knowledge, knowing and deep understanding? There is a risk here of epistemological superficiality as the educational enterprise focuses on the student's self-becoming.

In this complex of considerations, two further questions arise: what is to count as maturity on the part of the student? And, is it possible to derive a conception of learning spaces that, at once, addresses the three concerns of educational maturity, of knowing and understanding, and of potential ideological entrapment? I have suggested that a consideration of learning spaces as a *set* of ecologies may offer a way forward. This conception of learning spaces may turn out to be epistemologically, ontologically and practically efficacious. Learning spaces considered as a set of ecologies both opens up spaces and at the same time places severe epistemological burdens on the student as learner. The knowledge wanderings of students are still subject to the forms of life of academic disciplines, even as they find their own path through and form their own images of the world. Such a journey is precisely one means of achieving maturity as it opens up the prospect of the student coming into herself or himself in a totally new way; of 'finding' themselves, and of securing the personal resources through which to gain a genuine authenticity. And such a voyage of discovery, too, opens the prospect of a student engaging with the world and coming to form a care for the world. The sustainability of the world, the student and even of knowledges, can all be in evidence here.

Of course, the framing of curricula and the adoption of pedagogies that are going to do justice to all of these hopes is full of challenge. Fortunately, there are indications that such educational achievements are possible and, indeed, are already present. Not infrequently, students can be heard to say at graduation ceremonies, in introducing a tutor to the proud parents, not that 'I've gained a lot of knowledge on this course' or that 'I've acquired many skills on this course' but that 'this course has changed my life'. Is that not a shorthand and telling testimony to the presence of ecological learning spaces?

REFERENCES

Barnett, R. (2007). *A will to learn: Being a student in an age of uncertainty.* Maidenhead: McGraw-Hill/Open University Press.

Barnett, R. (2010). *Being a university.* Abingdon: Routledge.

Bauman, Z. (2000). *Liquid modernity.* Cambridge: Polity.

Berlin, I. (1969/1979). *Four essays on liberty.* Oxford: Oxford UniversityPress.

Bernstein, B. (1999). Vertical and horizontal discourse: An essay. *British Journal of Sociology of Education, 20*(2), 157–173.

Deleuze, G., & Guattari, F. (2007/1980). *A thousand plateaus: Capitalism and schizophrenia.* London: Continuum.

Foucault, M. (1991/1975). *Discipline and punish: The birth of the prison*. London: Penguin.

Heidegger, M. (1998/1962). *Being and time*. Oxford: Blackwell.

Kress, G., & Van Leeuwen, T. (2001). *Multimodal discourse: The modes and media of contemporary communication*. London: Arnold.

Lovlie, L., Mortenson, K. P., & Nordenbo, S. E. (2003). *Educating humanity: Bildung in postmodernity*. Blackwell: Oxford.

Maxwell, N. (2009). From knowledge to wisdom: The need for an academic revolution. In R. Barnett & N. Maxwell (Eds.), *Wisdom in the university*. Abingdon: Routledge.

Meyer, J. H. F., & Land, R. (Eds.). (2006). Threshold concepts and troublesome knowledge: Issues of liminality. *Overcoming barriers to student understanding: Threshold concepts and troublesome knowledge*. Abingdon: Routledge.

Savin-Baden, M. (2008). *Learning spaces: Creating opportunities for knowledge creation in academic life*. Maidenhead: McGraw-Hill/Open University Press.

Wheelahan, L. (2010). *Why knowledge matters in curriculum: A social realist argument*. Abingdon: Routledge.

Williams, B. (2008). *Ethics and the limits of philosophy*. Abingdon: Routledge.

ANNE BODDINGTON

14. DESIGNING EDUCATION AND RESHAPING LEARNING

'We become what we behold. We shape our tools
and then our tools shape us.'
(Marshall McLuhan, Understanding Media, 1964)

'We shape our buildings, and afterwards our buildings shape us.'
(Winston Churchill, 1943)

INTRODUCTION

This chapter begins with a glance in the rear view mirror, reflecting on the outcomes and more speculative ideas that emerged from the Centre for Excellence in Teaching and Learning through Design (CETLD) between 2005 and 2010. Structured in two parts, the first section will recount the ideas that underpinned the CETLD's formation and informed its aspirations, focusing on design education and learning spaces. The second section will speculate on its contribution to rethinking design, design learning and, in particular, how such ideas might contribute to broader conceptions of a *designed* and more sustainable education. It will also reflect on the potential for a more fundamental reshaping of university education in a volatile and changing world. The CETLD was the result of a rare opportunity for Universities in England. Funded by the Higher Education Funding Council for England (HEFCE)[1] the CETLD was one of 74 centres created to stimulate new ideas, dialogue and innovation in teaching and learning in the university sector. It was a unique collaboration between the University of Brighton, the Royal College of Art (RCA), the Royal Institute of British Architects (RIBA) and the Victoria and Albert Museum (V&A). Its key aim was to reinvigorate debate about the value of design learning and re-examine design education in some detail including where and how design learning happens, the roles different kinds of institutions play in the process, together with how they use their physical and digital resources.

PART ONE: OBJECT BASED LEARNING AND OBJECT SCHOLARSHIP

At the heart of the CETLD partnership was a shared interest in how to advance academic practice and research within design education; and how these were conceived and conducted differently in universities, museums, archives and professional organisations. Alongside these broad investigations, there was a specific

A. Boddington and J. Boys (eds.), Re-Shaping Learning: A Critical Reader: The Future of Learning Spaces in Post-Compulsory Education, 179–191.

focus on the development of object scholarship and object-based learning (Anderson, 1997). This was framed around a series of questions about the nature of objects, their physicality and provenance; and their role in design learning and in the student experience of designing and producing new objects. Across museum, educational and design communities there were also tacit assumptions of the rich knowledge that is embodied or 'locked' within every designed object. Yet despite a significant degree of agreement, there was little evidence as to how design education systematically employed encounters with objects in the process of learning. The CETLD proposed to explore these encounters based on the premise that if university and museum communities established a common understanding and shared educational language then this could stimulate and unlock new experiences and an appreciation of material objects and their role within post compulsory education and other learning communities. Equally it became clear that a collective examination of their strategic approaches to object scholarship across these different institutions would open up opportunities to share objectives and to re-examine the potential relationships between these different educational institutions and their future roles as part of a vital network of public learning spaces.

An Evolving Taxonomy

The initial CETLD proposal, written in 2004/2005, presented a series of conceptual and pedagogic challenges and propositions about the particularities of design learning. Responding to the national CETL initiative, the CETLD aimed to re-invigorate a dialogue about, and interest in, design learning across government sectors[2]. This had been obscured by rapid growth in student numbers, the development of research assessment[3] and the expansion of quality assurance regulation[4]. Significant emphasis had been placed on articulating and justifying the relationships between teaching and learning and between teaching and research, and much pedagogic research had become entirely divorced from the communities of practice that delivered subject knowledge. Consequently the CETLD aimed to explore design learning in its own language and to specifically examine the relationships between learning and research both in and through design. These relationships included the design of learning spaces and the transformative impact afforded by digital technologies and how these might disrupt, change and/or positively enhance learning experiences. Such early challenges align closely with the three domains and taxonomy proposed by Barnett (see Chapter 13): (a) material and physical space; (b) educational space; and (c) personal (psychic) space.

CETLD: Aspirations

The CETLD's primary vision sought to articulate the value, importance and potential of design education and its particular relevance in a changing educational world. Its objective was to explore the relationships between teaching, learning and research and to build bridges between pedagogic theories and their applicability for design education as both a participative and potentially transferrable model. In articulating its position the CETLD rejected what it described as 'deficit' educational models. These it characterised as envisioning students as 'half-empty vessels' in need of enlightenment and improvement; where academic practices are predominantly based on teaching as a form of instruction and transmission of information from teacher to student. It also questioned 'research-led teaching' as an extension of this transmission model, predicated principally on the inclusion of research content packaged within the curriculum and delivered through traditional means (Jenkins & Zetter, 2003). It sought instead to focus attention on the relationship between learning and research and how both might inform design and design education, positioning these ideas alongside more traditional disciplinary academic practices (Krippendorff, 1996). Importantly it also aimed to contribute to a wider examination of sustainability in the provision of education; and to explore how that might impact on physical, pedagogic and personal learning encounters and the spaces of these interactions.

The CETLD began from a proposition that the relationship between learning and research is a continuum built upon a spirit of enquiry. This enquiring spirit draws students and teachers together as one community, as explorers, learners and proto-researchers working together. This idea challenged traditional perceptions of two communities, of academics and students, one in the service of another, one as knowledge 'providers' and the other as 'receivers' and increasingly described as 'customers' or 'consumers'. Rather the CETLD proposed a co-operative model where the transfer, exchange and co-construction of knowledge are designed to occur through a series of negotiated and dynamic transactions. These included, but were not limited to, transmission, dialogue and debate where individual communities of practice have the potential to be invested in both the co-development of knowledge and new ideas, as well as how these are exchanged, developed and shared more publicly.

In considering physical learning spaces, the CETLD set out to explore emerging ideas about what our students had described as a 'learning home', a place they believed vital to their learning and wellbeing. This sense of a place, however modest, was a space that offered a symbolic counterpoint to notions of student communities as transient and solely virtual, as nomadic and detached from any sense of being part of a collective. Though there was considerable scepticism about the ability of overtly 'designed' spaces to impact on the quality of learning, the CETLD proposed to examine spatial relationships and the relative location of social and formal learning opportunities. Its initial focus was on how the concentration and cross-programming[5] of activities, types of space and resources that create 'conditions of possibility' for stimulating social and informal learning could be actively planned and developed to enhance the students idea of the 'learning home'. For example, the location and provision of a café alone is insufficient. In addition it would also require the affordances and adjacencies of wireless networks, gallery, external spaces and comfortable chairs to ensure that a vibrant learning environment could be assured. In this context the CETLD's key goal was to *design* a series of tangible and conceptual networks of spaces (physical and virtual) that enabled sustained conversation in real and asynchronous time. Their purpose was to create the 'learning home' and the 'conditions of possibility' that augment the utilitarian expectations of a university and the more formal dialogue and reflection that occurs in familiar academic settings whether online or within the classroom, studio, workshop or laboratory.

Strategically, what also underpinned the CETLD's unique partnership was the opportunity to re-consider the role and idea of the university as a place of learning with reference to other public educational institutions and environments. Given this challenge, the CETLD aimed to test the idea of the university as a 'learning home' and as a more permeable, but intensified hub within an extended and public 'learning landscape' (see Thody, Chapter 9). Its goal then, was to re-frame the university as a place, (a 'learning home') from which its community (staff and students) is encouraged and supported to venture out, seek knowledge and learn independently whether 'in the wild' or within other public institutions and spaces such as museums or archives.

The final thematic challenges for the CETLD focused on personal learning experiences in design education and on the relationships between the individual learner and the collective group of students *and* staff. Traditionally, design education has focused on developing individual, independent and innovative learners, and its pedagogies have principally been developed to support ideas that have included the rhetoric of risk and creativity, albeit without contestation or definition.

The CETLD questioned not only the validity of these long held assumptions, but also the nature of the institutional context and authority within which the expectation and evidence of learning remains principally measured by performance driven outputs and their assessment, rather than by evidence of the quality of learning and reflection. In turn these issues led to a series of projects exploring the role of trial and error and experimentation. These examined the disciplinary definitions of risk and failure. They looked particularly at how prescribed academic practices and/or environments may augment or inadvertently prevent learning opportunities; and how such activities might best be recognised and rewarded through the design and articulation of assessment. Importantly, underpinning all of these disciplinary investigations, our key challenge and question was whether such propositions for design were transferable, scalable and credible not only for those studying and researching more broadly within visual and performing arts and design, but also whether such ideas may have a more universal currency, applicable to advancing other disciplinary knowledge and pedagogies.

PART 2: CHANGING HORIZONS

While it would be impossible to try and succinctly capture the collective learning from over forty projects, the CETLD provided an evidence base for new propositions as well as generating foundational research to inform not only post compulsory education, but also learning in other public and private sector environments. In addition, it offered important insights and opportunities for understanding how large and complex institutions can collaborate and share ideas in the future through working together in innovative ways and with common goals. As with many large and complex projects, beyond the delivery of promised outputs, future innovation and insights often lie in what was learned peripherally, perhaps even accidentally, and how this may impact upon both its related communities as well as those beyond. The CETLD closed its doors in March 2010 at a sensitive political and economic moment, but also at a time when design is emerging as a subject of study and interest in many other fields including, for instance, computer studies, business, management, media and communications. This appears to be linked to how digital and social media have created new kinds of space and, over time, begun to 're-wire' and unsettle our thought processes and behaviour, transforming not only our personal and day-to-day lived experiences, but also calling into question the authority and stability of the current institutional infrastructures within which we live, work and learn.

The second part of this essay is therefore a personal attempt to present those emerging perspectives. These not only build upon the experience and ideas outlined in the first, but also aim to capture the spirit of informal but vital dialogue and the reflections that occurred both in the interstices of projects and since the CETLD's closure. I will offer some grounded speculations on how the convergence of design, design learning and design education drawn from those experiences has contributed to a series of emerging and interrelated themes, and how design (as both subject and process) might illuminate learning and post compulsory education in these changing times. At different conceptual scales I will explore the following, first, Expanding Design; second, Learning Design; and third, Sharing Design.

Expanding Design

Over the past two decades conceptions of what defines and constitutes design have been evolving and its processes and cultures have become a subject of growing interest to other disciplines. Curiously perhaps, design is less well conceptualised or articulated within the discipline (Krippendorff, 1996), i.e. within those subject communities or within undergraduate or postgraduate courses that carry the title of design. Instead design practice, design education and most notably design 'thinking' and/or design 'sensing', have all been adopted by more traditional fields such engineering, computer science, management and innovation studies each attempting to understand and articulate a field of activity that seems to persistently resist description. Given the aspiration of the CETLD and notwithstanding the many and varied theoretical texts that have emerged in the past decade, this short summary attempts to describe the convergence of a number of ideas in order to frame the characteristics and strengths that foreground and distinguish design, (its practices, processes, cultures and education) in ways that highlight its shared capabilities as distinct from the specific skills and knowledge of its many constituent communities, (e.g. architecture, fashion, product, industrial, textile, interior, graphic or service). The attraction of design for many is its facility and capacity to interrogate and unite disparate forms of knowledge irrespective of their discipline; and to balance the aesthetic contingencies of human and material conditions with those of time and place. As our cultures have grown arguably more visually literate through the everyday use of images and objects that transcend textual description, there has also been a growing, if grudging, recognition and understanding of sensory conditions that remain 'beyond text' and outside the linear textual spectrum. Design embraces ideas 'beyond text' because it is propositional and visceral. It demands a blueprint for engagement that unites the individual and collective self with the natural and the synthetic worlds we inhabit.

Design as an activity, aims to create conceptual clarity from complex fields knowledge and information. To achieve this, the designer draws together and distils both the contingent conditions that form the constituents of a design question or brief, and the array of external forces that may impact upon the design proposition as it evolves and exists in the world over time. Designers, then, are required to interrogate and to understand the 'DNA' of different systems of knowledge, values, information and conditions in order to devise ways in which these may be accommodated, aligned or conjoined through the design process. For students learning to design, for clients and even for practicing designers, the design process often appears confusing, uncomfortable and an unnerving experience precisely because its driving force is the dynamic generation and transformation of knowledge. Such confusion arises because design may appear contradictory, even contrary, in simultaneously offering a moment or moments of memorable clarity and certainty, but equally accepting and feeding upon an understanding and engagement with perpetual change and transformation. For all participants involved in the design process it is the tension, challenge and anticipation experienced in developing propositions that is core to the experience, and that attracts, unsettles and repels in equal measure.

Such instability presents pedagogic challenges as well as opportunities for design education and is perhaps why it has tended to remain embedded – and arguably buried – within its constituent subjects. In order to understand design better as an activity, it is important to distinguish its characteristics from the subject skills of its different communities of practice (the dominant conduits for design education). This is because design within its subject communities is predominantly represented through propositions or tangible artefacts that become *proxies for*, rather than *articulations of*, what it is to design.

These proxies, whether in the form of artefacts or proposals, serve to mask rather than reveal and communicate the nature of design. Consequently the overarching discourse within the wider design community has instead been occupied either by the discourse of other outside disciplines, or somewhat distorted by specificities of individual subject knowledge. Perhaps the greatest challenge now is to reveal what unites designers, and what constitutes the underpinning foundational knowledge, skills and understanding of design. This needs to be distilled from the collective practices of its constituent subjects, rather than from any single or specific mode of production, community of practice or conceptual position.

The challenge for design education beyond any specific subject, is to develop within each proto-designer and community of learners the confidence, determination and ability to work and thrive within increasingly unpredictable conditions, and to create from these compelling narratives and propositions. Such confidence is built upon self-awareness and a spirit of enquiry about the world and how it works; an optimism and reflection on how it might work better; and the ability to bring these together, supported by an underpinning scholarship and analytical rigour that can conceptualise and manage the complex arrays of information that any design brief demands. Building such a portfolio of skills over time is both the lifelong and life-lived experience of any active designer. Within 3 or 4 years, design education can therefore provide little more than a foundational framework to underpin design learning and an array of components and tools that enable proto-designers to begin to create narratives and propositions and situate them in the world in the form of 'prototypes' or 'sketch' designs.

What perhaps remains under or unacknowledged – although essential in the learning process – is the investment of theoretical, conceptual and enacted risk within any design process, as visceral and analytical activities are brought together. Design assimilation is all too often undertaken alone and can be challenging, frustrating, stimulating and rewarding. Learning how to manage these experiences as well as to work collaboratively is vital. Yet within education the dominant expectation remains that measures of success and assessment are achieved within the individual and within the final product, such that these become proxy indicators for design ability. It is at the point of assessment that outcomes and outputs often become conflated – and thus the process and effectiveness of design learning, and the quality of what is produced, become confused and confusing for both the student and for external audiences.

The educational difficulties here can be illustrated by any design project that attempts to extend the boundaries of knowledge in a number of ways simultaneously. For example, a design project may invent both a new product and a new material in parallel. For many reasons the material may fail technically, but the design idea remains robust and potentially groundbreaking. If this is predominantly assessed (which it would be professionally or commercially) on the success of the final output, then the overall result would be considered unsuccessful. Current assessment regimes tend to better reward a less adventurous design that meets all of the criteria, and so suppress rather than celebrate risk and advancement. While it is entirely possible to construct increasingly complex assessment algorithms that accommodate these concerns, the central question is whether our education system is designed to recognise and reward the contribution of different and integrated forms of knowledge, learning and experience (Robinson, 2008)?

These traits are deliberately accentuated here to reinforce the point that, as Robinson suggests, industrial rather than ecological and sustainable models of knowledge production predominantly underpin our educational infrastructures. Building in part on the issues inherent in the design of assessment outlined above, a significant future challenge that design education has yet to grasp is the balance between individual learning and the systematic development of the skills, challenges and imperatives of collective and collaborative practice. The emerging and future challenge for design education will be in learning the skills of collective, creative action, where outcomes, outputs and role of assessment will require considerable revision. Equally, however, this presents opportunities for new models of learning and highlights the importance in developing self-confidence and resilience alongside the skills of collaborative working, across disciplines, across institutions and increasingly across cultures, as the world in which we work becomes increasingly interconnected and geographically dispersed. In addition to improving its articulation to and for others, design education requires re-*designing*, such that it is sustainable, generative and begins to create the conditions that integrate aesthetic, conceptual and corporeal activities in order that they can be simultaneously recalled and enacted. It is the regular practice of this iterative experience and the choreographing of different forms of knowledge over time and in place, that inculcates the brokerage and intermediary role and that develops 'designerly knowledge'.

Through their interrogation of different kinds of knowledge and information designers have a long and largely unwritten tradition of continuously re-inventing and evolving their investigative tools, methods and devices (Potter, 1969). Each tool for each project is considered as bespoke, although developed from a series of components and devices. Investigative tools are devised and developed anew to help reveal, analyse, construct or reconstruct different ways of seeing and understanding the underlying 'DNA' of a specific context in order that can be assimilated, reshaped and designed. Perhaps because such practices are so deeply ingrained in the designers' psyche, design communities have tended to resist the systematic documentation of their underlying tactics and methods and have hence failed to reflect upon the status and potential of design when positioned alongside more traditional disciplines such as innovation studies and engineering.

Drawing both from the design theorist Horst Rittel[6] (Rittel and Webber, 1973) and from innovation studies and computer science, Jeff Conklin (2005) posits the idea that we are undergoing a period of cultural and conceptual transition, shifting from what he describes as an age of 'science' to an age of 'design' (1996/2001). He suggests that since the Enlightenment our recent past has been dominated by scientific logic and by description, focused on understanding and explaining the natural world as a predominantly linear process, transformed principally by technological solutions. His proposition is that this paradigm shift to an age of 'design' is not a rejection but the embracing of science, its descriptive modalities and its focus on the individual. His definition of an 'age of design' is expansive and centres on collective action and social creation, communicated through complex, nuanced narratives that are able to embrace contingencies, human conditions and to accommodate Rittel's 'wicked problems'. Taking Conklin's argument that design is essentially a process of collective action, it could also be argued that it is therefore entirely consistent that it has resisted, and continues to resist, the challenge of 'scientific' disciplinary description and, by implication, the linearity of text as its dominant means of communication and expression. In so doing it distinguishes itself from those subjects that attempt to colonise the intermediary and unstable territory it occupies.

Learning Design

Returning to the subjects of design learning and design education, the pedagogic model the CETLD proposed in 2005 for conjoining learning and research aligns well within the conceptions of design that Conklin and others (e.g. Leadbetter, 2008) propose, albeit from the different disciplinary worlds of ICT, business and management. With the benefit of hindsight what has also emerged is the imperative, and potential opportunities, for encouraging the pedagogic development of collaborative learning models that extend beyond both individuals and institutions. Bringing together students and academics as a single learning community and conceiving of the university as a co-operative or as an intellectual mutual, subsumes our current and arguably 'scientific' models of knowledge transmission and promotes instead an active investment in the process of learning. Such a proposal repositions both academics and students, as well as relocating the role of the curriculum as it has been traditionally constructed. It invites, rather than instructs the academic community (staff and students) to develop a collective approach to learning, teaching and research and to the co-generation of knowledge, not only peer-to-peer, but also between academics and students, as collaborators and as proto-researchers, and at all academic levels.

The research and propositions that have emerged through the debates about learning spaces and that make up the majority of this publication have reinforced the need for more socialised learning models. These need to be open and discursive, and to build communities of practice through which the co-construction of knowledge can be enacted. Co-designing learning also requires an understanding of the responsibilities for sustaining and contributing to the currency of the curriculum as a shared knowledge pool and as a legacy that is gifted from one cohort of learners to another. Such a conceptual educational shift will, over time, demand new and different kinds of expertise. These include the ability and agility to sustain and support conversations and to respond to and shape knowledge generation that is genuinely collectively thought and co-published. As part of an open system, the knowledge created will require enunciation and publication such that it can be shared between universities and other learning institutions, thereby ultimately enabling the formation of a shared 'knowledge pool', a 'design commons', that is by default current, dynamic and transformative.

Proposed and conducted under the auspices of design education, and within individual courses or learning environments, this proposition may at first appear relatively straightforward, precisely because it is underpinned and contained by the university infrastructures within which it is hosted. Perhaps more challenging is the potential implication of not only extending the idea of collaboration, co-design and co-construction to other or all disciplines in order to test its limits, but also to other elements of the intellectual and institutional infrastructure, beyond the campus. Here, it may have a more fundamental impact in reshaping the nature and culture of university education, its governance and the way in which such organisations learn and develop.

Perhaps the most exciting opportunities for post compulsory education lie in developing universities (and other public institutions) that have the capacity to learn; and that can extend beyond the teaching and delivery of education and research as product. Without the design and development of a more intelligent and sustainable institutional model, one that can learn and responsibly (and responsively) re-shape and develop learning, it would appear that there remains a curious irony at the core of our post compulsory education system; i.e. universities that do not have the capability to learn or to evolve. Perhaps it is now more vital than ever that university communities invest in the co-construction and transformation of disciplinary knowledge, and identify and analyse the skills and tools needed to effectively generate and share ideas, wisdom and experience in shaping the culture of our future learning.

At its heart, a future role for design within universities might be its ability to develop and reshape both the art and the craft of learning. In analysing user experiences, systems design and underlying educational infrastructures, design knowledge offers the skills to create progressive and evolutionary frameworks for the creative and intelligent development of learning. The implications for such infrastructural changes could be significant and far-reaching, extending beyond the academic structures within which we learn, to also address how best we construct, share and manage the future governance of knowledge production.

Sharing Design

Through the process of rethinking design education and design learning I have quite deliberately positioned each within an extended conceptual map, no longer bounded by their traditional or even their expanded taxonomies (Buchanan, 1992). Instead, both may be better conceived of as an active part of a 'life-lived' experience, of a reinvestment or restatement of learning as the craft of discovery and, as such, fundamental to the human condition, as an aesthetic rather than an anaesthetic experience. The value of design learning, then, extends far beyond the conceptions and idea of the university as either physically bounded or time limited by various forms of academic award.

As an experience, design learning could instead be described as the temporal convergence of a nexus of aligned minds with a nexus of contingent ideas in the formation of a utopian ideal, within which individuals may test their values and beliefs in dialogue with others. As such, it also aims to develop within each individual learner personalised and permeable learning spaces, repositories of knowledge and conceptual tools, and the ability to construct a kind of caravan or transitory 'learning home' that is resilient and that can traverse and engage with other disciplines and other kinds of learning spaces. As David Anderson recounts in his chapter on learning within the museum (Chapter 12), the idea of utopia is not without its ideological difficulties. But, in a contemporary world in continual flux, design learning could be a powerful intermediary in enabling the exchange of different kinds knowledge, practices and processes between institutions. In this context design learning is not about the contained relations of alternative pedagogies, about which much has already been written. Instead it is about rethinking the physical and the governing infrastructures within which those pedagogies are enacted or conducted; and examining whether they are fit for purpose, and can enhance and stimulate learning and advance knowledge.

In this recent email comment, the balance between the utilitarian vision for the physical learning environment of a university and the creative potential and collective imagination of any educational community is laid out in sharp contrast:

Accommodation Planning colleagues here in Estates & Facilities Management advised us that the normal provision within pooled rooms consists of a projector, screen and a whiteboard.[7]

Reflecting on the quotations from McLuhan and Churchill at the beginning of this chapter, and the agency of our institutional contexts, I am arguing that design education and design learning are potent intermediaries that can help us radically rethink, rather than merely believe our own rhetoric about what it is we do, how, and indeed where we do it. Applying design learning to our own circumstances offers us a chance to become 'disenthralled' (Robinson, 2010), to think, learn and act as designers and consider how, from within our learned institutions – be they universities or museums – we can develop institutions that can learn and that create the capacity for sustainable transformation. This will require the creation of new models that recognise, as Anderson does, the necessity for utopian dreams and for the defence of culture and public space. Equally, though we will not only have to listen and learn individually, but perhaps to learn, or re-learn how to think, trust and act collectively, not as divided communities of students, academics or researchers but as a single if temporal, community of learners, scholars and citizens.

Clay Shirky (2005) has suggested we are undergoing an evolutionary process of change, brought about by the emergence of the World Wide Web and social media that has resulted in growth of new forms of co-operative structures and strategies. Our traditional, predominantly 19th century institutional models and their resulting cultures and structures are under increasing pressure, socially, culturally and economically. Shirky does not propose any extreme or radical (re) action, but instead suggests we work with, and to begin to understand, the implications of where and how co-operative models interface with institutional ones. Whether post-compulsory education, in all its forms, has the capacity to make the transition from one to the other remains to be seen. The opportunity to create inclusive and permeable learning spaces and re-map our learning is a potent design challenge, one that should help us sustain and intensify the quality of our local 'learning home' within the university, alongside developing the spirit of generosity that is the global commons.

CONCLUSION

In the context of the above, rethinking and reshaping the idea and purpose of a university or a museum is not a marketing or 'identity' question about what distinguishes one institution from another. Instead it is about a wider relational network for learning, where each nexus, each institutional concentration, serves to shape and play a role in questioning, revitalising and advancing our cultural inheritance. In other words, other cultural institutions, like the communities of practice and the bodies of knowledge they generate, can also become part of that global commons, but only if they are prepared to evolve and to rethink their values, authority and internal social coherence. Likewise, within any such learning network, universities will need to reconsider and re-design their relational position and take on (or perhaps take back) their role as agoras, as key public spaces, where the arts of rhetoric and of co-operative and collective action may be learned (or re-learned), where disciplines can be formed and transformed and civilised debate sustained.

Most potent, however, in any such proposition is not how individual institutions position or reposition themselves, be they museums, universities or other educational provision. More importantly, it is where and how they touch one another and learn as organisations to engage and collaborate as complementary entities that are intelligent enough to recognise and respect the multiple identities of learners and to design the kinds of learning spaces they will increasingly choose to inhabit both physically and virtually. Designing our learning is now critical in terms of how we might create a more vital co-operative model of knowledge generation and exchange. We can reconstruct discovery as our craft, and the world, albeit one we have had a significant hand in re-designing, as our classroom, and as a truly public sphere within which to reshape and invigorate our future learning, our research and our spirit of enquiry.

NOTES

[1] Centres for Excellence in Teaching and Learning were one of the key initiatives that emerged from 'The Future of Higher Education' 2003, published by the Department for Education and Skills. The report identified an £8 billion historic under-investment in teaching and research in Higher Education and specifically pledged a series of initiatives to stimulate and share good practice in teaching and learning, including the creation of a series of Centres for Excellence.

[2] Because of its partnership this project set out to explore the common ground and differences in approaches to learning as articulated by Department for Education and Skills (DfES) and the Department for Culture, Media and Sport (DCMS).

[3] The growth of the Research Assessment Exercise (RAE) and its relative importance for the Arts & Humanities, created behaviour change within Higher Education institutes and tended to shift the focus of attention away from teaching and learning.

[4] The impact of the Quality Assurance Agency (QAA) (founded in 1997) and a growth of institutional and subject-based review changed the educational framework for many subject cultures including those in architecture, art and design.

[5] This term refers to the work of the architect Bernard Tschumi who argues for no fixed relationship between architectural form and the events that take place within it but instead champions a proactive architecture that can permit questions and responses rather than one that fixes extant social structures. See for example: Tschumi, B. (1994). *Architecture and disjunction*. Cambridge, MA: MIT Press (and Boys, Chapter 4).

[6] Horst Rittel (with Melvin Webber) is credited with developing the term 'wicked problem'. It is used to describe a problem that is difficult or impossible to solve because of incomplete, contradictory and changing requirements that are often difficult to recognise. Moreover, because of complex inter-dependencies, the effort to solve one aspect of a wicked problem may reveal or create other problems.

[7] Extract from an internal university email about learning spaces (June 2010).

REFERENCES

Anderson, D. (1997). *A common wealth: Museums and learning in the United Kingdom*. A report to the Department of National Heritage. Department of National Heritage. London: Her Majesty's Stationery Office.

Buchanan, R. (1992). Wicked problems in design thinking. *Design Issues, 8*(2), 5–21.

Buchanan, R. (2000). Myth and maturity: Towards a new order in the decade of design. In V. Margolin & R. Buchanan (Eds.), *The idea of design*. Cambridge, MA: MIT Press.

Conklin, J. (1996/2001). *The age of design*. Retrieved from http://www.cognexus.org/ageofdesign.pdf

Conklin, J. (2005). *Dialogue mapping: Building shared understanding of wicked problems*. Wiley. See also Rittel, H., & Webber, M. (1973). Dilemmas in a general theory of planning. In *Policy sciences* (Vol. 4, pp. 155–169). Amsterdam: Elsevier Scientific Publishing Company, Inc., 1973. [Reprinted in N. Cross (Ed.). (1984). *Developments in design methodology* (pp. 135–144). Chichester: J. Wiley & Sons. Retrieved from http://www.uctc.net/mwebber/Rittel+Webber+Dilemmas+General_Theory_of_Planning.pdf

Jenkins, A., & Zetter, R. (2003). *Linking research and teaching in departments*. London: LTSN Generic Centre.

Krippendorff, K. (1996). On the essential contexts of artefacts or on the proposition that 'design is making sense (of things)'. In V. B. Margolin & R. Buchanan (Eds.), *The idea of design* (pp. 156–186). London: MIT Press.

Leadbeater, C. (2008). *We-think: Mass innovation not mass production*. London: Profile Books Ltd. Retrieved from http://www.ted.com/talks/clay_shirky_on_institutions_versus_collaboration.html

Potter, N. (1969). *What is a designer: Things, places, messages*. London: Hyphen Press, UK.

Robinson, K. (2008). *Changing paradigms*. RSA lecture given following the award of the Benjamin Franklin Medal 2008. Retrieved from http://www.thersa.org/events/vision/archive/sir-ken-robinson

Robinson, K. (2010). *Bring on the learning revolution*. TEDtalks. Retrieved from http://www.ted.com/talks/sir_ken_robinson_bring_on_the_revolution.html

Shirky, C. 'insitutions v. collaboration'. (2005). TEDtalks. Retrieved from http://www.ted.com/talks/clay_shirky_on_institutions_versus_collaboration.html (posted 2008).

ETIENNE WENGER

15. SOCIAL LEARNING CAPACITY

Four Essays on Innovation and Learning in Social Systems

INTRODUCTION: CONTEXT

The following essays contain some reflections on my involvement with the EQUAL initiative[1], funded through the European Social Fund, which aimed to foster social innovation. As a way to support the spread of social innovation across projects, EQUAL started a number of communities of practice and organised events for participants to learn together. This capability to organise learning across a complex social system is itself an important achievement. It is less visible than the 188 projects and 320 codified solutions that were heralded as the outcomes of the initiative. And it is still a fledgling capability, to be sure. But if it provides a foundation for new projects and initiatives aimed at social innovation, within the context of the European Social Funds and beyond, it may well be the deepest legacy of EQUAL.

I will use the case of social innovation to reflect on some key elements of social learning capacity. I will draw on the case of the EQUAL initiative as well as on my broader experience with large-scale social learning systems in the private and public sectors. I am basing my reflection on my own sense of what the initiative was trying to accomplish without claiming that everything I describe here was fully realised (though it was a good start and much more would have been done had the initiative been continued). The elements of learning capacity I highlight are relevant to social innovation, the goal of EQUAL, but also to all large-scale social learning challenges, whether in business organisations or in the public sector, including government, education, health or international development.

ESSAY 1: SOCIAL LEARNING SPACES

Social innovation requires investigation of what works in practice. Which ideas are worth pursuing? What difference do they make? What potential do they hold for other places of application? Peer-to-peer learning focused on practice allows participants to sort out which innovations to adopt on a large scale while remaining sensitive to each context. The negotiation required depends on what I will call 'social learning spaces'. These are social containers that enable genuine interactions among participants, who can bring to the learning table both their experience of practice and their experience of themselves in that practice.

A. Boddington and J. Boys (eds.), Re-Shaping Learning: A Critical Reader: The Future of Learning Spaces in Post-Compulsory Education, 193–210.
© *2011 Sense Publishers. All rights reserved.*

Variety of Social Learning Spaces

Social learning spaces can take a variety of forms. The effort of the EQUAL initiative in developing a series of communities of practice was meant to create learning spaces across the projects and the countries involved. Communities of practice, when they work well, are quintessential examples of social learning spaces. The learning space of a community is built through a history of learning together over time. Commitment derives from identification with a shared domain of interest and with others who share that identification with the domain. There is enough continuity to develop a shared repertoire of language, concepts and communication tools that make practice discussable. All this contributes to building relationships and trust that enable a joint inquiry into practice. Similar characteristics, however, can be found in other types of spaces, which may require less intensity of commitment. Some may be short-lived, like a good conversation or a well-designed workshop. For instance, we ran a workshop for community leaders in EQUAL where the main driver of learning was a reflection on practice that connected the participants through their own experience with their communities. The value of learning together in this way helped the participants deepen their understanding of the social learning spaces they were trying to foster. Sometimes, when relationships are more diffuse, social learning spaces happen in pockets. For example, the 'social reporters' at the final EQUAL conference were attempting to create social learning spaces in parallel with the formal conference programme. They were using new media technologies to enable direct conversations with and among participants in the hallways and publish them immediately on the web in the hope to foster further conversations.

Not all contexts for learning amount to social learning spaces. An instructional space is structured by an instructor and a predefined curriculum. An academic project tends to take knowledge as something to be objectified. Informational spaces, like reports, books, or static websites, support the documentation of practice (so-called 'best practice') rather than interactions among participants. Service encounters with professionals can foster learning, but it is usually one-way. All these learning contexts can create value but they rarely constitute a meeting between learning partners. Note that under the right circumstances they can also become a social learning spaces: a classroom run by a very good teacher can be so engaging that the students and teachers create a social learning space; a service encounter can become a two-way learning partnership; a website can be interactive to the point of enabling participants to experience each other as co-learners. Whether a learning context does or should constitute a social learning space is something that can only be decided pragmatically in each case.

Rigor of Inquiry in a Social Learning Space

Terms like experience and practice often seem to be associated with a lack of rigor. Producing knowledge that is livable in the experience of practice entails a different accountability than traditional research-based knowledge, but there is a rigor to it.

It involves a discipline of inquiry that takes practice as the place of knowledge and the person as the vehicle for knowledgeability. It is useful to start by exploring this dual rigor of social learning spaces:

- Knowing as practice
- A social learning space is not a detached inquiry that only succeeds if it objectifies knowledge or formally 'documents' practice. Knowledge is not a separate object from the people who produced it or even the process of producing it. It is part of the mutual engagement through which participants refine and expand their experience of practice. Note that the focus on practice in social learning spaces is not defined in opposition to documentation or research-based knowledge. The evaluation of social innovation, for instance, often requires systematic data collection and analysis of the research-based kind. Practitioners themselves often produce reflective documents, concepts, and other reification. If objectified knowledge or documented practice is incorporated into the inquiry of a social learning space, however, it has to be integrated into the experience of practice. In other words, its significance depends on the participants' ability to negotiate its relevance to contexts of practice.
- Knowing as identity
- A focus on practice means that knowledge is part of engagement in the world. Knowing is a lived experience. It is personal, not in the sense of being less valid or objective, but in the sense of requiring a person's experience of engagement. The ability to engage depends on both skills and position in the world. Knowledgeability is therefore a form of identity anchored in practice. In a social learning space, participants engage their identity in the inquiry. They use their very beings—their personal history, relationships, and aspirations—as vehicles for learning. They pursue learning as a change in their ability to participate in the world, as a transformation of their identity. To bring a rigor of inquiry in any social learning space, this dual focus on practice and identity has to manifest in two ways: in the accountability of learning to the experience of participants (the lived experience that learning needs to enable) and in the expressibility of experience (how the actual experience of participants can become engaged in the learning process).

Accountability

The inquiry process in social learning spaces has to produce livable knowledge, that is, knowledge that is meaningful because it enables new forms of engagement in the world. This accountability to livable knowledge includes both the relevance of knowledge to practice and the ability to become the person who will do the knowing:

- Accountability to practice
  Learning becomes knowledge to the extent that it responds to and changes the experience of engagement in practice. In this sense, practice acts as the curriculum of a social learning space: challenges of practice are the driver of learning and experiences of practice provide resources to learning.

- Accountability to identity

An accountability to practice may seem to put the emphasis on 'practical' aspects—on instrumental and technical knowledge. But this is a very narrow view of practice. In real life, being able to engage in practice involves a much broader set of requirements, which includes the ability to find meaning in activities and to engage competently with other people involved. Learning in a social learning space covers all the aspects of knowing relevant to a person who can behaving and talking. It involves issues such as efficacy, legitimacy, values, connections and power, typical of engagement in the human world.

Expressibility

Achieving the accountability associated with social learning spaces requires a corresponding rigor of expressibility: participants must be able to express their experience of practice and who they are in that experience, so this can serve as the substance of learning:

- Expressibility of practice

Participants must be able to bring their experience of practice into the learning space and give each other access to that experience. Engagement in practice is complex, dynamic, and improvisational. It includes narrative episodes and moments of experience that do not form a coherent body of knowledge. It has many tacit elements. Tacit here does not mean inexpressible; but it means that communication requires enough mutual engagement to negotiate a shared context of experience. This can be easy if participants already share much context, or require substantial work if their contexts are very different. With enough shared context, few words can express huge amounts. Imagine two violinists discussing the vibrato of a student or two technicians analysing the smell of a malfunctioning machine. They may be together, on the phone, or online. It is the shared experience that serves as the main communication resource. Only then can participants start exploring what they know, what they don't know, what they only half-know, and what they could learn together. The expressibility of lived experience as a form of social engagement is therefore central to the rigor of inquiry in a social learning space

- Expressibility of identity

Knowledgeability in practice is always a personal experience, which includes physicality and emotions as well as cognition. The level of personal involvement varies across contexts of practice, to be sure. But it affects our sense of self as we always locate what we are doing in the experience of life more broadly. There is a discipline to making this experience discussable. Furthermore, our identity is defined across many contexts, which are never simply turned off. It is impossible to predict in any simple way which of these contexts are going to be relevant and where significant insights are going to come from. Actually new insights often come from remixing perspectives, crossing boundaries between contexts, and thus seeing things in new ways. So expressibility of the full identity of participants, in all their areas of experience and identification, is an important condition for the richness and meaningfulness of the inquiry.

Accountability and expressibility can be in conflict. In a given social learning space a strong connection in one area may crowd out or seem to forbid expressibility of other areas of one's identity and accountability to other contexts. Two scientists having a strong experience of learning about a problem may find it difficult to express their experience as musicians or parents because the intensity of the scientific connection crowds out the musician or parent, or literally excludes it, even in cases when it has the potential of being a relevant source of insights. This rigor suggests two questions to keep in mind for the development of any social learning space. First, what experience must the inquiry be able to induce in order to open meaningful possibilities for engagement in practice? Second, how can the space render expressible all the aspects of participants' lives that can potentially contribute to the inquiry as it unfolds?

Learning as Partnership

In order to achieve a high level of mutual expressibility and accountability, participants in a social learning space need to recognise each other as learning partners through the experience they bring to the space. They need to recognise the practitioner in each other. Whether or not they have equal mastery of the topic, they should be able to negotiate the mutual relevance of their respective experience. They are 'peers' in a very broad, practical sense of the term. This recognition forms the basis of a mutual commitment to learning. This commitment can be made explicit but more often than not it will remain implicit, expressed in the doing of it.

Commitment to Candor: The Value of Practice-Oriented Trust

The expressibility of practice requires a lot of candor and such practice-based candor is a pillar of the discipline of social learning space. But it is not necessarily easy. Theory and policy are clean, but practice is messy, improvised, and always requiring judgment. It is made up of fragments of experience that are not necessarily coherent. This is a condition for its effectiveness, but also something that makes it more difficult to share, not only because of the difficulty to express what really happens, but also because there is a personal vulnerability inherent in opening the door of reflection on the messiness of practice. One's identity may easily seem at stake. Engaging with knowledge as lived in practice requires a lot of trust. Practice is always complex and dynamic. It is difficult and challenging. In practice, there are no smooth-sailing superheroes. So when practitioners become less guarded with one another, when they recognise each other as co-practitioners, candor becomes almost a relief. There is a comfortable discomfort in the shared refuge of authenticity. Candor can then become a mutual aspiration. It is a form of togetherness – candor reinforced by its mutuality, by its effects on the partnership, and the possibility of learning together. I have seen communities of practice thaw from a terror about exposing one's practice to fellow practitioners and over time shift to a full commitment to candor. This shift was based on the quality of conversations that were possible once candor had opened a window onto practice. They had experienced how sharing the actual challenges they face in their practice was the best way to trigger significant collective learning. Admittedly, this often takes the leadership of some courageous individuals to start the process. But over time, trust becomes a property of the social learning space, not merely of individuals toward each other.

Commitment to Openness: Reframing Stories of Practice

Social learning spaces involve an open-ended learning process. Participants contribute their perspectives in the hope that something will come out of the mix. No single person can direct the process because there is no knowing where significant insights are going to come from. When engagement in practice is the curriculum, the learning process has to unfold out of the interactions among participants. Mutual engagement and negotiation become ways for people to build a shared and deepened understanding of the situation at hand. By listening and giving voice to multiple experiences of practice, the interplay of diverse perspectives often reframes the initial stories. In such cases, the conversation of practitioners goes beyond sharing tips or good practices. It becomes a shared commitment to an open inquiry. Pushing the inquiry in this way means leaving our zone of comfort. We identify strongly with our experience of practice and its interpretation. It becomes part of who we are. Reframing our stories is also reframing who we are. Learning, and the attendant need for unlearning, is a journey of the self, with birth and death, resistance and willingness, doubts and inspiration. But again, this commitment to re-understand practice and discover new perspectives through interactions can be reinforced when it is mutual. The spirit of inquiry is contagious when it takes off. It becomes a property of the social learning space. Opening and sustaining successful social learning spaces with such a depth of reflection is not an easy thing to do. Conversations can easily remain superficial and uni-dimensional. Difficult topics can degenerate into conflicts. Many communities of practice struggle to create enough commitment and some simply fail. There are many psychological, social and organisational obstacles. The next essays explore further aspects that I have found to be key success factors.

ESSAY 2: LEARNING CITIZENSHIP

Learning is not just something that happens in our heads. It happens in social spaces and across social spaces. As we engage in and move across learning spaces, we carry who we are. Our journey forms a trajectory of identity, which involves both participation in specific spaces and connections across these spaces. People and social spaces both have histories, but these histories are not parallel. They crisscross in a kind of social weave. Social learning spaces and individual trajectories are two distinct dynamics of learning, but they are in interplay. Their dynamic complementarity is key to the learning capacity and innovation potential of a social system.

Learning as Citizenship

As we participate in various social learning spaces, our actions affect the nature of these spaces. They also affect the people we interact with, who in turn belong to further social spaces. So our own learning behaviour can affect the learning capacity of a whole landscape of social learning spaces. How we manage our participation in and across learning spaces is what I call 'learning citizenship.' Learning citizenship can take multiple forms:

– *Engagement.* At its most basic, learning citizenship is expressed through the quality of our engagement in the learning spaces we participate in. In some spaces we are central players; others, we barely touch. In some we are experts; in others we are beginners. We act as learning citizens whether we ask a pertinent question, present an interesting case, probe an assumption, or talk about something relevant we just read. As we bring our experience to the table, we push the learning and build relationships with others. The extent and quality of our engagement in various learning spaces is the most obvious way in which we can influence learning, ours and that of others.

– *Moving on.* The decision to disengage from a learning space is as significant as entering and engaging. It lets us move on with our lives. It affects both our own trajectory and the learning space we leave behind. Unlearning and letting go are an essential part of the ability to journey forward and innovate.

– *Brokering.* We all participate in multiple social learning spaces. We affect the relationships between spaces as we carry (or do not carry) our learning from one space to another. In some cases we play a key brokering role by importing or exporting significant insights or challenges across the boundaries between spaces. Such brokering can even reshape these boundaries when, for instance, it triggers substantial interactions between the spaces involved. Brokering is important because it thickens the weave of a social system. Innovation often happens at boundaries when things are combined in new ways.

– *Convening.* Sometimes we are in a unique position to see the potential for a social learning space that does not exist yet; and our position also gives us the legitimacy to step in and create it. We start a conversation, we call a meeting, or we convene a community that needs to come into existence. Convening is one of the most significant acts of learning citizenship in terms of opening new possibilities for learning and legitimizing the need to care about an issue.

Our stance toward learning citizenship affects the spaces we enter, create, connect, or leave as well as our own learning. This remains true whether or not we have a choice in our participation and its form; and whether we are just a participant or take leadership in making things happen. Learning citizenship matters in all cases. The actual quality of our engagement (even if it starts as submission or rebellion) is something that we can modulate – with deep effects on the learning potential of social spaces.

Ethics of Identity

With the term 'learning citizenship' I want to emphasise that learning has an ethical dimension: our participation has both local and systemic effects. I do not use the term citizenship to suggest that some are citizens and some are not, that learning citizenship is an elite club. We are all learning citizens, just as we are all citizens of the world, whether we let this reality guide our actions or not. Claiming that there is an ethical dimension to learning is not assuming that learning depends on altruism. Some altruism may be involved, but engagement in social learning spaces is for our benefit as well as our contribution. Pushing our learning, building a reputation, forging relationships, all are part and parcel of the process. When it comes to learning citizenship, the distinction between contributing and benefitting is not so clear. More often than not, the two go together.

If our moves have learning consequences for ourselves and for the social systems in which we live, our trajectory is part of the weaving of these systems. Learning citizenship is situated right at the crossroads between social learning spaces and trajectories of identity. As learning citizens, we proceed from who we are – our personal histories, connections, networks, vision, aspirations and position in the landscape of practice – to find forms of participation that increase learning capacity. When we seize opportunities to participate in social learning spaces, to bridge a boundary, to convene a community that needs to exist, it is because we understand the learning potential of our location in the world and act upon it. It is also because we understand our limitations as just one person. With this under-standing, we can invest who we are in enabling learning. We can invest the pers-pective, capacity, legitimacy, and accountability that we derive from our unique trajectory, where we have been, where we are going, and what that makes us. In this sense, learning citizenship involves a recognition that our identity, as a dynamic location in the social landscape, is a unique learning resource. As learning citizens, we are investing and developing that resource, for ourselves and for the world.

Fostering Learning Citizenship

Recognising the ethical dimension of learning is important because the behaviour of a learning citizen it is not something that can be mandated. You cannot mandate learning of the kind that happens in social learning spaces because it requires an authenticity that cannot be perfunctory. No one knows in advance what it will look like. If one could know what to mandate, then a social learning space would not be necessary; a course or a book would do. The process of bringing the experience of practice into a social learning space can only be shaped by those who are doing it. The result of this kind of mutual engagement is never predictable. Even if you tried to mandate such learning and people did what you ask them to do, the result would probably not be what you wanted in the first place. Because learning citizenship is fundamentally voluntary, but with broad effects for individuals and collectives, the ethical dimension of learning is inescapable. People are going to act as learning citizens out of their own experience of the meaning and value of doing so.

That learning citizenship cannot be dictated does not mean that it cannot be fostered, however. While it involves a sense of personal responsibility and initiative, it is not merely an individual experience. It is in fact very sensitive to context. It is easily thwarted by obtuse bureaucracy or conflicting demands; those in charge of organising the context have to be very careful that it does not inadvertently discourage learning citizenship. At the same time, learning citizenship is also very contagious when it thrives; leading by example can therefore be quite effective. Manipulative rewards are usually counterproductive for the same reason that mandates do not work in that they assume that one knows what to reward in advance. Recognition after the fact works better. Some organisations have started to recognise acts of learning citizenship explicitly as part of one's contribution to organisational goals. This puts some teeth to the assertion that learning is valued, which can seem empty when people's schedules are crowded with operational demands and project deadlines. If our ability to innovate and spread innovation depends on learning citizenship, then learning how to foster this citizenship, recognise it, and make it count is an urgent challenge for increasing the learning capacity of our social systems.

ESSAY 3: SOCIAL ARTISTS

Enabling social learning spaces is an art. And so is inspiring the learning citizenship these spaces depend on. Among the many factors that account for the success or failure of the process, I have seen again and again that one of the key ingredients is the energy and skills of those who take leadership in making it all happen. I call the people who excel at doing this 'social artists.' The name may be surprising, but it is quite apt. Artists create beautiful pieces of art that inspire us: songs, paintings, movies, sculptures, poems, dances. The presence of this art shapes the world around us and enriches our lives. Similarly social artists create social spaces where meaningful learning can take place. When these social learning spaces work well, they are magnificent pieces of art – social art – that change the way we experience the world and ourselves.

Social Artists as Leaders

Social artists are leaders, but the kind of leadership they exercise is subtle. It does not engender or depend on followership. Rather it invites participation. It is a mixture of understanding what makes learning socially engaging and living the process yourself. It is not a formula; it is creative, improvised, intelligently adaptive and socially attuned. I find the magic of this artistry difficult to describe, though I know it when I see it:
– *Opening learning spaces*
  Social artists have a good understanding, sometimes completely implicit and intuitive, of the social discipline that makes social learning spaces productive. They have a knack for making people feel comfortable and engaged. They generate social energy among participants. They have a nose for the cultural and personal clues to social dynamics. They produce a climate of high trust and aspirations.
– *Inviting learning citizenship*
  Social artists help us experience ourselves as learning citizens. They know how to bring out our passions. They make us care to the point of engaging our whole

person in a social learning space. Or rather they help us discover we care and channel that care into learning citizenship.

This dual focus is important. Social artists are not just good pedagogues who can help people learn something. They have a natural instinct for leveraging the complementarity of learning spaces and individual trajectories. They help people experience learning spaces as part of their own trajectories so that collective and individual learning blend.

An Exercise in Paradoxes

Like all artists, social artists are unique. They vary in style. Some are flamboyant and some prefer to operate almost invisibly. Some are jovial and some are sharp-edged. Some will make you laugh and emphasise the fun of learning; some will make you feel serious about the challenge. What they all seem to have in common is an ability to embrace successfully a number of paradoxes:

- *Social yet intentional.* Social artists are of course, by definition, social. Their personal touch is a cornerstone of their artistry. They connect with people and they connect people. They are natural networkers. But they are not generic networkers. They network because there is something they care about, some new learning they want to enable. Their social artistry is suffused with purpose. Yet it is not the case that they are disingenuous or manipulative in using their social connections to serve their purpose. On the contrary, they combine the two to help others identify with what they care about and become partners in the aspiration. Their ability to enlist engagement in social learning spaces is precisely due to the fact that it reflects a genuine intention to create a collective learning process.

- *Collaborative yet wilful.* Social artists tend to be collaborative. They care that people feel ownership of their learning space. They listen to others and are very good at including multiple voices. They create social containers that turn conflict into learning opportunities. They are patient with social processes. They do not seek control and are comfortable with a high level of uncertainty. They can tolerate chaos, dissension, and negotiation. Given these characteristics, it might be easy to assume that social artists are easy-going or consensus-seekers. But my experience is that they are extremely wilful even if this wilfulness is expressed in collaborative ways. They care about making things happen. They will (gently) twist arms if need be. They will inspire people to do things these people never thought they would do and end up feeling good about doing. In the social expression of their wilfulness social artists help others discover new part of themselves.

- *Idealistic yet pragmatic.* Social artists tend to be activists. They do not accept the status quo. They are not impressed by arguments that 'this is the way things have always been done.' They have visions and aspirations even when they are quiet about them. But they are also practical. They may have strong opinions, but they are not ideologues. While they too visionary and socially attuned to be political beasts, they are politically astute. They are able to navigate the complex politics of communities and organisations to promote and protect the learning spaces they care about. Learning can be threatening; energized learning spaces are not always welcome in organisational contexts. Social artists pay careful attention to all the factors, internal and external, that can contribute to the success or failure of a learning space. In this sense, their idealism is of a very pragmatic kind.

Above all, social artists live what they seek to bring about. Like all artists, they use themselves, their own experience and identity, as a source of inspiration. They are themselves learning citizens of great intensity. This is how they can embrace the paradoxes of their work without falling, like the rest of us would, into an easy, but fatal resolution on one side or the other. We can all be learning citizens in our own ways, but we are not all social artists. That would be an unrealistic and unnecessary expectation. I am sometimes hired to train people to lead communities of practice—aspiring social artists as it were. It is always a special occasion for me. I prepare a workshop agenda, with presentations and activities. I am always amazed by the amount of learning taking place. But in my heart of hearts, I know that the real secret ingredient, what is really going to make a difference in enabling a community, is not something I can teach. It is not a technique or something that can be reduced to skills, even when some techniques and skills are involved. It has to do with the heart as well as the mind, with passion and commitment. It has to do with the person, with identity as a social resource. The key is the ability of social artists to use who they are as a vehicle for inviting others into inspiring social spaces. The intensity of their own passion is the powerhouse of their artistry. Their livingness and spirit of inquiry are contagious. They infuse social learning spaces with their soul, their humanity, their restlessness, their optimism, their courage and their own focus. If this makes it sound 'soft,' nothing could be further from the truth. A social learning space is an ideal context to address thorny issues of strategic importance. And it is hard work. A social learning space can be infinitely demanding of attention. I think most social artists love what they do; but it is the most delicate and consuming work I can imagine.

Recognizing Social Artists

One thing about the type of leadership exercised by social artists is that it often seems to be of a less visible kind. This is unfortunate at a time when learning and knowledge are recognised as critical to organisations and society. My experience is that this recognition has heightened appreciation for the role of experts and specialists. Experts and specialists are key players indeed, but we seem better equipped culturally and organisationally to appreciate their role. I want to shine a light on social artists because I believe their role is only going to grow in importance. The world is becoming so complex that any expertise worth caring about is too extensive for any one person to handle. Social learning spaces are indispensable – and so is the work of social artists as the key ingredient. By helping people come together and discover their own learning citizenship, social artists build up the learning capacity of social systems. I have met a number of them in my work and I have grown a profound respect for who they are and what they do. It is of extraordinary beauty and usefulness. Still social artists tend to be invisible because we do not have good frameworks and language to appreciate their contributions. I hope writing about them can help make their work more visible. Whether they do what they do because of professional responsibilities or just as extraordinary learning citizens, their role is of utmost importance. We need to learn to recognise, support, and celebrate their work. Their contribution is especially critical today when humankind faces unprecedented challenges that will place increasing demands on our ability to learn together.

ESSAY 4: LEARNING GOVERNANCE

The EQUAL initiative is an example of a fairly complex social system. It includes a constellation of learning spaces operating within an institutional context, which consists of an overall sponsor, the European Social Funds, and a multiplicity of decentralised administrative units and local governments across numerous countries. In creating social learning spaces across innovation projects, the intent of EQUAL was to increase the learning capacity of the overall system. The intentional weaving of independent projects into a learning system is a key role for the central sponsor, which differs from the role of managing the projects themselves and requires an additional layer of accountability and governance oriented to learning across the board. Everything I have said so far about the dynamics of social learning spaces, the voluntary nature of learning citizenship and the paradoxical work of social artists suggests that increasing learning capacity in a social system is a lot more complex than increasing, say, efficiency or even coordination. In addition to local factors, it is necessary to look at systemic factors such as governance and account- ability that affect learning capacity. I will proceed in three phases. First I will discuss governance processes oriented to learning itself. Then I will add the complication of accountability structures typical of organisational contexts. Finally, I will explore how the two interact to foster or inhibit social learning capacity.

Emergent and Stewarding Governance

Issues of governance are crucial to learning in social contexts. First, learning in social systems is inherently political. It involves decisions about what matters, about what counts as learning, about the direction to move toward. To the extent that learning suggests doing something better, then the definition of 'better' is a contes- table terrain. Second, learning capacity has both local and systemic dimensions. Governance processes propagate decisions among these levels. Governance oriented to social learning capacity must reflect two fundamental characteristics of socials systems. On the one hand, our imagination gives us the ability to project what we care about, individually and collectively, into the future and across social spaces. On the other hand, our knowledge and our visions are limited. Each of us is just one node in a network. We need to respond to and embrace the unexpected as part of our learning. This suggests two types of governance processes that contribute to social learning capacity:

– *Stewarding governance.*
This type of governance derives from a concerted effort to move a social system in a given direction. Championing a cause or pushing an issue is a typical example. Stewarding governance is a process of seeking agreement and alignment across a social system in order to achieve certain goals.
– *Emergent governance.*
This type of governance bubbles up from a distributed system of interactions involving local decisions. Market mechanisms are the quintessential example of emergent governance in that they produce decisions like prices of goods that emerge out of many transactions. Similarly, aspects of learning capacity emerge as the cumulative effect of local decisions negotiated in learning spaces and spread by participants.

The two types of processes interact. What is stewarding at one level of scale can be emergent at another. Stewarding governance in individual social learning spaces can result in emergent governance at the system level. Furthermore, emergent and stewarding governance have complementary strengths and weaknesses in their effects on learning.

Participants in local learning spaces may not be aware of systemic effects. A constellation of local experiments can lock the system in unproductive patterns that are not visible or manageable from local spaces or individual action. Some things we care about cannot be dealt merely through local decisions because they require too much coordination. Sometimes we need to recognise our interdependence and act in concert to bring about the learning we need. It takes stewarding governance to nurture the imagination of people so they can see themselves as participants in broader systems and align their actions accordingly. From a learning capacity perspective, however, stewarding governance can be the victim of its success. As the saying goes, be careful what you wish for; you might get it. The alignment and agreement sought under stewarding governance are like fire or knives: very effective but dangerous. Our designs have unintended consequences. To the extent that we inevitably act from our own perspectives, our efforts at stewarding governance require a degree of humility. Emergent governance is a learning safeguard against overreach. Given this complementarity, it is necessary to consider both types of governance processes when learning capacity is concerned. It is the combination of the two that can maximise the learning capacity of social systems.

Vertical and Horizontal Accountability

When one considers institutional contexts, the story becomes a bit more complicated. Social learning spaces often function in the context of institutional accountability structures. Institutional structures tend to be based on what can be called vertical accountability. In organisations, for instance, governance is usually implemented with hierarchical relationships configured to ensure, at least in theory, that the organisation achieves its goals. Systems of government also create vertical accountability through positions of authority, legislation, policies and enforcement mechanisms. By contrast, the kind of accountability I have described for social learning spaces and learning citizenship could be defined as horizontal in that it exists in mutual relationships among participants. To the extent that social learning spaces are expected to play a role in organisations, it is important to recognise both types of accountability:

- *Vertical accountability*, associated with traditional hierarchies; decisional authority; the management of resources; bureaucracies; policies and regulations; accounting; prescriptions; and audit inspections;
- *Horizontal accountability*, associated with engagement in joint activities; negotiation of mutual relevance; standards of practice; peer recognition; identity and reputation; and commitment to collective learning.

A common mistake in organisations is to assume that horizontal relationships lack accountability – and therefore that the only way to create accountability is to overlay vertical structures. A well functioning community of practice can give rise to very strong horizontal accountability among members through a mutual commitment to collective learning. Even a good conversation creates accountability, albeit of a temporal and tacit nature. Participants are held to an expectation of mutual relevance: they can't just go off into irrelevant topics or statements without violating such expectation. In its own ways, the horizontal accountability inherent in social learning spaces is no less binding and operative than formal vertical accountability. Horizontal accountability has to be the primary axis of social learning spaces, even when they operate in the context of institutions. Without a strong sense of mutual accountability, the learning potential of these spaces cannot be realised since genuine peer engagement and learning citizenship cannot be dictated. Social learning spaces must place governance in the hands of participants because it is the only way that learning can fully engage and reflect who they are.

Vertical accountability structures are usually not primarily geared to learning but they can deeply affect social learning capacity. In fact, my experience is that learning capacity is often a casualty of institutional accountability structures. Vertical accountability privileges the perspective of those to whom it gives more power to affect a system. From this perspective, if power corrupts, it is among other things because it can make horizontal accountability less expressible and thus decrease learning capacity. From these observations, another common mistake is to demonise vertical accountability and romanticise local engagement in practice. A self-governed social learning space is not heaven. It can reproduce all sorts of undesirable things, such as racism or corruption. It can be a place of collective mediocrity or contribute to systemically counterproductive patterns. When a system becomes too complex for negotiating governance issues directly, horizontal account-ability is not always the best means of fostering systemic learning capacity. It is useful to have certain things that are non-negotiable across a social system to limit the effects of local dysfunctions and myopia. Vertical accountability can help structure and simplify local engagement. We don't need to each decide at every moment on which side of the road to drive or whether it is a good idea to grab someone's wallet. Not everything has to be negotiable and decided anew every time. There is more productive use of our learning capacity.

Even though vertical and horizontal accountability structures can both be useful, there is an inherent tension between them. Vertical accountability is based on compliance; power and expressibility tend to be one-way. By contrast, horizontal accountability is based on negotiation and tends to involve mutual expressibility. (Note that this mutual expressibility does not necessarily imply equality. For instance, when an expert interacts with a novice, their relationships may be mutual without denying a difference in knowledge and power.) Coexisting vertical and horizontal systems of accountability can create conflicting demands, for instance, in the use of time. Compliance requirements can be at odds with the conclusions of engaged intelligence. It is not uncommon for practitioners to be caught in the two and have to choose between their own understanding of a situation and the demands of a policy. Finally, the two types of accountability are not easily visible to each other. The delivery of policies typically does not convey the full process by which they come into existence. Similarly, measures for auditing compliance are proxies because they need to be extractable from local practice, and in the process they inevitably lose much of the richness of the situations they are about.

The respective characteristics of vertical and horizontal accountability make the tension between them an inherent trait of institutional contexts. The tension is not to be removed or resolved; it has to be managed productively. The point is not to choose between vertical and horizontal accountability, but to configure the two so as to enable learning capacity through both emergent and stewarding governance.

Configuring Social Learning Capacity

Learning governance and accountability structures interact. For instance, a stewarding stance can be expressed vertically or horizontally, and in both cases meet emergent governance. Organisations typically seek stewarding governance through vertical accountability structures, but emergent governance still operates in practice. First hierarchies are never total. They inevitably rely on local decisions. Second, attempts at bureaucratic control have unintended consequences in the local responses they generate—unexpected situations, compliance to the letter rather than the spirit, workarounds, appearance of compliance, improvised interpretations. From a purely vertical perspective, unintended consequences are bugs to iron out (or ignore). From a learning perspective, they are data that reflect local intelligence.

Social artists also take a stewarding stance by promoting what they are passionate about and enabling the necessary social learning spaces, but they typically act horizontally. Participants in social learning spaces usually do not report to them formally and they have no vertical authority over them. In expressing their stewarding, they are masters at engendering horizontal accountability. But the negotiated nature of their social work also involves a lot of emergent governance. Good social artists embrace the complexity of social learning spaces to calibrate their own stewarding. They leverage the complementarity of social spaces and individual trajectories to let unexpected encounters and emerging processes shape the learning they care about. The interaction of learning governance and accountability structure is summarized in Table 15.1.

A similar table can frame the intentional use of vertical and horizontal accountability to realise stewarding and emergent governance (Table 15.2).

Table 15.1. Configuring social learning capacity - structural interactions between governance and accountability

Governance accountability	Stewarding	Emergent
Vertical	Hierarchies Policies and legislation Prescriptions Compliance audits	Gaps in prescriptions Local responses to design Unintended consequences Workarounds
Horizontal	Collective 'self-design' in social learning spaces The passions and caring of learning citizens The wilfulness of social artists	Unpredictable interactions between learning spaces and individual trajectories Cumulative systemic effects of local negotiations

Table 15.2. Configuring social learning capacity - creating patterns of vertical and horizontal accountability

Governance accountability	Stewarding	Emergent
Vertical	Enforcing non-negotiable alignment around what is certain; i.e. clearly known or desirable Making the local accountable to systemic effects	Unlocking clearly dysfunctional patterns to revitalise learning Legitimising voices that might be silenced locally
Horizontal	Inspiration Local initiative Grass-root leadership	Engaged improvisation Joint reflection-in-action Increasing movement of people

I outline these principles because I believe we need a language to take into consideration the learning implications of the governance and accountability systems we design. For instance, if a topic of stewarding governance is going to be non-negotiable through vertical accountability, it had better be something that is worth the possible cost in learning capacity: curtailing learning experiments and improvisation, privileging the stewarding perspective of those who enforce it and usually reducing the expressibility of other perspectives. More generally social learning capacity can be hindered in two opposite ways:

- If a uniform policy or 'best practice' imposes compliance on all localities in a social system, the learning capacity of the system is decreased because experimentation is curtailed (at least of a visible and sharable kind).

– Conversely, if governance is purely local and everyone acts completely independently, the learning capacity of the system is not fully achieved because experimentation, risk-taking, success and failure remain local.

Maximising learning capacity requires a variety of learning experiments that are independent, yet woven together with appropriate communication channels, commitment to learning, support and distribution of risk. The beauty of this principle of interwoven learning experiments is that it does not homogenize practice, as a uniform policy would, and yet it does interconnect contexts of practice by generating learning interdependence among the participants. This principle of independent but interwoven learning experiments suggests a new role for a centralised function in social systems. It is neither control nor *laissez-faire*, but an instance of stewarding governance aimed directly at fostering learning capacity.

In the space defined by the tables above, maximizing learning capacity requires all sorts of transversal processes that cut across dimensions:

– Vertical accountability structures make explicit room for social learning spaces without 'colonizing' these spaces with vertical accountability. For instance, projects may be structured to include activities for cross-project learning. Communities of practice may have a budget.
– The role of social artists is recognised and they can engage directly with hierarchical power structures to give voice to the learning they care about and draw attention to key learning spaces.
– Learning citizenship is encouraged and valued as a carrier of learning capacity within and across social learning spaces. For instance, the time people dedicate time and the contributions they make significant to their learning spaces are recognised in the vertical systems in which their performance is evaluated.
– People in the hierarchy act as learning citizens in their own ways and capacities. An executive can decide to sponsor a community of practice or to open a series of conversations as a way to steward an issue.
– Systemic patterns are made visible so they can become actionable through local interpretations.
– Ideas generated in a social learning space become proposals for new directions to be implemented across the board.

The configuration of horizontal and vertical accountability to support learning governance is key to the learning capacity of a social system. But it paradoxical and dynamic character challenges traditional organisational structures. It requires transversal processes. It cannot be fully formalised and intelligence cannot be designed out through bureaucracy. Learning governance requires strategic conversations with a focus on substance rather than form. The configuration of a productive interface between horizontal and vertical accountability is perhaps the central challenge for 21st-century organisations in all sectors that are concerned with systemic learning and innovative capacity.

CONCLUSION: A SHIFT IN MINDSET ABOUT LEARNING

What I have said here about these four factors of social learning capacity is not really new. It has always been happening in small pockets. What is new is a need to become more intentional and systematic about fostering social learning capacity as well as a need to do so at higher levels of scale and complexity. The learning capacity that EQUAL was trying to promote across a diversity of projects, cultures and nationalities is something we are only beginning to learn how to do. Still I am aware of a number of contexts where ideas like the ones presented here are influencing attempts at organising for learning, including businesses, governments, school improvement programmes, healthcare systems, and regional and international development agencies. I believe that a shift in mindset about learning is in the air – from a view of learning as a formal process caused by instruction to learning an essential aspect of everyday life and thus a capacity inherent in social systems. I see people in a position to make a difference all over the world becoming attuned to this reality and interested in taking action. To move forward, we need two things: (a) more examples to serve as living laboratories; and (b) better conceptual frameworks of the type I have tried to outline here to interpret these experiments and learn from them. This combination of practical experiments and conceptual framework is an urgent need today when the world is full of pressing large-scale learning imperatives. It is what will give us the models we need to accelerate the learning of our small planet.

NOTES

[1] For more information about the EQUAL initiative, see http://ec.europa.eu/employment_social/equal/index_en.cfm

LIST OF CONTRIBUTORS

David Anderson, Director General, National Museum Wales
David was born in Belfast and studied Irish history at Edinburgh University. After working as a history teacher in a state school, he became Education Officer at the Royal Pavilion Art Gallery and Museums, Brighton (1979) then Head of Education at the National Maritime Museum in Greenwich (1985). He joined the Victoria & Albert Museum as Head of Education in 1990. As Director of Learning and Interpretation at the V&A for 10 years he managed the V&A's learning services, community programmes, and audience research and gallery interpretation; he also had responsibility for cultural policy, diversity and external partnerships across the V&A. His publications include *A Common Wealth*, a report for the Government on the development of museums and learning in the United Kingdom (1997, second edition 1999) and (as co-author) *A Netful of Jewels*, a review of the potential for digital learning through museums for the UK Conference of National Museum Directors (1999).

Ronald Barnett, Emeritus Professor of Higher Education, Institute of Education, University of London
Ronald was previously Pro-Director (Longer-Term Strategy) and Professor of Higher Education at the Institute of Education, London. Through his writings, he has become known as an international authority on the conceptual understanding of higher education and the university. Prior to joining the Institute in 1990, he worked mostly in academic administration, especially at the former Council for National Academic Awards. While an administrator, he became interested as a part-time research student in the ways in which theoretical perspectives might illuminate our understanding of higher education and, since 1990, with his first book (a national prize winner) *The Idea of Higher Education*, has been engaged in trying to work out a response to the question: 'What is – and what might be – a university in the current age?' Other books and edited collections include: *Realizing the University in an Age of Supercomplexity* (2000), *Beyond All Reason: Living with Ideology in the University* (2003), *Reshaping the University: New Relationships between Research, Teaching and Scholarship* (2005), *A Will to Learn: Being a Student in an Age of Uncertainty*, (with John Strain and Peter Jarvis) *Universities, Ethics and Professions* (2009), and *Being a University* (2011).

Dr Brett Bligh, Researcher, Learning Sciences Research Institute (LSRI), University of Nottingham
Brett's work centres on the spatial implications of new technologies for learning. He was part of the JISC-funded project *A study of Effective Evaluation Models and Practices for Technology Supported Physical Learning Spaces* which investigated how Learning Spaces are evaluated. He has investigated how Multi-Display Learning Spaces can support small group learning by providing rich visual resources as part of the *Visual Learning Lab*, a HEFCE-funded Centre for Excellence in

Teaching and Learning. A Computer Scientist by background, Brett is currently interested in spatial context for Technology Enhanced Learning and how activity-focussed investigations can inform processes of Learning Space design.

Anne Boddington, CETLD Director, Dean of Faculty of Arts, University of Brighton and Co-Director of the Higher Education Academy's National Subject Centre for Art Design & Media (ADM HEA).
Anne was Director of the Centre for Excellence in Teaching and Learning through Design (CETLD) between 2005 and 2010. Educated as an architect and later as a cultural geographer, she leads a Faculty of around 3900 students and an academic portfolio that includes the Visual and Performing Arts, Architecture, Design, Media, Literature, Languages and Humanities. It is located in the heart of Brighton's cultural quarter and has an international reputation for high-quality research and creative interdisciplinary education.

Dr Jos Boys, Senior Research Fellow, Learning Spaces, Centre for Excellence in Teaching and Learning through Design (CETLD) University of Brighton
Jos joined the CETLD in 2007 as an academic developer and researcher. Her background is in architecture and she has taught at various institutions, including the Architectural Association, London Metropolitan University and at the University of Brighton. Jos has also been involved in teaching and learning research; both as an academic developer in art and design at De Monfort University and as under-graduate course leader at DMU Milton Keynes, leading an innovative BA in Architecture and Urban Studies, which completely integrated online and face-to-face learning. Her research interests lie in the social aspects of architecture, and the intersections of space and power. Jos is author of '*Towards Creative Learning Spaces: re-thinking the architecture of post-compulsory education*' (2010) and is currently teaching design in Moscow.

Fiona Duggan, Director of FiD Ltd
Fiona works with educational institutions involved in building projects. Using a combined background in architecture and psychology, she helps institutions articulate their organisational requirements and translate them into spatial requirements. She is particularly interested in how space can be used to support (or hinder) learning and working practices. Her focus is on developing client briefs that facilitate movement from 'the way we are now' to 'the way we believe we could be'.

Dr Clare Melhuish, Independent Researcher
Clare conducted research into staff and student perceptions of new learning spaces, and their impact on the teaching and learning process, for CETLD, University of Brighton and InQbate (CETL in Creativity) Universities of Sussex and Brighton. She is Visiting Research Fellow in Anthropology at Brunel University, specialising in the study of the modern built environment as social setting, and an architecture critic and writer. She ran the newly founded cross-disciplinary journal *Home Cultures* (Berg) from 2004 to 2008, and has a wide range of publications to her name.

Ian Pearshouse, Researcher, Learning Sciences Research Institute (LSRI),
University of Nottingham
Research at the Institute explores the cognitive, social and cultural aspects of learning and designs innovative technologies and environments for learners. Ian has over 20 years experience in developing and managing innovative IT systems for Higher Education including 12 years in the field of learning technology. He leads the 'Technology Enhanced Learning Spaces' strand of research at the LSRI and was principal investigator for the JISC funded study *"A study of Effective Evaluation Models and Practices for Technology Supported Physical Learning Spaces"* (JELS).

Dr. Olivia Sagan, Head of MSc. Psychoanalytic Developmental Psychology
(PDP) at University College London
Her PhD won the 2009 Director's prize for Best Doctoral Research at the Institute of Education, University of London, and was a longitudinal, psychosocial study of mentally ill adults' community auto/biographic practices. A firm believer in the role of first-person narratives in counter-balancing 'culturally sanctioned stories', Olivia makes extensive use of biographic narrative in her research, and uses psychosocial theory to explore the quandaries of learning and creativity.

Professor Maggi Savin-Baden, Professor of Higher Education Research,
University of Coventry
Maggi and has always been interested in innovation and change. Her interest in learning has been the focus of her research for many years. Her current research is focusing on the impact of virtual worlds on learning and teaching, through a large Leverhulme funded project. Further, over the last 3 years she has been developing the method of qualitative research synthesis. To date she has published six books on problem-based learning; and another entitled *Learning Spaces* (McGraw Hill). In 2010 she published three books *An Introduction to Qualitative Research Synthesis* (Routledge) in January; *New Approaches to Qualitative Research: Wisdom and Uncertainty* (Routledge) in April and *A Practical Guide to using Second Life in Higher Education* (McGraw Hill) in June. In her spare time she has been doing an MSc. in e-learning at the University of Edinburgh and learning to snowboard.

Susan Sherringham, Senior Lecturer and Course Director in Interior Design,
Faculty of Design Architecture and Building, University of Technology,
Sydney (UTS)
Susan is the Project Leader on an Australian Learning and Teaching Council (ATLC) Priority Project concerning the design and evaluation of learning spaces and is the Chair of the working party on Teaching and Learning Space Improvement at UTS. She has over 20 years of industry experience as a designer, as a director of a multidisciplinary design practice and in her own multidisciplinary design practice, primarily designing for the commercial sector including research and development projects. Her current post-graduate research focuses on adaptive expertise, systems

thinking, organisational learning and life-long learning in the design industry: an aspect of which is conceptualising the workplace as a learning environment.

Hilary Smith, Researcher, Centre of Excellence in Teaching and Learning through Design (CETLD) University of Brighton.
Hilary's background is in human-computer interaction stemming from a Bachelors degree in Psychology and Computer Science (University of Dundee, 1994) and a Masters from University of Sussex (1997). Over the last 10 years she has researched technology support for teaching and learning in primary and secondary school contexts, including in maths, science and reading skills. At CETLD she worked with members of the Arts faculty to understand how space can impact on art materials practice in higher education learning contexts.

Dr Susan Stewart, Director of Design Studies, School of Design, University of Technology, Sydney (UTS)
Susan is currently acting Course Director for the Masters in Design at UTS. She is passionate about teaching and in particular the development of curriculum, curriculum delivery and support infrastructures. Her research interests include design studies, design engagement with ethical dilemmas, actor network theory, hermeneutics and cross-cultural negotiation in design, the cultivation of judgment in practice and interior design research strategies. Susan practiced architecture for 6 years before returning to full time study, gaining her doctoral qualification in 1999.

Dr Paul Temple, Reader in Higher Education Management, Centre for Higher Education Studies, Institute of Education, University of London, UK
Paul is Co-Director of the Institute of Education's Centre for Higher Education Studies, where he also co-directs the MBA programme in higher education management. He has recently worked on two large research projects examining aspects of university-enterprise relations in different European countries, and contributed to the book describing the work of one of these projects, *Entrepreneurialism in Universities and the Knowledge Economy* (2009). He is currently directing a long-term project providing support for management development in the Romanian university system. He has written on various aspects of university planning and management, and is Executive Editor of the London Review of Education. He is currently editing 'Universities in the Knowledge Economy' for the Routledge Studies in International Higher Education series.

Angela Thody, Emeritus Professor, Centre for Educational Research and Development (CERD), University of Lincoln
Angela was a member of the Learning Landscapes, HEFCE funded, research project, 2007–2009, with 10 universities and private sector partners, led by the University of Lincoln. Now Emeritus Professor, Angela supervises doctoral students and researches emeriti roles, writing and presenting research and nineteenth century history of education management [AT1]. Her core discipline is education

leadership, both UK and international and she has written five books, edited or co-authored five more, 50-plus articles in professional and academic journals and various chapters and research reports. Angela edited Management in Education for 7 years, was President of the Commonwealth Council for Educational Administration for 6 years, has lectured in every continent except Antarctica and is a Senior Fellow of the Higher Education Academy.

Etienne Wenger, International Education Consultant
Etienne Wenger is a globally recognized thought leader in the field of communities of practice, who was featured by *Training Magazine* in their *A New Breed of Visionaries* series. A pioneer of the 'communities of practice' research, he is author and co-author of seminal articles and books on the topic, including *Situated Learning* (1991), where the term was coined, *Communities of Practice: Learning, Meaning, and Identity* (1998), where he lays out a theory of learning based on the concept of communities of practice, and *Cultivating Communities of Practice: a Guide to Managing Knowledge* (2002), addressed to practitioners in organisations. His work as researcher, author, and consultant has influenced both thinking and practice in a wide variety of fields, including business, education, government and social theory. His new research project, 'Learning for a small planet' (http://www.ewenger.com/research/index.htm) is a cross-sectoral investigation of the nature of learning practices and institutions at the dawn of the new millennium.

INDEX

A
Aalto, A., 22
Abbott, E., 124
Abertay, University, vii, 36, 40–41
Aberystwyth, University, 37
absence of borders, 170
academic community, 187
academic content, 8
academic developers, 15
academic disciplines, 61, 177
academic effectiveness, 139, 143
academic fictions, 3
academic freedom, 171
academic infrastructures, xxi
academic offices, 124
academic settings, 139, 182
academics lives, 100
academic structures, 188
academic timetable, 61
academic workplaces, 36
accessibility, 110, 125
accommodation planning, 189
accountability, 160, 194–197, 200,
    204–209
accountability structures, 204–207,
    209
action-learning, 125
activation of space, 50
active learning, 37, 89, 111, 126
activity checklists, 11
activity-scapes, 113, 116
Activity Support approaches, 6,
    10–12
Actor Network Theory, xvii, 214
adjacencies, 181
Adjaye, D., 38, 44
adult education, xi, xxi, 38, 72
adult learning, 73, 130
advanced levels, 57
advertisements, 59
advisory groups, 151

aesthetics, xii, xx
affordances, xv, 10, 12, 23, 181
agency, 55, 81, 189, 190n4
agoras, 190
aha! moments, 99
Akhtar, S., 75
Aldrich, C.T., 127
algorithms, 185
alienation, 125
Allen, P., 129
allocation models, 140
allocation schedules, 43
ALTC Priority Project, xv, 116n3
alternative pedagogies, 188
ambience, 43, 82, 84
Amin, A, 139, 141
analysis techniques, 15
analytical methods, 5
analytical rigour, 185
anthropological studies, 24
anthropology, xii, xiv, 3, 19, 24, 42,
    212
anytime access, 42
appearances, 35, 41, 43, 49, 53, 126,
    158, 207
appraisal evaluations, 5
archetypes, 6, 58
architectural rhetoric, 43
archives, 40, 59, 179, 182
Arias, S., 53
Arnold, T., 127, 130
art and design, 212
artefacts, 58, 102, 105, 112, 127, 184
Arthur, M., 126
artists, xvi, 37, 42, 71, 161, 163,
    201–204, 207, 209
artists commissions, 37
art schools, 156
arts environment, 70
Ashley, W.J., 124
assessment algorithms, 185

assessment criteria, 61
assessment framework, 9
assessment regimes, 185
Astin, A.W., 8
asymmetric furniture layouts, 36, 42
Atkinson, P., 25
attention levels, 86
auditing, 206, 207
Augoyard, J.-F., 25, 53
Austerlitz, N., 52
authenticity, 144, 176, 177, 197, 200
authentic learning, 106, 109, 116,
   116*n*2
autobiography, 159
autonomy, 20, 176
avant-garde, 54

B
Bain, A., 127
Baldridge, J. V., 125
Banks, M., 112
Banning, J., 143
Bann, S., 163
Barnes, C.R., 127
Barnett, R., xii, xvi, xviii, 53, 54, 62,
   73, 76, 77, 123, 126, 143, 144,
   167–177, 180, 211
Baron, S., 144
Baudrillard, J., 54
Bauman, Z., 173
Bayne, S., 76
Becher, T., 121
Beck, T., 129
Beetham, H., 19–21
behavioural patterns, 24, 27
behaviourist paradigmatic methods,
   26
Belanger, C, 138
Bel Geddes, N., 106
Bell, D.L., 75
belonging, xvi, xx, 72, 91, 121,
   127–128, 131, 149
Benjamin, W., 123
Bennett, S., 138
Berlin Free University, 22

Berlin, I., 22, 168
Berman, P, 122
Bernstein, B., 172
best-fit, 148
Bhabha, H.K., 53, 60
Bielaczyc, K., 10, 11, 14
biotechnology, 42
Birmingham, University, 35
Black History Month, 162
Black, R., 129
blended learning, 21, 130
Bligh, D.A., 111
Blomberg, J., 111
body language, 114
bonding places, 153
booking systems, 153
Boudon, P., 42
Boughey, C., 98
boundaries model, 152
boundary conditions, 114
boundary crossings, 53
boundary spaces, 139
bounded curricula, 168
Bourdieu, P., xvii, 24, 60, 72, 107
Brady, T., 122, 131
brainstorming, 86
branding and identity, 13
Brennan, J., 125, 126
bridging model, 152
Brighton University, xiii, 81, 83, 86,
   179, 212, 214
Brink, L., 122
British Architects RIBA, xiii, 179
British Library London, 40
Britzman, D., 70, 73
brokering, 199
Brooks, D.C., 8
Brown, E, 4–7, 9–12, 15, 16, 21, 91*n*4
Bruns, A., 102
Buchanan, R., 188
building types, 38, 60
bureaucracy, 24, 200, 209
bureaucratic control, 207
Burrowes, G., 105
business start-up, 41

C
Cairns, A., 35
Cambridge, University, 37, 139
Cameron, J.M., 123
Campbell, L., 124
Campus Mapping Profile, 12
canteens and cafés, 61
capitalism, 24, 138
care empowerment policy, 97
cartographers, 130
Castaldi, B., 129
Castells, M., 95
casual lounge setting, 42
CCTV cameras, 160
central atrium, 39
Centre for Educational Research and
    Development (CERD), 123, 124,
    126, 130, 214
Centre for Excellence in Teaching
    and Learning through Design
    (CETLD), xiii, xvi, 81, 84, 85, 87,
    88, 91n1, 91n2, 179–183, 186,
    212, 214
Centres for Excellence, 81, 91n1,
    190n1
Centres for Excellence in Teaching
    and Learning (CETL), 81, 180,
    212
CETLD partnership, 179
CETLD space, 87, 180–182
CETL in Creativity, 36, 212
Chapman, M., 76, 138, 140
checklists, 11, 20
Chicago, Illinois, University of, 127
childrens learning, 127
choreography, xix
citizen-learners, xvi
citizenship, xvi, 198–204, 206, 209
civic pride, 138
civility, 155
Clark, H., 130
classroom as cafè, 42
classroom as nightclub, 41
client groups, 129
client influence, 129

client perspectives, 129
Clifford, J., 26, 27
closed access, 83
clustering, 6, 37, 38, 45, 107
Coats, D., 143
Cobban, A., 139
co-construction, 181, 187, 188
co-creation, 71
co-designing learning, 187
co-development, 181
cognitive learning, 24
Cohen, S., 143
cohesiveness, 141
co-learners, 194
collaborative learning, 10, 130, 187
collaborative projects, 129
collaborative spaces, 96–97
collecting data, 6, 10
collective memory, 149
collective self-design, 208
collective sense-making, 147
Colorado, University of, 122
comfortable discomfort, 197
commercial practice, 62
commercial pressures, 160
commercial purpose, 158
Committee for Architecture and the
    Built Environment (CABE), 129,
    130
communications technologies, 20
communicative interactions, 121,
    122
communities of practice, xvii, 52,
    56–59, 61, 150, 153, 180, 181,
    184, 187, 189, 193, 194, 197, 198,
    203, 209, 215
community arts centres, 160
community-building, 142
community cohesiveness, 141
community facilities, 39
community formation, 140
community involvement, 122
community learning, 131, 187
community projects, 151
comparative methods, xviii

competitive market, 89, 150
complex institutions, 182
complex interactions, 143
complex settings, 112
complex variables, 45
compliance audits, 208
concentration levels, 87
condition survey, 148
Conklin, J., 186, 187
Conole, G, 20
consciousness raising, 97
consensus-seekers, 202
conserving tradition, 123
constituencies, xv
construction projects, 149
consumer practice, 20
contemporary architecture, 62
contemporary curricula, 171
contemporary learning experiences, 19
contemporary students, 108
contemporary theories, xiv, 50, 53
contextual factors, 12
contingencies, 183, 186
conventional facilities, 13
co-operative models, 189
Copenhagen, University of, 142
co-presence, 150
corporate plan, 148
corporate universities, 127
corporations, 176
corridor spaces, 83
cost constraints, 90
Cousin, G., 45
Cowling, M., 143
Creanor, L., 19
creating place, 141–143
creating writing, 98, 99
creative learning, xxi, 99, 212
creative professionals, 161
creative sociability, 43
creative technologies, 40
Crellin, G., 3, 7–10, 12–15, 33, 35, 125
Criddle, S., 122

criticality, 96, 102
Crook, C., 10, 12
cross-disciplinary, xii, 212
crowds, 46n1, 123, 197
culinary arts, 107
cultural affordances, 10
cultural behaviours, 27
cultural capital, 72
cultural contexts, 24
cultural democracy, 163
cultural diversity, 23
cultural education, 160
cultural heritage, 162
cultural institutions, 160, 189
cultural phenomenology, 22
cultural spaces, 160
cultural theory, xix
culture of scholarship, 109
Cumbria, University of, 35
current architectural theory, 50
curricula aims, 176
curricula construction, 174
curricula spaces, 169
Cutright, M., 123
Czordas, T., 22

D
Darby, J., 20
databases, 59
data collection, 5, 7, 9, 15, 195
Davis, R. H., 129
Day-Sclater, S., xiv, 69
DCSF, 129
Dealty, R., 124
De Certeau, M., xvii, 25
decision-makers, 55
decision- making, 28, 57, 63, 110, 111, 129, 149, 154
deconstruction, 54
deep learning, 69, 111
deficit educational models, 181
DEGW, ix, 116n4, 122
de Laat, M., 20
Deleuze, G., xix, 51, 75, 173
democracy, 123, 163

democratic society, 155
demonstrations, 5, 151
dentistry, 20
Denver Public Schools, 122
Denzin, N.K., 26
deprivation, 43
Derbyshire, A., 142
Derrida, J., 51, 54
de-schooling, 128
descriptive evaluation, 11
descriptive modalities, 186
design communities, 180, 184, 186
design culture, 109
designed affordances, 10
design education, xii, 156, 179–189
designer as celebrity, 106
designerly activity, xvi
designerly knowledge, 186
design examples, 37
design features, 21, 141, 142, 144
designing education, 179–190
designing learning, 33, 41–44
design intentions, 25, 35, 45, 55
design language, 35, 38, 40
design learning, 8, 33, 34, 179, 180,
    183, 185–189
design practices, 63, 153, 161, 183,
    213
design principles, 11, 142
design scenarios, 112
design schools, 42, 109, 129, 130
design spaces, 3, 4, 8, 10–13, 16, 25,
    33, 38, 41, 50, 53, 57, 58, 63, 109,
    110, 112, 139, 171, 212
determinism, 10
developing briefs, 112
developing evidence, 33
developing protocols, 110, 116n3
developing relationships, 143
developing universities, 187
DfEE, 129
DfES, 129, 190n2
dialogic spaces, 98
diaspora, 124
differential abilities, 129

difficult knowledge, 70, 77
digital learners, 19
digital spaces, xi, 160
digital technologies, 105, 180
Dillon, T., 20
disabilities, 21, 96, 97
disciplinary boundaries, 84, 139
disciplinary perspectives, 173
disciplinary worlds, 187
discipline-specific, 106, 152
discourse analysis, 27
discussion space, 101
disembodied attention, 109
disenfranchised group, 97
disjunctive space, 75
Disney, 124, 158
distance learning, 69, 124
distributed learning, 126
diverse learners, 5
diversity programmes, 162
divided communities, 189
Dobbin, G., 8, 9
Dober, R., 37, 138
Dombrovsky, Y., 159
domestic space, 24, 44n2
dominant elites, 163
dominant ideologies, 176
dominant interests, 171
Dovey, K., xvii, 138, 141
Dudek, M., 22, 23, 129
Duffy, F, 43
Durrett, C., 125
dynamism, 50, 161
dystopias, 155, 159

E
early learning, 71
early mirroring, 72
early years, 125, 156
eclecticism, 141
ecological considerations, 15
ecological landscape, 175
ecological learning, 177
ecologies, xx, 13, 123, 175–177
ecology model, 6, 12–13

Economic and Social Research
　Council (ESRC), 96
economic benefits, 143
economic capital, 97
economic studies, 143
economy, xxi, 13, 171, 175, 177,
　214
ecosystem, 16, 127
Edinburgh, University of, 37, 130,
　131, 211, 213
Edmunds, R., 130
educational agenda, 54
educational difficulties, 185
educational discourse, xiv, 69
educational doctrines, 168
educational enterprise, 177
educational infrastructure, xi, 185,
　188
educational language, 180
educational philosophies, 170, 171
educational power, 172
educational radicalism, 168
education space, xvii
education system, 94, 185, 188
Edwards, R., 75, 127, 137
effective evaluation, 4, 21, 211, 213
effective refurbishment, 41
effective research spaces, 101
effective teaching, 127
e-learners, 20
e-learning, 19, 20, 122, 124, 127,
　130, 174, 213, xi
e-learning architectures, 122
e-learning environment, 20
e-learning resources, 20
e-learning tools, 127
Elliott-Burns, R., 129, 130
e-mail, 20
embedded meanings, 98
embodied environmental awareness,
　23
embodied experiences, 50, 51, 107,
　114
embodied knowledge, 142
embodied space, 23–25

emerging perspectives, 183
emerging technologies, 102
employability, 84, 174
employability skills, 84
employment patterns, 173
empowered students, 89
empowerment policy, 97
encounter management approach,
　141
enforcement mechanisms, 205
engineering courses, 87
enterprise initiatives, 150
environmental awareness, 23
environmental behaviour, 57
environmental conditions, 22, 24,
　114
environmental influences, 8
environmental psychology, xiv, 22, 24
ephemeralism, 170
epistemic tools, 113
epistemological burdens, 177
epistemological implications, 172
epistemological space, 77, 169
epistemological superficiality, 177
e-portfolios, 19, 122
equal access, 124
Erickson, F., 24
Eriksen, T.H., 95, 102
ESRC. See Economic and Social
　Research Council
Essex, University of, 35, 37
estate management, xii, 148
estates departments, 15
estates planning, 33, xi
estates refurbishment, 4
estate strategy, 148
e-structures, 122
ethical dimension, 175, 199, 200
ethnic minority neighbourhoods, 137
ethnographic methodologies, 3, 26
ethnographic practice, 27
ethnomethodology, 60
e-university project, 128
European Social Fund, x, xvi, 193,
　204

European universities, 127
evaluating activities, 6, 10
evaluating learning, 3, 11
Evaluating Scenario Provision, 10
evaluating spaces, 4, 6
evaluation criteria, 171
evaluation evidence, 35, 37
evaluation fatigue, 15
evaluation milestones, 14
evaluation models, 4, 5, 21, 211, 213
evaluation outcomes, 5
evaluation outputs, 16
evaluation practices, 4
evaluation questions, 5
evaluation strategies, 15
evaluation support, 37
evaluation tools, 154
evaluation types, 5
everyday life, 42, 64n2, 97, 210
evidence base, 33, 182
evolutionary frameworks, 188
exclusivity, 82–85, 90
expanded taxonomies, 188
expressibility, 195–197, 207, 208
extended university, 127
external spaces, 181
extra-curricular, 75

F
face-to-face, 19, 124, 150, 152, 153, 212
facilities management, 33, 189
Featherstone, M., 129
feudalism, 123
Field, J., 144
Fields, G., 143
financial cuts, 100
fine art, 26, 70
fitness for purpose, xi
Fitzwilliam College Cambridge, 37
flexible work spaces, 122
Florida, R., 141
fluidity, xiv, 75
Flutter, J., 129

focus groups, 9, 12, 81, 82, 90, 91n2, 109–111
Fonagy, P., 74
formality, 41, 121
formal learning, 33, 45, 50, 56, 61, 62, 167, 181
fostering learning, 200–201, 209
Foucault, M., xvii, 60, 72, 75, 171
foundational framework, 185
foundational knowledge, 184
foundation degrees, 69
foundation level, xiv, 69
founding fathers, 157
fragility, 170
Francis, R., 122, 126, 130
Fraser, K., 11
free market, 83
free university, 22
Freire, P., 97
Frenay, M., 125
French, R., 76
french structuralism, 25
Frost, L., 71
Fry, T., 106
fulfilling workplace, xi
functional analyses, 27
functional concerns, 91
functional implications, 86
functional patterns, 61
funding bodies, 14
funding decisions, 14
funding timescales, 7
furniture choices, 129
furniture layouts, 36, 42
future governance, 188
future innovation, 183
future learning, 112, 188, 190
future planning, 3, 5
future roles, 180, 188
future society, 157

G
Gabrielsen, M., 138, 142
Gadamer, H.G., 108
gallery management, 151

Gans, H., 24
Garfinkel, H., 60
Gaver, W.H., 112
Geertz, C., xviii, 25, 57
geertzian school, 25
gender, 23, 71, 129
generative dialogues, 106
generative narratives, 112
genuine learning, 175
geography, xiv, 24, 121, 163, 168
Gibbs, G., 111
Gibson, J.J., 23
Giddens, A., 107
Gilbert, A.D., 123, 124
Gladwell, M., 140
Glasgow Caledonian University, 20,
    35, 36
Glasgow, University of, 157
global commons, 189
globalisation, 163
globalised learning economy, 171
Gluch, P., 112, 113
Goffman, E., 22
Goliber, M.J., 13
Gordon, T., 129
Gore, C., 123
Gore, E., 123
Gosso, S., 72
governance and accountability, 204,
    207–209
governance issues, 204
governance processes, 204, 205
governance structures, xxi, 207, 208
government policies, 148
government sectors, 180, 193
Gowan, D., 19
Graber, R., 4–7, 9–12, 14–16, 21,
    91n4
graduation ceremonies, 177
Graetz, K.A., 13
graphic designers, 152
Greene, M., 125
Greenhalgh, P., 73
group working, 87
Guattari, F., xix, 51, 75, 173

H
Hain, D., 115
hairdressing, 36
Hall, E.T., 22
Hamel, G., 141
Hamilton, D., xix, 28, 57
Hammersley, M., 25
Hanson, J., 137, 140, 142
Harper, D., 112
Harrison, A., 35–36, 123, 126, 127
Harrison, R., 21–23
Harte, N., 139
Hartnell-Young, E., 4–7, 9–12,
    14–16, 21, 91n4
Harvey, D., 64n1
Hayden, D., 137
Haywood, J., 122
Hazelwood, A., 122
healthcare, 19, 26, 210
healthcare studies, 26–27
HEFCE. See Higher Education
    Funding Council for England
hegemony, 171
Heidegger, M., 107, 174
Heimstra, R., 111
Henderson, K., 113
Henley, B., 124
Herrington, J., 106, 116n2
Hertzberger, H., 22
heterogeneous evaluations, 5
hierarchical learning, 22, 69, 209
hierarchical power, 209
hierarchical relationships, 205
Higher Education Funding Council
    for England (HEFCE), ix, 148,
    179, 211, 214
Hillier, B., xvii, 3, 13, 137, 140, 142
Hirsch, E., 22
historic buildings, 124, 128, 138,
    157
historicism, 158
history, 39, 69, 77, 123, 137, 163,
    194, 195, 211, 214
Hoggett, P., 71
HOK Architects, 36

holding environment, 46*n*2, 53, 73, 74
holism, 125
Holston, J., 42
homelands, 153
Hooke, M.T., 75
Hooper-Greenhill, E., 51, 58
horizontal relationships, 53, 206
horizontal systems, 207
housing projects, 25
Houston, M., 131
Howells, C., 19
human behaviours, 24, 62
human-computer interaction, xi, 214
human-computer interface, xii
human condition, xvii, 183, 186, 188
human consciousness, 121
human embodiment, 23
human experience, 22, 59, 112
human geographies, 60
human intention, 27
human interaction, 23
humanities, 172, 190*n*3, 203, 212
human motivation, 106
human rights, 162
human scale, xv, 140
human settlements, 140
Hunley, S., 9
Hurdley, R., 75, 77
Hurworth, R., 112
Hutchinson, D., xvii, 121, 125, 127, 128, 130
hybrid architecture, 54, 62
hybridity, 50
hybrid societies, 158
Hyerle, D., 115
hyper modernity, 170

I
iconic buildings, 138
iconic university, 138
idealism, 203
ideal society, 157, 159
ideal type-form, 105
identity of place, 142

identity question, 189
ideological difficulties, 188
ideological terrain, 177
ideologies, 55, 60, 93, 163, 173, 176, 211
Illich, I.D., 125
illuminative evaluation, 28
imaginary space, xix
immersive landscape, 127
immersive learning environment, 127
impact studies, 101
improving behaviour, 129
improving efficiency, 149
improving learning, xii, 16
improving space, xii, 16, 45, 124
improvisation, 151, 169, 196, 208
inclusion and exclusion, 174
inclusive conversations, 106
inclusive learning, 69, 189
inclusive learning environments, 76
individual creativity, 22
individual experience, 200
individual institutions, 190
individual learners, 58, 182, 188
industrial design, 156
inefficient spaces, 7
informal design typology, 41
informal/formal learning, 56, 63, 130
informal learning, xiii, xiv, 12, 33, 34, 38–41, 44, 49, 56, 63, 86, 126, 130, 170, 181
informal modes, 46
informal networks, 20
informal setting, 44, 46*n*3
informal space, 84
information-gathering, 28
information-sharing, 20, 57, 58
infrastructures, xi, xxi, 10, 11, 81, 89, 110, 153, 183, 185, 187, 188, 214
innocent spatiality, 60
innovation studies, 183, 186
innovative design, xii, 10, 35, 85, 106, 110, 112, 213
innovative learners, 182

innovative pedagogy, 10
innovative space, xiv, 6, 10, 13, 15,
    33, 62, 89, 106, 111, 112, 122
innovative university, 130, 148
input-process-output, 140
InQbate Creativity Zone, 81, 82, 87
instant messaging, 20
institutional accountability, 205, 206
institutional agendas, xii, xv, 90
institutional boundaries, 90
institutional culture, 143
institutional effectiveness, 140–141
institutional evaluations, 8, 9, 15
institutional hierarchies, 16, 83
institutional identities, xiv, xv–xvi,
    xviii, 4, 61, 114
institutional infrastructure, 183, 187
institutional intentions, 91
institutional knowledge, 141
institutional learning, 109
institutional memory, 11
institutional prestige, 13
institutional priorities, 105
institutional space, xix, 8, 76, 77, 86,
    89, 110, 160
institutional tradition, 105
institutional values, 13, 110
Institution's vision, 13
instructional space, 194
instrumentality, 101
intellectual agendas, 139
intellectual property, 101
intelligent models, xxi, 187
intensifying behaviours, 21
intentional spaces, 169, 174
interactionism, 26
interactive classroom, 36
interactive learning, 44, 50, 58, 62,
    89, 194
interactive spaces, 49, 76, 90, 95
interactivity, 5, 42, 86–89
interconnectedness, 122, 125–127,
    174, 175
intercultural exchange, 155

interdependencies, 121, 190n6, 205,
    209
interdisciplinary enquiry, 16
interface designers, xii
interior design, 44, 57, 124, 213–214
interior space, xviii, 22, 169
interior worlds, 125
internalisation, 172
Interpretative Phenomenology
    Approach (IPA), 19, 26, 27
interpretative strategies, 58
intersecting spaces, 51
invisibilities, xvi, 60, 85, 89, 167,
    174
invisible governance, xx
IPA. *See* Interpretative
    Phenomenology Approach
iterative experience, 186

J
Jackson, N.J., 72
Jamieson, P., 3, 12, 15, 33, 41, 42,
    143
Jarman, M., 27
Jary, D., 125
Jenkins, A., 111, 181
JISC. *See* Joint Information Systems
    Committee
Johnson, A.F., 127
Joint Information Systems
    Committee (JISC), ix, 4, 19–21,
    33, 35–36, 127, 211, 213
Jones, A., 143
journalism, 108

K
Kalz, M., 122
Katz, C., 24
Kaynar, I., 13
Kelly, A.V., 123
Kensing, F., 111
Kerr, I., 123, 125, 126
Kiley, M., 99
Kinzie, J., 140
knowledge architectures, 127

knowledge articulation, 131
knowledge creation, 58, 62
knowledge ecology, 175
knowledge exchange, 58
knowledge-intensive companies, 141
knowledge management, 122
Kolb, D.A., 125
Kolb, Y., 112
Kolko, J., 115
Koolhaas, R., 50
Kress, G., 173
Krippendorff, K., 181, 183
Kuh, G., 140
Kumar, K., 158, 163

L
laboratories, xiii, 43, 61, 152, 182,
    210
Laguerre, M., 24
Lahelma, E., 129
landmark elements, 36, 42
Land, R., xx, 44, 45, 52, 99, 175
landscapes principles, 130
landscape terminology, 121–123
Lasdun, D., 22
Latour, B., xvii
Lave, J., xvii, xx, 52, 59, 61, 62,
    64n2, 69, 116n2
Lawrence-Zuniga, D., 24
leadership modes, 76
leadership styles, 76
learned skills, 106
learner-centred activity, 70
learner-centred evaluation, 20
learner collaboration, 126
learner experience, 19, 21
learners assumptions, 105
Learners' Experience of e-Learning
    programme, JISC, 4, ix
learners lives, 19
learners perceptions, 19–21
learning achievements, 151, 193
Learning as Citizenship, 199
Learning as Partnership, 197
Learning by Working, 151–153

learning challenges, xvii, 193
learning citizens, 199–201, 203, 204,
    208, 209
learning disabilities, 96, 97
learning ecologies, xx, 175, 176
learning economy, 171, 175, 177
learning governance, xvi, 204–209
learning interdependence, 209
learning journeys, xx, 52, 99, 167,
    174
learning landscapes, ix, xv, xx, 13,
    116n4, 121–131, 148, 182, 214
learning methods, 13, 62, 83
learning modalities, 175
learning networks, 20, 189
learning nooks, 36, 42
learning outcomes, 6, 8, 9, 61, 126,
    171
learning platforms, 151, 152
learning scenarios, 8, 10, 106, 111,
    114, 116
learning skills, 19, 151, 185
learning streets, 36, 37
learning styles, 10, 58, 173
learning theories, xiii, 3, 4, 16, 121,
    125–128
Learning through LANDSCAPES,
    122
Lebeau, Y., 131
Leeds, J., 129
Lee, N., 143
Lefebvre, H., xvii, xviii, 24, 53,
    55–58, 63, 76, 94, 137
legitimate peripheral participation
    (LPP), 52, 53
Leigh, J., 127
Lesser, E.L., 140
Levi-Strauss, C., 24
Lewthwaite, S., 4–7, 9–12, 14–16,
    21, 91n4
Lex project, 19, 20
librarians, 152
libraries, 12, 20, 35–40, 61, 105,
    122, 126, 150, 152, 153, 160, 174
library centres, 36

lifelong learning, 74, 130, 214
life-long learning opportunities, 150
life skills, 161
lifestyles, 24, 99, 122
liminality, 170
liminal space, 53, 75, 76, 106, 112
Lincoln Learning Landscapes
    Project, 128
Lincoln, University of, ix, 116*n*4,
    126, 128, 148, 214
Lindsay, V.J., 126
linearity, 101, 186
linguistic capital, 97
linguistics, 20, 27
linguistic theory, 54
liquid learning, 173
literacy, 70
literary theory, 25
livable knowledge, 194, 195
Liverpool University, 37
local businesses, 40
local communities, 40, 150
local dysfunctions, 206
local fauna, 158
local government, 141, 204
local history, 39
local identity, 141
localities, 208
local spaces, 205
locational capital, 143, 144
Loewy, R., 106
Lofland, L., 22
London School of Economics (LSE),
    127
loose-fit, 22, 107
Lorenz, K., 12, 15
Loughborough, University of, 148,
    149
Lovlie, L., 169
Low, S.M., 24
LPP. *See* legitimate peripheral
    participation
LSE. *See* London School of
    Economics
Lyn, H., 22

Lyons, J.B., 129
Lyons, M., 141
Lyotard, J.-F., 64*n*1
Lytras, M.D., 130

M
Macdonalds, 124
MacIntyre, A., 107
maintenance issues, 13
major building projects, 151
Major, C., 101
management approach, 141
management challenge, 141
management perspectives, 45
management statistics, 148
management structures, 148
management training, 122
managing time, 95
Managing Value Delivery, 149
Manchester, University of, 138
Mandelstam, N., 159
mapping learning, 131
mapping techniques, 128, 130–131
Marchall, N., 122
Marcus, G., 26, 27
market calculations, 6
marketing, 151, 189
market mechanisms, 205
marketplace, 140, 141, 152
market trends, 148
Martin, S.H., 129
marxist urbanists, 24
Maskell, D., 123
Mason, W., 129
Massey, D., 139
masterpieces, 158
master-planning, 141
material culture, xvi, 90
mathematics, 108, 139
Maughan, B., 143
Maxwell, N., 174
Mayes, T., 19
McGregor, J., 75
McLuhan, M., 179, 189
Mcwilliam, E., 127

meaningful learning, 108, 201
meaning-making, 50, 52, 55
measurement and prediction, 28
media technologies, 194
meeting places, 128
Meier, P. S., 112
metaphorical image, 42
metaphorical intentions, 42
metaphorical references, 44
metaphorical validation, 72
metaphors, xiv, xvi, xix, xx, 14,
    34–36, 41–45, 46n1, 46n2, 46n3,
    49, 53, 76, 102, 103, 121, 170
Meyer, J.H.F., xx, 44, 45, 52, 99,
    175
Miami, University of, 140
micro-design, 11, 12
micro-utopias, xvi, 159
mirroring, 71–75
Mitchell, G., 10, 12
mobile lives, 128
models for triangulation, 6
modern age, 158
modern cities, 141
modernist design, 42
modern shopping, 140
Moher, T.G., 127
Morris, W., 156, 157, 159
Mortenson, K.P., 169
Mortimore, P., 143
Mosher, A., 111
Mount, J., 138
Muller, M.J., 11
multi-focal environment, 87
multiple identities, 190
multi-purpose environments, 22
multi-user experience, 127
museum communities, 180
museum experience, 156
museums collections, 156, 158, 160,
    161
museums education, xii
museum studies, xi
museum utopians, 158
musicians, 197

Muthesius, S., 141
mutual accountability, 206
myopia, 206

N
Naeve, A., 130
Namioka, A., 111
narratives, 112, 184–186, 213
narrative space, 139
national CETL initiative, 180
National Student Survey, 9
Natural Learning Landscapes for
    Schools, 122
natural sciences, 172
Neary, M., 4, 7–10, 12–15, 33, 35,
    125
neighbourhoods, 137, 158
Nelson, J.R., 129
neutral environment, 105
Newcastle, University of, 123
Newman, J.H., 123, 125, 126
no-go areas, 169
nomadic learner, 169
nomadism, 173
non-designed, 44
Nordenbo, S.E., 169
normalisation, 60
normative representations, 55
Northumberland Learning
    Landscapes, 122
Northumberland, University of, 122
nostalgia, 155
notation, 25
Nottingham, University of, 37, 211,
    213
Noyes, A., 121

O
objective measures, 7, 27
object scholarship, 180–182
Oblinger, D.G., 33
O'Brien, R., 19–21
observation-based methods, 6
occupant density, 6
occupants satisfaction, 9

off-campus learning spaces, 121
office allocation, 43
Office for Economic Co-operation
    and Development (OECD), 127,
    129
office spaces, 93
off-limits, 174
Ogden, T.H., 74
Oliver, R., 106, 116*n*2
ontological quest, 172
ontological risk, 73
ontological space, 77, 169
Oosterling, H., 107
open-access, 150, 152, 153
open air, 158
open-door, 130
open learning, 69
open plan, 13, 20
open spaces, 160, 168, 171, 175
operational costs, 150
operational demands, 201
operational insights, 3
operationalising outcomes, 9
opportunity costs, 7
oppositional analogies, 51
optimism, 185, 203
organisational contexts, 203, 204
organisational culture, 143
organisational developments, 139
organisational features, 86
organisational layout, 53
organisational obstacles, 198
Ormes, S., 122
Osborne, M., 27
O'Sullivan, F., 125
Ouston, J., 143
outcomes model, 6, 8–9, 16
outdoor learning, 122
outdoor playing, 109
outdoor spaces, 110
ownership, 89, 90, 101, 115, 129,
    130, 152, 202
Oxford Brookes University, 126,
    128, 130
Oxford University, 126, 128, 130

P
Paechter, C.F., 21–23, 69
paradigmatic methods, 26
Parekh, N., 3, 7–10, 12–15, 33, 35
parenting practice, 107
Parlett, M.R., xix, 28, 57
Parman, A.T., 112
participatory processes, 106, 116
participatory tools, 112
partnership boards, 97
Pascarella, E.T., 126, 131
passive students, 33
Passmore, J., 115
patchwriting, 99
pathetic fallacy, 137
Payne, G.C., 60
Pearson, E., 129
pedagogical aspirations, 13
pedagogical paradigms, 13
pedagogic challenges, 73, 180, 184
pedagogic control, 171
pedagogic practices, 76
pedagogic space, 74, 77
pedagogic theories, xii, 180
pedagogy of air, 168
peer-based learning, 150
peer critique, 101
peer groups, 84, 87, 101
peer support, 20
peoples stories, 93
performance measures, 38
performativity, 103
performing arts venues, 160
peripheral participation, 52, 53
permeable learning, 188, 189
Personal academic offices, 124
personal histories, 195, 200
personalised budgets, 97
personalised e-learning, 122
personalised learning, 20, 122
personal perspectives, 125
personal technologies, 20
person-environment interaction, 9
phenomenology, 19, 22, 26
philosophy, 170

photography, 97
physical access, 83
physical adjustments, 87
physical affordances, 12
physical boundaries, xx, 139
physical capital, 143, 144
physical interactivity, 86
physical invisibility, 89
physical mobility, 86
physical presence, 138
physical properties, 29, 83
physiological wellbeing, 129
Pinder, D., 24
Pitt, A., 70, 73
place-making, 86
place-shaping, 141
planning initiatives, 25
play and creativity, 74–76
play and security, 71
playful behaviour, 87
playful environment, 35
playgrounds, 160
playing fields, 109
Policies and legislation, 205, 208
policy and management, xi, 15, 214
policy drivers, 97
policy goals, 160
political imperatives, 121, 124
pooled rooms, 189
Popper, K., 158
positive mirroring, 72
positive psychology, 115
postgraduate, 99, 152, 183, 213
Postman, N., 155, 158
post-modern, 50, 71, 128, 138, 170
post-modernist campus, 128
post-occupancy, 14
post-occupancy evaluations, 89
post-structuralist, 56, 72
potential spaces, 73–75
Potter, N., 186
Pouloudi, A., 130
poverty, 43
Powell, D., 5, 6, 11, 14
Powell, K., 43

power dynamics, 96
power structures, 76, 176, 209
practical spaces, 169
practical systems, 130
practical timescales, 14
practical ventures, 169
practice theory, 106–108, 110, 116, 166n2
pragmatic constraints, 3
pre-liminal, 45
Prencipe, A., 122
pre-school, 70, 73
prestige projects, 138
Preston, J., 140
private sector environments, 182
private space, 140, 159
private wealth, 138
privileged places, 100
professional communities, 58
professional education, 174
professional formations, xxi
professional guidelines, 4
professional learning, xiii
professional organisations, 179
professional practices, 83, 84, 107
professional vocabularies, 111
professorial systems, 123
prototypes, 185
psychic space, 169, 180
psychoanalysis, 72
psychoanalytic theory, xvii, 72
psychological overload, 167
psychology, xiv, 19, 22, 24, 26, 115, 212–214
public cultural spaces, 160, 162
public display, 43
public education, 156, 182
public funding, xv, 160
public institutions, 182, 187
public learning, 180, 182
public places, 139
public policy, 160
public sector, 193
Putnam, R.D., 144

Q
qualitative methodologies, 20
qualitative research synthesis, 101, 213
quality assurance, 180, 190n4
quantitative analysis, 6
quasi-utopias, 158
questionnaires, 27
Quinn, J.B., 121, 122

R
racism, 206
Radcliffe, D., 7, 11, 14
radical architecture, 54
radicalism, 168
Raftery, J., 122, 126, 130
Ramsden, P., 111
Rapoport, A., 22
rationalism, 26, 64n1
reading groups, 101
real-world knowledge, 40
reciprocal learning, 114
Reckwitz, A., 107
recruitment, 138
rectilinear spaces, 90
reflection-in-action, 208
reflective framework, 53
reflexivity, 102
refurbishment, 4, 41
reification, 59, 60, 195
relaxation areas, 40
repertoire, 42, 57–61, 63, 194
repositories, 188
representational aspects, 42
representational qualities, 44
representational spaces, 94
research-led teaching, 181
residence patterns, 131
resilience, 73, 171, 185
resistance, 27, 198
resource allocation, 140
resource management, 124
resource requirements, 153
reverse engineering, 6, 15
revolutionary change, 105

rhetoric, 43, 174, 182, 189, 190
rhetoric of risk, 182
Richardson, J.T.E, 130
Richards, V., 71, 130
Riddle, M., 127, 130
Roberts, S., 4, 5, 9, 14, 15
Robinson, I., 123
Robinson, K., 185, 189
Robinson, L. B., 112
Rogers, A, 24
Rose, G., 76
Roussos, M, 127
Royal College of Art, London (RCA), xiii 179
Royal Institute of British Architects (RIBA), xiii, 179
Rudduck, J., 129
Russell, R., 122
Rutter, M., 143
Ryave, A.L., 60

S
Sackler Centre for Arts Education, V&A Museum, London, xvi, 42, 161
Sacks, H., 60
safe environment, 72
Saint, A., 42
Saltire Centre, University of Glasgow, 35, 36
Sanders, E.B.N., 111
Sandoval, W.A., 11, 12
sandpits, 96
Sarles, H., 123
satisfaction surveys, 138
Saugstad, T., 138, 142
scaffolded learning, 69
scales and granularity, xviii
scenarios, 10, 111, 112, 114, 116, 125
scepticism, 90, 157, 181
Schaeffer, T. N., 122
Schaller, M., 9
Schatzki, T., 107
Schenkein, J.N., 60

Schofield, J., 140
school learning, 24, 125
schools sectors, 37
Schuh, J., 140
Schuler, D., 111
scientific models, 187
scientific-objective approach, 25
scientific truths, 26
Scott-Webber, L., 57–60
Scruton, R., 123, 124
sculptures, 201
Seamon, D., 26
secondary levels, 62
secondary school design, 42
seduction, 73
Segal, H., 74
self-authorship, 171
self-awareness, 184
self-becoming, 176, 177
self-confidence, 185
self-design, 208
self-directed study, 61
self-help, 173
self-image, 87
self-learning, 173
self-presentation, 171
self-reflection, 154
self-regulation, 72
self-sabotage, 70
semiotics, 27
Sennett, R., 76, 139, 141
sense-making, 147, 154
sense of place, xvii, 37, 131, 139,
    143
Serafin, E., 127
service environment, 113
service evaluation, 9
settlements, 140
Shattock, M., 138
Sheffield Information Commons, 11
Shirky, C., 189
Shulman, L., 70
silent majority, 163
Silver, H., 143
Silverstone, R., 22

site management, 131
site-specific, xviii
situated learning, 62, 215
Skeggs, B., 72
Smith, D., 125, 127
Smith, J. A, 26
Smith, L., 27
social anthropology, xiv, 19, 24
social architecture, 93
social artists, xvi, 201–204, 207–209
social behaviour, 137
social capital, xvi, 138–144
social classes, 127
social coherence, 189
social construction, 115
social deprivation, 43
social environments, 126
social factors, 90
social funds, 193, 204
social identities, 10
social infrastructure, 11
social innovation, xvi, 193, 195
socialisation, 24
socialised learning, 187
social learning, xi, xvi, 36, 39, 46n1,
    60, 150, 193–210
social meanings, xvii, 61
social media, 183, 189
social networking, 21, 42
social reformers, 163
social reproduction, 125
social rituals, 24
social scientists, 112
social spaces, 72, 193, 194,
    198–201, 203, 204, 207
social systems, xvii, 193, 200, 201,
    203–205, 209, 210
social theory, 24, 107, 213, 215
social work, 71, 207
societal norms, 55
sociological investigations, 25
sociological topography, 125
socio-political perspectives, 128
socio-spatial practices, xx, 51–54,
    56, 57, 60, 61, 63

Softroom Architects, 42
Soja, E. W., 60
SOLSTICE, 9
SOMUL, 130
space-for-being, 73
space guidelines, 151
space-in-use, 154
Space Management Group (SMG),
    7, 8, 148
space metrics, 6
space models, 153–154
space ownership, 152
space planners, 137
space provision, 6, 40
space requirements, 147, 148, 151
spaces-in-between, 59, 62
spaces literature, 13, 50
space syntax, 13
space types, 4, 12
space usage, 124
space values, 149
spaciousness, xvi, 171
spatial affordances, xv
spatial analogies, 52
spatial arrangements, 154
spatial causality, 8
spatial determinism, 10
spatial ecology, 6, 12–13
spatial factors, 87, 90
spatial language, 69
spatial layouts, 36
spatial norms, 4
spatial relationships, xx, xviii, 44,
    143, 181
spatial settings, 24, 87
spatial zones, 169
Spitz, E. H., 69
SpotPLUS, 130
staff costs, 7, 137, 152
staff elites, 125
staff experiences, 90
staff involvement, 14, 131
staff offices, 61, 130
staff perceptions, 81, 90

staff support, 9, 11, 15, 61, 150, 152,
    153
stakeholders, 3, 14, 61, 105, 106,
    110–116, 123, 130, 131, 149, 154,
    160
stakeholders and designers, 115, 116
stakeholders and facilities, 110
stakeholders and users, 3, 61, 114,
    131, 160
stakeholders values, 149
standard-setting, 142
Starik, M., 122, 123, 126
state-sponsored, 24
statistics, 6, 148
stay-at-home, 169
Strange, C., 143
Strathclyde, University of, 148
streetscape, 162
striated spaces, 173
structural interactions, 208
structuralism, 25
structuralist analysis, 24
structured learning, 126
structured settings, 174
stuckness, 99
student behaviours, 12
student-centred approach, 21
student communities, 181
student control, 127
student diversity, 93, 123
student evaluations, 9
student focus, 82, 91n3
student numbers, xv, 93, 100, 180
student satisfaction, 9, 91, 138, 148,
    171
student services, 36, 37
students identities, 125
students lives, 168
students self-becoming, 177
studio workspace, 161
study environments, 20
Styhre, A., 112, 113
subject communities, 183, 184
subject disciplines, 171
subjectivity, 71, 173

subject knowledge, 62, 84, 180, 184
subject positions, 72
subject skills, 184
subject specialisms, 142
sub-optimal locations, 143
suburban estates, 43
summative analysis, xviii
supporting citizen-learners, xvi
supporting collaboration, 149
supporting evaluation, 35
support systems, 101
surrounding spaces, 12
Sussex, University of, 36, 81, 82,
    214
sustainability, 64n3, 175, 177, 181
Swenton-Wall, P.,
Sydney, University of Technology,
    116n3, 213, 214
Syed, S., 138
symbolic capital, 97
symbolic elements, 24
symbolic identity, 90
symbolic interactionism, 26
syncretism, 26
synthetic worlds, 184
systems design, 188

T
tacit elements, 196
tax-payers, 123
Taylor, P., 127
teachers concerns, 111
teaching employability, 84
teaching relationships, 84
teaching theories, 131
technical education, 158
technicians, 196
technological infrastructure, 81, 89
technological innovation, 81
technological solutions, 186
technologies, xv, 4–6, 8, 10, 12, 15,
    19–23, 33, 36, 40, 42, 64n1, 81,
    83, 89, 90, 95, 102, 105, 110, 112,
    114, 116, 116n2, 116n3, 121, 122,
    124, 127, 148, 150, 153, 160, 163,
    168, 180, 194, 211–214
technology-rich environments, 33,
    36
technology-supported learning, 89
telepresence, 102
television, 99
Tell, F., 122
Terenzini, P.T., 126, 131
Tertiary Education Facilities
    Management Association
    (TEFMA), 33
Texas, University of, 128
texting, 20
therapy, 36
Thody, A.M., ix, xii, xv, 14, 38, 71,
    121, 125, 130, 182, 214
Thomas, G., 37, 129
Thomas, H., 3, 4, 9, 14
threshold concepts, 44, 45, 69, 99
Thrift, N., 43, 52, 102, 139, 141
time and space, 7, 43, 51, 55, 75,
    127, 158, 159, 173
time-management skills, 19
timetabling, 148
topography, 125
Torelli, L., 125
Tosh, D., 122
traditional disciplines, 186
traditional facilities, 127
traditional hierarchies, 206
traditional learning, 3, 127
traditional psychology, 26
traditional space, 151
training workshops, 122
transformative spaces, 94
transitional journey, 44
transitional movement, 52
transitional object, 72, 73
transitional spaces, xiv, 53, 69–74,
    77
transitory learning, 188
transmission model, 21, 181
triangulation, 6, 16
Trosten-Bloom, A.,

troublesome knowledge, 45, 52
Trowler, P.R., 121
Tschumi, B., 50, 190n5
typologies, 5–15, 33, 37–39, 41, 42, 45, 131

U
unemployment, 124
universal accessibility, 125
universal public education, 156
university culture, 143
University Grant Committees, 4
university infrastructures, 187
university landscapes, 121, 125, 130
University of Abertay, 36, 40–41
University of Brighton, xiii, 81, 83, 86, 179, 212, 214
University of Cambridge, 37, 139
University of Chicago, 139
University of Colorado, 122
University of Copenhagen, 142
University of Edinburgh, 130, 131, 213
University of Essex, 37
University of Lincoln, ix, 128, 148, 214
University of Liverpool, 37
University of London, 36, 139, 211, 213, 214
University of Manchester, 138
University of Strathclyde, 148
University of Sussex, 36, 81, 82, 214
University of Texas, 128
University of Warwick, 36
University of York, 141, 142
university regulations, 100
university typologies, 39
unsettled spaces, 74–77
unspoken interactions, 52
unstructured settings, 174
unsuccessful space, 23
unusual furnishings, 127
users, xii, 6, 20, 43, 82–84, 88, 89, 97, 121, 125, 137, 143, 147–153, 155, 160

users and designers, 149
Usher, R., 75, 127, 137
utilisation surveys, 148
utilisation targets, 7
utilitarian, 182, 189
utopian thinking, 158–160
utopian visions, 156, 157

V
valorisation, 26
vandalism, 129
Van Leeuwen, T., 173
Van Note Chism, N., 3, 14
Vasilakis, C.A., 127
ventilation, 36
vertical accountability, 205–209
vertical structures, 206
vertigo, 75
Vertovec, S., 24
Victoria and Albert (V&A) Museum, London, ix, 211
Vince, A., 140
Virilio, P., 102, 103
virtual architecture, 121
virtual classrooms, 127
virtual communication, 153
virtual ecosystems, 127
virtual learning, 76, 122, 127
Virtual Learning Environment (VLE), 76
virtual reality, 127
virtual space, xx, 21, 23, 64n3
visualisation, 56
vocabularies, xv, 36, 45, 57, 61, 72, 111, 121–131
Vygotsky, L.S., 69

W
Wales, University of, 37
Warf, B., 53
Warger, T., 8, 9
Warwick, University of, 36, 123
Watson, L., 10, 11, 13, 14, 20, 35
way-finding, 13
Weaver, M., 4, 5, 9, 14, 15

Web 2.0 technologies, 21
Web 2.0 world, 21
wellbeing, xv, 46*n*2, 108, 129, 181
Werdmuller, B., 122
Wheelahan, L., 172
Whitney, D.A., 115
Whitt, E., 140
wicked problems, 186, 190*n*6
Williams, B., 176
Williams, L., 143
Williams, T., 139
Wilson, H., 12, 40, 44
windowless rooms, 109
Winnicott, D.W., 69, 71, 74, xiv
Winn, J., 125
wired alcoves, 130
wireless networks, 181
Wisker, G., 9

Wittgenstein, L., 107
Wolverhampton, University of, 124
Wood, E., 125
Woolf, V., 99
working-class, 137
workplace-based learning, 61
workplaces, ix, xi, 36, 61, 64*n*2, 111,
    116*n*3, 148, 151, 214
work spaces, 40, 50, 57, 122, 124,
    153, 154, 161, 201, 204
writing grant applications, 97, 98
writing retreats, 99, 101
writing spaces, 94, 98–100
Yamamura, E., 143
York, University of, 141, 142
Yost, B., 122

Z
Zetter, R., 181
Zizek, S., 71

Lightning Source UK Ltd.
Milton Keynes UK
UKOW07f1823081214

242841UK00009BA/632/P